BUDDHA SHAKYAMUNI

Manjushri

༄༅། ཀུན་མཁྱེན་འཇམ་མགོན་མི་ཕམ་རྒྱ་མཚོའི་རྣམ་ཐར་དོ་མཚར་
བདུད་རྩིའི་སྣང་བ་དང་ཁོང་གི་སྐོང་ཕྲིན་མེད་གཉིའི་ང་རོ་དང་
གསུང་དུམ་ཚན་འགའ་ཞིག་བཞུགས་སོ། །

པདྨ་ཀུ་རའི་སྤྲ་བསྐྱར་མཐུན་ཚོགས་ནས
སྤྲ་བསྐྱར་ཞུས།

The Padmakara Translation Group gratefully acknowledges the generous support of the Tsadra Foundation in sponsoring the translation and preparation of this book.

Lion of Speech

The Life of Mipham Rinpoche

Dilgo Khyentse

TRANSLATED BY THE
Padmakara Translation Group

SHAMBHALA

Shambhala Publications, Inc.
4720 Walnut Street
Boulder, Colorado 80301
www.shambhala.com

Page 225 constitutes a continuation of the copyright page.

Cover art: Thangka of Mipham Rinpoche from the private collection of
Orgyen Chowang Rinpoche

9 8 7 6 5 4 3 2 1

First Edition
Printed in the United States of America

♾ This edition is printed on acid-free paper that meets the
American National Standards Institute z39.48 Standard.
♻ Shambhala Publications makes every effort to print on recycled paper.
For more information please visit www.shambhala.com.
Shambhala Publications is distributed worldwide by
Penguin Random House, Inc., and its subsidiaries.

LIBRARY OF CONGRESS CATALOGING-IN-PUBLICATION DATA
Names: Rab-gsal-zla-ba, Dil-mgo Mkhyen-brtse, 1910–1991, author. |
Comité de traduction Padmakara, translator.
Title: Lion of speech: the life of Mipham Rinpoche / Dilgo Khyentse;
translated by the Padmakara Translation Group.
Other titles: Title in Tibetan: kun mkhyen 'jam mgon mi pham rgya
mtsho'i rnam thar ngo mtshar bdud rtsi'i snang ba dang khong gi stong
thun seng ge'i nga ro dang gsung dum tshan 'g'a zhig bzhugs so
Description: First edition. | Boulder: Shambhala, 2020. | Includes
bibliographical references and index.
Identifiers: LCCN 2019056509 | ISBN 9781559394949 (hardback)
Subjects: LCSH: Mi-pham-rgya-mtsho, 'Jam-mgon 'Ju, 1846–1912. |
Rnying-ma-pa lamas—China—Tibet Autonomous Region—Biography. |
Mādhyamika (Buddhism)—Doctrines. | Rnying-ma-pa (Sect)—Doctrines.
Classification: LCC BQ972.I457 R33 2020 | DDC 294.3/923092 [B]—dc23
LC record available at https://lccn.loc.gov/2019056509

CONTENTS

Foreword by Alak Zenkar Rinpoche

Mipham Rinpoche was a master of the most wondrous qualities of study, reflection, and meditation. Through his activities of explanation, debate, and composition, he did an unsurpassed service to the Buddha's teaching of both transmission and realization. Even if hundreds of scholars were to discourse on his achievements for an entire kalpa, there would still be more to say.

Adorned with every glorious quality, the noble being Mipham Jamyang Namgyal Gyatso Pelzangpo was Manjushri in person, appearing in the form of a teacher in this degenerate age. And since the story of his life is so difficult for us to comprehend, it is here set forth by the vajra master and lord of refuge Dilgo Khyentse Rinpoche, Rabsel Dawa—the very life tree of the most secret teachings of the Old Translation school—a master as learned as he was accomplished, a lord of all enlightened families and of an infinity of mandalas, whose name (but for the present necessity) I scarcely dare even to pronounce. He has composed an essential distillation of the life of Mipham Rinpoche, to which he gave the name *The Light of Wondrous Nectar.* And since he has revealed therein its quintessential significance, as though he had refined the purest gold, the text itself is perfect and adorned with a glory of poetic metaphor. It is the life story of a truly extraordinary master; it is utterly immaculate both in content and expression; it is free of the slightest imperfection.

I believe that to translate this most precious gem, this biography so replete with meaning, into other languages will without a doubt be of service to the Doctrine. It will kindle faith and devotion in the hearts of many and will plant therein the seed of liberation. So it is with an immense joy that I received the news that the life story of this great master has been translated into English. What an excellent, what an extremely excellent, what a supremely excellent thing to do! Joining my hands before the chakra of my heart, I cast upon this book a hundred times the flowers of my joy.

This was written by Thubten Nyima, otherwise known as Zenkar Tulku, for the publication both in French and English of *Lion of Speech*, the condensed biography of the omniscient Mipham Rinpoche.

Translators' Introduction

Dilgo Khyentse Rinpoche composed his biography of Jamgön Mipham in 1939 at the behest of Jamyang Khyentse Chökyi Lodrö and Jedrung Karma Chökyi Nyinje. Incorporating much of the material gathered in an earlier biography by Khenpo Kunzang Pelden,[1] one of Mipham's closest disciples, Khyentse Rinpoche enlarged and enriched his account from two important sources: oral accounts preserved in notes kept by his elder brother Shedrup Tendzin and, most especially, the personal recollections of Lama Ösel Jalü Dorje, who had been Mipham's devoted personal attendant for thirty-seven years.

With the passage of time, the unpublished manuscript was displaced among its author's papers and disappeared. Left behind in Tibet when Khyentse Rinpoche went into exile in 1959, it was not included in his collected works when these were assembled and published thirty-five years later in 1994. To all intents and purposes, the biography was lost beyond recovery and, were it not for a single chance occurrence, would have passed completely out of memory. In the winter of 1986–87, Dilgo Khyentse Rinpoche himself presided over the publication of Mipham Rinpoche's collected works. One day, as he was perusing Kunzang Pelden's biography of Mipham, which was to be included in the seventh volume of the collection,[2] he casually remarked to Dakpo Tulku, one of his students who happened to be standing close by, that he himself had written a biography of Mipham many years before, which while containing most of the information supplied by Kunzang Pelden but with added supplements, was actually more detailed.[3] There, for the time being, the matter rested. Khyentse Rinpoche died a few years later in 1991 and, apart from the startling piece of information received by Dakpo Tulku, no one had either seen or heard of the long lost biography.

By an extraordinary stroke of good fortune, however, the text came to light in 2010. Brought to Larung Gar in Serta by an old monk from Gyarong, it was offered to Khenpo Chime Rigdzin, one of the professors there. The manuscript was circulated among several readers, but seeing that the author had identified himself simply as Tashi Paljor, no one recognized its provenance. Eventually, however, it came into the hands of Gelong Gyurme Senge, a young monk of Shechen in Kham, who at the time was a student at Larung Gar. He immediately realized that Tashi Paljor was the personal name of Dilgo Khyentse Rinpoche—given to him shortly after his birth by Mipham himself. A copy of the text was sent to Nepal to Dakpo Tulku, by then the distinguished editor of the new and definitive edition of the Rinchen Terdzö, the collection of Nyingma treasure texts. After careful examination by several scholars, it was unanimously decided that the text was indeed the long lost biography of Mipham composed by Khyentse Rinpoche seventy years before. It was brought to Shechen Rabjam Rinpoche, Khyentse Rinpoche's grandson, who immediately arranged for it to be published, just in time for it to be distributed during the reading transmission of Mipham's works, which Rabjam Rinpoche himself gave at Bodhgaya in India in 2013 to mark the centenary anniversary of Mipham's death.

Khyentse Rinpoche's biography of Mipham is in many ways a traditional *namthar*, an account of the "life and liberation" of a man who is widely considered to be among the greatest scholars and accomplished masters in the history of Tibetan Buddhism. Profoundly reverential in tone, the text is composed in a rich, honorific, literary style, filled with the kind of poetic elegance for which its author is famous. It is rare to find references to even quite ordinary events, persons, and places that are unaccompanied by at least some kind of rhetorical flourish. According to the dictates of polite Tibetan protocol, for instance, no person of note is referred to merely by name without some additional expression of fulsome

Dilgo Khyentse Rinpoche as a young monk. This picture was taken
a few years after the composition of his biography of Mipham.
Shechen archives, used with permission.

praise. The text is arranged in long, complex periods, beautifully
constructed according to the canons of traditional literary composition but often difficult to construe and certainly quite foreign
to the taste and practices of twenty-first-century English. But even
though a measure of simplification is inevitable when casting the
translation into shorter English sentences, it would nonetheless
have been undesirable, as well as impossible, to try to disguise the
style and linguistic register of the text and to attempt to rewrite
it in simpler form. On the contrary, it is hoped that, in the final

result, the reader will have a biography that while being clear in sense, will preserve many of the rhetorical features and reflect the majestic power of the original.

As an indication of the origins of the nirmanakaya that appeared in the form of Mipham Namgyal, the first chapter of the text is a rhapsodic celebration of the nature and role of Manjushri within the vast supramundane context of Mahayana Buddhism.[4] Conceived in terms of multiple universal systems in the course of immense lapses of cosmic time, the account is presented with all the mind-numbing hyperbole of the Mahayana scriptures, the purpose of which seems to be to bring the minds of the readers into a state of silent wonder by forcing their imaginative powers literally to their breaking point. The nature and exploits of Manjushri, paradoxically both the sire and disciple of all the buddhas, are considered from the beginningless past, through the present, and on into the horizonless future until the very emptying of samsara. This stupendous backstory is not simply an expression of hagiographical reverence dictated by tradition. It sets the scene for the life of a man who is widely regarded as one of the defining figures of his home tradition, a scholar and master of meditation who, despite the lateness of his appearance on the historical scene, is often placed on the same level as the greatest personages in Tibetan history—Longchenpa, Sakya Pandita, Tsongkhapa, and so on—all of whom have been traditionally regarded as manifestations of Manjushri.

Be that as it may, the vision is gradually scaled down until, by the end of the first chapter, we reach the manageable dimensions of a human being—even if a man of superlative gifts—whom the author encountered while he was still a baby in arms, and whose memory lived on powerfully in the recollections of a whole generation of scholars and meditators whom the author knew personally. Thanks to the testimony of these witnesses, Khyentse Rinpoche has bequeathed to us a vivid, almost firsthand description of Mipham's extraordinary qualities as a scholar, teacher, and spiritual master—marks of greatness that were plain for all to see. "It is thus," he says, "that, on the basis of the valid cognition of direct perception, we know with certainty the causes that made him a noble and sublime bodhisattva. In this life, his qualities of elimination and realization were immaculate—and this is something I find even more amazing than the record of his many hundreds of incarnations in times gone by."

The ensuing biography focuses very much on the man: the strong and courageous boy of good family, full of promise and already marked for greatness by his place of birth and illustrious pedigree; the young monk and diligent student who with astonishing precocity would rapidly blossom into a scholar, teacher, and author of truly spectacular genius; and the dedicated practitioner of many years of solitary retreat.

As the previous quotation indicates, one of the striking features of Khyentse Rinpoche's account is a marked tendency, despite its opening chapter, to downplay the "miraculous" aspects of Mipham's life and activities—perhaps as a means of bringing into sharper focus the impact in human terms that he had on his contemporaries as a spiritual master, scholar, and teacher. It is entirely plausible that, as a tantric yogi of high accomplishment, Mipham acquired all manner of preternatural powers. But, from the age of thirty, we are told that he became extremely secretive about his own inner dealings and very rarely manifested or even spoke of them even to his closest attendants. As we learn from the biography, he once composed a whole volume describing his yogic exploits and signs of accomplishment, only to consign it to the flames before it could be published. In any case, it was Mipham's supreme intelligence and scholarship, coupled with amazing diligence and integrity as a master of meditation, that was for Khyentse Rinpoche the real miracle of his life—an unquenchable source of inspiration for disciples like himself. By comparison, "simply to talk according to our common perceptions about a great being such as this—whether in terms of the deities that he beheld or the minor miracles that he worked—is to do only what is liable to lead childish beings astray."

Another aspect that the biographer does not dwell on in any great detail, but that is sure to impress the Western reader, is that the achievements of Mipham's later life were played out against a background of relentless pain, the result of a serious and gradually worsening illness (apparently some kind of acute neuralgia), which, as some of his verses suggest, sometimes drove him almost to the brink of madness. Perceived in traditional terms, this illness was indeed a reflection of the declining merit and virtue of a decadent age—severely hampering, to our great and irreparable loss, the composition of his works.

Nevertheless, particularly in the springtime of his adult life, Mipham was closely involved in the rime, or nonsectarian, movement inaugurated by his teachers, notably Jamyang Khyentse Wangpo (1820–92), Jamgön Kongtrul Lodrö Thaye (1813–99), Patrul Rinpoche (1808–87), and others. The purpose of this extraordinary and much-discussed initiative was to preserve and invigorate the vast range of teachings and practices of the Tibetan Buddhist tradition—particularly those of the older schools— that, by the late nineteenth century, had largely fallen into abeyance, principally for social and political reasons, and were in an advanced state of decline. New centers of learning were founded and older establishments were restored. Great collections of texts were assembled, edited, published, and transmitted. And in the attempt to overcome the spirit of sectarian intolerance that for centuries had crippled the intellectual and spiritual life of Tibet, conscious efforts were made to create an atmosphere of tolerance and exchange in which members of all schools were encouraged to study and deepen their understanding and practice of their own traditions, coexisting with others in a climate of open inquiry and mutual respect. To this collective effort, Mipham gave his wholehearted support and made an unparalleled contribution to the revival of the teaching tradition of his own Nyingma school, reaching back through the writings of Longchenpa and Rongzom Pandita to the heroic age of the founding fathers of the Tibetan tradition (Guru Rinpoche, Abbot Shantarakshita, and the dharma king Trisong Deutsen). He produced a range of commentaries on all the main sutra topics, thus creating an unprecedented body of philosophical textbooks that have since provided the core curriculum for the modern *shedra*, or commentarial colleges, of the Nyingma school.

On the sutra level, he wrote commentaries on the Abhidharma compendia of both Asanga and Vasubandhu. In the area of logic and epistemology, he explained the classic texts of Dignaga, Dharmakirti, and Sakya Pandita. His work on Madhyamaka included commentaries on the writings of Nagarjuna, Shantarakshita, Chandrakirti, and Shantideva. Finally, he composed important presentations of the five Yogachara texts of Maitreya-Asanga.

These endeavors by no means exhausted Mipham's energies. For he also composed numerous important works on tantric topics such as his famous overview of *Dispelling the Darkness in the Ten Directions*, Longchenpa's great commentary on the *Guhyagarbha Tantra*. One should also mention his *Discourse on the Eight Great Mandalas*, and of course his immense two-volume commentary on the *Kalachakra Tantra*. He also produced important works on the Great Perfection, notably his *Trilogy of the Uncontrived Mind* (which though unfinished was completed from notes taken by his disciples) together with his vast collection of essential pith instructions for practitioners. Mipham also took a particular interest in the epic of Gesar of Ling and attempted to reconcile its different versions. Recognizing the importance of Gesar to the folkloric identity of Tibet and especially of Kham, where to this day he occupies an important position in the collective imagination, Mipham composed liturgical rituals based on him and devised a sacred dance sequence in his honor.

These are just a few examples taken from the vast corpus of a master whom Gene Smith described as "one of the most imaginative and versatile minds to appear in the Tibetan tradition."[5] His *Ka'bum* (collected works) is one of the largest in Tibetan literature and reflects the interests of a truly universal scholar. In addition to religious and philosophical topics, Mipham's interests extended also to all the secular sciences, including medicine, politics, poetics, technology, divination, and even sorcery.

Mipham spent almost his entire life in remote hermitages in the wilds of Kham, the eastern province of greater Tibet that borders upon the Chinese provinces of Yunnan and Sichuan. Reading the biography, which focuses exclusively on the details of his scholarly and spiritual life, one would scarcely guess that Mipham lived through a period of catastrophic social and political unrest—in China and Tibet and particularly in Kham, which in the latter half of the nineteenth century must have been in a state of almost permanent crisis. The civil conflict in Nyarong (1863–66), provoked by the warlord Gonpo Namgyal and eventually crushed by the direct intervention of the Lhasa government, is scarcely mentioned. We hear only of the unusual displacement of nomads from Golok and the fact that, in order to avoid potential danger, it was thought expedient for the eighteen-year-old Mipham to make a pilgrimage to the holy places of central and southern Tibet—a journey that brought him to Lhasa and the great monastery of Ganden, where he witnessed with admiration the teaching and debating practice of the Geluk school.

Mipham was almost an exact contemporary of the Dowager Empress Ci Xi (and for that matter Queen Victoria). He lived through a period that saw the collapse of the Ming dynasty, which brought to a calamitous conclusion two thousand years of Chinese imperial rule. The signs of impending change were everywhere apparent as the modern world pressed in on all sides. In China itself, there had been the opium wars and the Boxer Rebellion. And in the early years of the twentieth century, Tibet itself was disturbed by the British military expedition to Lhasa in 1903, soon to be followed by an invasion of Chinese forces, provoking the flight of the thirteenth Dalai Lama, first to Mongolia and China, and then to India. Having little direct impact upon Mipham himself, who in any case spent most of his adult life in retreat in the remote fastness of the mountains, these momentous events are passed over in silence or are referred to by Khyentse Rinpoche only in the most oblique terms.

Provoked by a Tibetan uprising in Kham in 1905, the Ming government sent a punitive expedition that restored order through a campaign of unprecedented brutality. On the orders of its leader, Zhao Erh Feng, monasteries were destroyed and large numbers of monks and lamas were summarily executed. The Chinese soldiers mentioned in the biography,[6] whose presence in Chamdo so alarmed Lama Ösel, almost certainly belonged to this ferocious army, even if they are not so identified. And when the Chinese battalion, passing along the valley road far below Mipham's hermitage, encountered the mysterious opposing force, perhaps it was the horse of Butcher Feng himself that lay down and refused to move. We shall never know. Likewise the identity of the mysterious foreigners, whose saddlebags, filled with what seem to have been geological samples, were scattered in the snow, remains a matter of complete surmise. Could the hapless travelers have belonged to the expedition of William Rockhill, the American explorer, whose journey through western China and Kham in the early 1890s brought him to the neighborhood of Dzogchen and Derge?[7]

Mipham was of course aware of the general atmosphere of social decay. He had noticed, perhaps more than most, the lengthening shadows. But when he spoke of the decadence of his time, he was referring not so much to social and political upheavals as to the decline of the Buddhist tradition: to the progressive loss and diminution of authentic and effective practice, to the misinterpretation of key doctrines, and to the divisions and sectarian intolerance that existed between the various schools, casting a pall of suspicion and discord over the sacred land. These same sentiments are echoed in the reactions of Khyentse Rinpoche himself, who on several occasions pauses to reflect with amazement on the fact that a scholar of such magnitude and a master of such perfect integrity as Mipham should have appeared in these end-times.

To be sure, Mipham, his teachers, and his immediate disciples, including the author of the biography himself, were imbued with a tradition and worldview that had remained virtually unchanged for more than a thousand years. And by the end of the nineteenth century they were living, so to speak, in a parallel universe. Their world of ancient tradition, of learning and intense spiritual endeavor, and

the coarse environment of modern politics and international rela-
tions were merely juxtaposed. They touched but did not interpen-
etrate. The hidden kingdom of Shambhala of the North was a far
more pressing reality to Mipham than, say, the machinations of the
Kuomintang, which, in the very year of his death, would usher in
the short-lived Chinese Republic, itself destined to fall, within a
few years, to the followers of Mao Tse-tung.

Which of these parallel worlds was the more real? From the point
of view of modern history, it is impossible to overlook the existence
of the forces that within decades were to overwhelm and sweep
away forever the traditional life of Tibet. And yet for Mipham,
Jamyang Khyentse Wangpo, Jamgön Kongtrul, and others—that
entire generation of great tantric masters and the generation that
followed—what we take for reality is nothing but a tissue of shift-
ing appearances, where the truth of the Dharma either shines or is
obscured, depending on the fluctuating merit of beings. The world
that seems to us so clear and solid is for such great yogis no more
than a cinematic projection on a screen that, however opaque, is as
thin as paper. For them, and even for the ordinary disciples who
frequented and still frequent their presence, the screen itself may at
times become diaphanous and no longer a barrier between this and
other dimensions. By way of illustration, we may conclude with a
story about Mipham himself, passed down in oral tradition but
not included in Khyentse Rinpoche's account. Early one morning,
during one of Mipham's retreats in the hermitage of Gothi, Lama
Ösel, busy with his daily duties, suddenly entered his master's quar-
ters unannounced. There, on the table, he was astonished to see a
beautiful fresh blue flower and asked in amazement where it had
come from. For it was in the dead of winter, and all around the
hermitage, the blanket of snow that had fallen in the night was
deep and undisturbed. Surprised perhaps by the sudden appearance of his attendant, which had left him no time to conceal the
prodigy, Mipham replied, after what one imagines to have been a
slight pause, "I have just returned from Shambhala. The flower is
a gift from the king."

THE SELECTION OF WRITINGS BY JAMGÖN MIPHAM

On the several occasions in the biography when Khyentse Rinpoche expresses his profound admiration for Mipham's commentaries, he speaks in tantalizingly general terms. In the hope of satisfying, if only partially, the curiosity of the reader thus aroused, and in the belief that the character and personality of authors are often made manifest in their writings, we have made a small selection of sample texts taken from Mipham's collected works. The texts in question cover both sutra and tantra topics. Some have been newly translated for the present occasion (*The Lion's Roar* and a pith instruction entitled *A Lamp to Dispel the Dark*), while others have been taken from texts already translated and published.[8] Needless to say, this supplement is not intended as an adequate reflection of Mipham's work as a whole, for it is only a tiny fragment of his vast and varied output. Nevertheless, we hope that it will afford the reader a taste of the clarity, precision, and eloquence of Mipham's style. Intended as a humble complement to Khyentse Rinpoche's biography, the texts in question address profound issues and are in some places inescapably technical.

In keeping with the identification of Mipham as an emanation of Manjushri, the lion of speech, these selected writings have as their centerpiece a new translation of *The Lion's Roar: A Comprehensive Discourse on the Buddha-Nature*. The doctrine of the buddha-nature (Skt. *sugatagarbha*) is one of the central unifying themes of Mahayana Buddhism, with important ramifications on the level of both the sutra and tantra teachings. The passages chosen to accompany *The Lion's Roar*—the texts on Madhyamaka that precede it and the passages of a tantric nature that follow—are intended to reflect this twofold orientation.

Mipham's position on this important doctrine goes to the heart of his complex and nuanced presentation of the Nyingma view, in which he fully aligns himself with the teachings of the two great luminaries of the Old Translation school, Rongzom Pandita (1012–88) and Longchen Rabjam (1308–63). One of the most striking features of Mipham's compositions is their thematic unity: the fact that whatever may be their level or variety of subject matter—sutra, tantra, Madhyamaka, Yogachara, and so on—they seem invariably to be conceived within the parameters of an overarching and cohesive system. Adopting the position and outlook of whichever text he is commenting on, Mipham is at all times careful to emphasize their complementarity, pointing out ways in which the various facets of Buddhist doctrine, correctly understood and assigned to their proper position, are interrelated—even those that at first sight seem unconnected and even contradictory. Contrasting categories such as Hinayana and Mahayana, the three turnings of the dharma wheel, Madhyamaka and Yogachara, Svatantrika and Prasangika, sutra and tantra, and so on are all brought together into a perfectly concordant unity. Where other scholars have seen differences leading to fragmentation, Mipham emphasizes relatedness and harmonious consistency.

As well as serving to exemplify a compositional style, the selected passages also illustrate this remarkable gift for synthesis. The important ideas discussed in the excerpts from Mipham's Madhyamaka commentaries prepare the way for, and naturally lead into, his characteristically Nyingma understanding of the buddha-nature as expounded in *The Lion's Roar*. Subsequently, the Madhyamaka teachings (belonging to the scriptures of the second turning of the dharma wheel) and the doctrine of the buddha-nature (belonging to the third turning), brought together in synthesis, form the natural basis for the view of the Vajrayana. This is clearly evoked in the excerpt from the *White Lotus*, Mipham's profound and beautiful commentary on the Seven-Line Prayer to Guru Padmasambhava. Finally, in the teachings of the Great Perfection, exemplified in the concluding pith instruction, the buddha-nature—cleansed through the teachings on emptiness of any possible reification as a truly existent entity—is equated with awareness, or *rigpa*.

The texts on Madhyamaka are taken from Mipham's magisterial commentary on Shantarakshita's *Madhyamakalankara* and from the *Ketaka Jewel*, his shorter explanation of the ninth chapter of

Shantideva's *Bodhicharyavatara* (*The Way of the Bodhisattva*). Of these two compositions, it was the second that proved particularly controversial. Mipham's Nyingma interpretation of this well-known scripture provoked sharp critiques from several Gelukpa scholars who sent him written refutations and challenges to debate. To two of these, Mipham composed brilliant and incisive replies, thus entering into a polemical exchange that, at first sight, seems strangely at odds with his commitment to the nonsectarian movement. For this reason, we have chosen as the first item in the supplement what might be regarded as Mipham's rime manifesto. It is the opening preamble of his reply to the critique of Drakar Tulku of Drepung Loseling, in which he explains the reasons for his allegiance to the Nyingma tradition and his natural desire to express and defend its view. In this preface to his tightly argued riposte, Mipham enunciates one of the essential aims of the nonsectarian movement as he saw it: the cultivation of an environment of tolerance and mutual respect in which contending positions could be freely aired and debated before the tribunal of impartial reason unclouded by sectarian animosity—and without fear of opprobrium or persecution. Disagreement, Mipham contends, may be respectful and need not imply denigration. And he sums up his remarks by stating very clearly that his rejection of Tsongkhapa's Madhyamaka teaching does not in any way call into question the sincerity of his admiration for, and devotion toward, the "Jewel Ornament of the Land of Snow."

The history of the development of Madhyamaka in India and Tibet is long and fascinating, but it would be out of place here to attempt even a summary account of the twists and turns of its complicated evolution. Fortunately, there exists a large and ever-growing literature on Madhyamaka in the English language: original texts in translation as well as a rich supportive secondary literature, to which interested readers can easily refer.[9]

In the passages selected, the reader will need to take account of three important points. The first is the distinction—which Mipham emphasizes but did not invent—between two kinds of ultimate truth: the *nonfigurative ultimate* and the *figurative*, or *concordant, ultimate*. The nonfigurative ultimate is the ultimate truth in itself—a state of sublime realization experienced in meditation and characterized by a profound mental silence, the freedom from all conceptual elaboration. By contrast, the figurative ultimate is an idea, a state of intellectual understanding of the ultimate truth, which arises discursively in the mind on the basis of hearing and reflecting on the teachings as well as on the study of texts. Even though the figurative ultimate is described as secondary and of a lesser kind, its importance—as a stepping-stone to the ultimate in itself—is obvious when one reflects that the majority of people need to be introduced to the doctrine of the two truths by intellectual means. The conceptual understanding that results from this, enhanced by careful reflection and supported by considerable reserves of merit, produces a profound sense of intellectual certainty that lays the ground for the direct meditative experience of the ultimate truth in itself.

The second point that the reader should notice is that the distinction between the figurative and nonfigurative ultimates constitutes for Mipham the principal criterion of difference between the Svatantrika and Prasangika subschools of the Madhyamaka tradition. Rejecting the opinion of Tsongkhapa that the Svatantrikas and Prasangikas are divided by a divergence of view (the former being considered inferior to the latter), Mipham affirms that the real difference between them is a matter of pedagogical method. He contends that, in expounding the Madhyamaka teachings, Svatantrikas like Shantarakshita stress the figurative ultimate and cater to those who need a gradual approach to the ultimate in itself. By contrast, Prasangikas like Chandrakirti speak directly in terms of the nonfigurative ultimate in a manner suited to those who are able to enter directly into the state of freedom from conceptual elaboration. Moreover, since pedagogical methods are devised according to the needs of disciples and do not reflect the understanding of their proponents, Mipham does not hesitate to declare that, in terms of individual realization, the views of Shantarakshita and Chandrakirti are exactly the same.

Be that as it may, while in no way questioning the excellence of Chandrakirti as a commentator, Mipham considered that among all the great Madhyamaka masters, Shantarakshita occupied a position of particular eminence. For his Madhyamaka-Yogachara synthesis—the last major development of Buddhist philosophy in India—brought the two tenet systems of the Great Vehicle together into a meaningful and harmonious relation. And since, according to the traditional classification, Madhyamaka and Yogachara correspond respectively to the teachings of the second and third turnings of the dharma wheel, Shantarakshita's synthesis also points to the equal importance and complementarity of these two streams of Mahayana doctrine. Bringing together the traditions of Nagarjuna and Asanga, and also the logico-epistemological tradition of Dignaga and Dharmakirti, Shantarakshita was, in Mipham's estimate, the third great charioteer of the Mahayana. This positive assessment of Yogachara, and also of both the second and third turnings of the dharma wheel, are important features of Nyingma teaching, affecting not only its presentation of Madhyamaka but also, as the reader will discover, its approach to the doctrine of the buddha-nature. As Mipham says in *The Lion's Roar*, "The omniscient Longchen Rabjam held that the meanings of both the second and the third turnings—together and without separation—constituted the definitive teaching, and this is precisely the position that we too should hold."[10]

The third point that the reader should be aware of is Mipham's strenuous rejection of the position, held by Tsongkhapa, that the realization of the actual ultimate truth corresponds to a "nonimplicative negation"—that is, the simple refutation of phenomenal existence. For such a refutation is, in Mipham's view, an essentially intellectual position. It is in fact the figurative ultimate—the outcome of reasoned analysis performed by the discursive intellect. Admittedly, it is of great importance in that it constitutes the refutation of the first—but only the first—of the four ontological extremes (existence, nonexistence, both, and neither) delineated by Nagarjuna in his famous *catuskoti*, or *tetralemma*. It is not, however, the nonfigurative ultimate in itself, since freedom from conceptual elaboration can occur only when all four ontological extremes are simultaneously refuted. Only then does a state of realization manifest in which the discursive intellect is stilled, the nature of the mind revealed, and the path of seeing attained. It is at this point, moreover, that self-cognizing primordial wisdom arises; and this, in Mipham's view, is none other than the buddha-nature itself.

As the reader of *The Lion's Roar* will discover, the interpretation of the doctrine of the buddha-nature by the various Tibetan schools was just as controversial as their views on Madhyamaka. Briefly stated, Mipham's Nyingma presentation plots a middle course between the definition of the buddha-nature as mere "emptiness" and the view that reifies it as an ultimately existing entity, empty of extraneous characteristics but not empty in itself. *The Lion's Roar* is an extremely interesting and truly masterful extrapolation of a single stanza taken from the *Sublime Continuum*, the text known in Sanskrit as either the *Uttaratantrashastra* or *Ratnagotravibhaga*. Mipham's purpose is to show that whereas it is only in the state of final enlightenment that the buddha-nature is fully manifest and activated, nevertheless, this same buddha-nature (being a permanent and immutable state of perfection) is necessarily present, fully accomplished and primordially endowed with the qualities of enlightenment, even in sentient beings. It is present and yet completely hidden by the obscuring veils of adventitious defilement. Therefore, what seems to be a step-by-step acquisition of realization and accomplishment on the path is in fact the removal of obscurations that adventitiously conceal an already present—indeed, primordially present—state of perfection. Through scriptural authority and reasoning, Mipham endeavors to demonstrate the truth of this characteristic position of the Nyingma school. On the side of scripture, he appeals to the sutras and shastras of the third turning of the dharma wheel but also to texts such as

Nagarjuna's *Praise of the Dharmadhatu* (*Dharmadhatu-stava*). His appeal to reasoning is somewhat more complicated. Rational proof is necessarily based on evidence, and evidence is a matter of valid cognition. Of course, for ordinary beings, the presence of the buddha-nature is not something that is directly perceived; its presence must be inferred on the basis of reliable evidence. Mipham proceeds accordingly but adds that the kind of reasoning that *incontrovertibly* establishes the primordial and fully accomplished buddha-nature is grounded in the "valid perception of pure vision"—that is, the valid cognition operative in the postmeditative experience of bodhisattvas who are on the grounds of realization. The doctrine of the sugatagarbha is extremely profound. And since, in the final analysis, it is difficult to fathom even for great bodhisattvas on the path of vision and above, it is hardly necessary to say that in practice it lies beyond the scope of ordinary beings. "It was for this reason," Mipham says, "that the Buddha told his disciples to trust his teaching, saying that it was undeceiving, however difficult it was for them to understand it using their own strength."[11]

Nevertheless, Mipham's demonstration of the doctrine of the buddha-nature primordially endowed with the qualities of enlightenment is of vital importance, since in the manner in which he presents it, the sugatagarbha is simply the nature of the mind itself. Spanning both the sutra and the tantra vehicles, it is in fact none other than the "ground tantra," the unchanging continuum that becomes manifest as obscurations are purified and the result attained.

In conclusion, the reader should note that in the excerpts taken from Mipham's commentaries on the *Madhyamakalankara* and on the Seven-Line Prayer to Guru Rinpoche, (figuring in *Adornment of the Middle Way* and *White Lotus*, respectively) the wording has occasionally been modified for the sake of editorial consistency in the present publication. The reader should also note that in the interests of typographical consistency, diacritics and other forms of accentuation have been reduced to a minimum. Readers unfamiliar with the phonetic rendering of Tibetan words should be aware that the final letter *e* is never mute but is always pronounced separately. For example, *nyingje* and *rime* are consequently words of two syllables, "nying-je" and "ri-me," and are not pronounced as if they rhymed with *cringe* and *time*, respectively.

ACKNOWLEDGMENTS

As so often, it is our first duty to thank Pema Wangyal Rinpoche, who requested the translation of Khyentse Rinpoche's recently published biography of Mipham, and to express our gratitude for his patient assistance in negotiating the often elaborate Tibetan of the original. We must also record our thanks to Khenchen Pema Sherab of Namdroling in Mysore, India, without whose help we would have been unable to bring this project to completion. The translation of *The Lion's Roar on the Buddha-Nature* was greatly assisted by the wonderful exposition of this text given by Khenpo Namdrol, masterfully translated by Gyurme Avertin, at the Rigpa Shedra in December 2008. We record our appreciation and thanks to Khenpo Namdrol, to his translator, and to the Rigpa Wiki for generously making it available online. Our thanks are due also to Gelong Konchok Tendzin (Matthieu Ricard) for his permission to use photographs of Mipham's hermitages and for his helpful suggestions in the composition of the translators' introduction. We would also like to thank our friend and colleague Anne Benson of the Padmakara Translation Group for kindly allowing us to see the manuscript of her translation of the biography into French.

This book was translated by Wulstan Fletcher of the Padmakara Translation Group, with the much-appreciated assistance of Helena Blankleder.

Dordogne, France
The fifteenth day of the Saga month,
the feast of the mahaparinirvana of Shakyamuni Buddha,
June 16, 2019

THE LIGHT OF
WONDROUS NECTAR

*The Essential Biography of the Omniscient
Mipham Jamyang Namgyal Gyatso,
the Fearless Lion of Eloquence and
Charioteer of the Teaching of
the Great Secret*

PROLOGUE

Light of primal wisdom, banishing
For evermore the dark root of samsara, ignorance,
You set the lotus garden of the perfect path in flower.
Youthful Sun of Speech, the glory of the dawn
And springtime of the great and lesser marks of buddhahood,
Bestow on us both excellence and virtue!

Perfect moon, young girl of sixteen years,
Arising from the ocean of delight, the music of the teachings,
Saraswati, radiance of the nectar of Manjushri's mind supreme,
Within the garden of night-flowering lilies, my faith a
    hundredfold, I honor you.

To the wonder spread upon the sky, the cloudy garlands
Of the perfect spotless lives of infinite victorious ones[12] together
    with their heirs,
And to the threefold secret of Manjushri, diamond keenly sharp,
I bow down in my dance of wondrous joy.

Deep is the ocean of the causal and resultant vehicles,
Encircled by a range of golden mountains,
Learned and accomplished masters—
A fence endowed with six activities of freedom—
This tradition of the lake-born Victor is a marvelous wonder.

Like the conflagration that destroys the kalpa
Is the high tradition of the supreme charioteers.
Fanned by winds of scripture, reasoning, and oral teaching,

It consumes the tangled desolation of false doctrine.
Rongzom and Longchenpa and the knowledge-holding masters
Of the threefold lineage, to you the victory!

When the citadel of evil views—
The darkness of this age of dregs—
Was damaging the supreme Doctrine,
You, the sovereign of the fastness of the supreme vehicle,
Destroyed it with the vajra weapon[13]
Of your swift and sharpened reasoning.
Such was your amazing kindness, fearless master Mipham,
Marvelously adorned with jewels
Of speech, of wisdom, and of love!
Knowing this, I join my palms together at my heart.

To the host of teachers and their sons,
Lodro Gyatso, Ösel Dorje, Situ Panchen, and the rest,
Empowered as regents who might open without limit
The doors of your instruction, I reverently bow.

The essential riches of the secret of the teachings deep and vast—
My mind is powerless to grasp them as they are,
But knowing that a simple fragment will dispel
The pain of both samsara and nirvana,
With an attitude of faith, I set it forth.

The sovereign lord, the master Mipham Jamyang Namgyal Gyatso, arose as the very embodiment of the primordial wisdom of the great and nonreferential love of the venerable Manjushri ever youthful, holder of the secret treasure of great, all-knowing wisdom—the one and only sire of unnumbered buddhas and their bodhisattva heirs. The three worlds are adorned with the sounding drumbeat of his name. This brief account of his life is divided into eight parts. The first is a general description of the excellence of the ground of his emanation. This is followed by an account of how, through the power of his bodhichitta, he took birth in this sphere of existence. The third and fourth parts tell of how he entered the door of the Dharma and then relied on qualified teachers for his study and reflection. The fifth part then describes how the precious Mipham hoisted the banner of practice of the profound teachings, while the sixth part goes on to give some indication of his secret life. The seventh part continues with a description of Mipham Rinpoche's activities for the sake of the Doctrine and beings, and the eighth part concludes with an account of how his emanated form was gathered back into the ultimate expanse.

I

THE GROUND OF EMANATION

When the spontaneously present appearances of primordial radiance manifest outwardly from the luminosity of the original ground, that which recognizes them as the self-experience of primordial wisdom[14] and achieves enlightenment marked by six special characteristics[15] is the dharmakaya, Samantabhadra, the primordial lord and glory of samsara and nirvana. Samantabhadra is beyond all dualistic discursive thought, and yet by the power of the self-arisen cognitive potency that is his compassion, which reaches out impartially to beings who pervade the whole of space without end, his effortless activities are permanent, omnipresent, and spontaneous. In order to bring benefit throughout the three times to all beings to be guided, he manifests in the three families of the wisdom deities of the enlightened body, speech, and mind and displays the spontaneous lamps of the five kayas. It is thus that the lord Mipham appeared—one in whom all the victorious ones were made manifest in a single wisdom body, inseparable from the expanse of primordial wisdom of Manjushri, the venerable Wheel of Stability. For indeed it is through the infinite and glorious qualities of this great hero that the immaculate lives of all the buddhas—from whom, in truth he is never parted—are adorned and made beautiful.[16]

It is written in the *Tantra of Great Self-Arisen Awareness*,[17]

> Profound and vast, Manjushri's name is hard to fathom.
> The qualities of Manjushri are utterly sublime.
> From Manjushri does perfect bliss arise.
> Of Manjushri there is no end, no emptying.

As this text describes, Manjushri is the nature of the ultimate expanse of the dharmakaya, the inconceivable freedom from conceptual elaboration. He is suchness, ultimate reality. He is the youthful vase body beyond the ordinary intellect, the knowing aspect of the wisdom of inner luminosity, and for this reason, he can never be parted from the immaculate qualities of the result. So it is that he personifies the great state of union, the state of great equality that permeates the whole of samsara and nirvana. He is inexpressible, ineffable, and inconceivable.

We find also in the *Net of Illusory Manifestations of Manjushri*,[18]

> Arisen from space and self-arisen,
> Great fire of knowledge and of wisdom,
> Great all-illuminating light,
> The brilliant radiance of wisdom.

Never stirring, even slightly, from the state of ultimate reality, Manjushri, the self-experience of wisdom, spontaneous and perfect, is the sovereign lord of the five enlightened kayas in the pure field of the indestructible vajra expanse. He reveals himself in beauteous and splendid form, beyond all movement and change, as the sambhogakaya mandala of the net of illusory manifestation endowed with the seven qualities of union[19] and stainless bliss—clouds of the five perfections, or certainties, of the five peaceful families and forms of wrathful subjugation.

As the *Net of Illusory Manifestations of Manjushri* declares,

> Manjushri, the great light of wisdom and of knowledge—
> From him the lights project, all empty in their nature.
> This has been explained as the great mandala of Manjushri.

In terms of his own benefit, Manjushri remains in the ground, or level, of buddhahood, the ultimate result. Nevertheless, through the power of his compassion, he appears for the sake of beings as numerous as the sky is vast. And for as long as samsara endures, he guides them according to their need in an array of countless illusory appearances. Effortlessly, and at every moment, he bestows on them the glorious states of benefit and happiness appropriate to their aspirations.

As the *Net of Illusory Manifestations of Manjushri* declares,

> Manjushri's wisdom emanations—
> Just as they are viewed, so too do they appear.
> And yet Manjushri is beyond substantial being;
> Ultimate Manjushri is primordial wisdom in itself.

———

In keeping with the teachings of the Tathagata, I will briefly explain the inconceivable way in which, while never being separate from the dharmadhatu, the ultimate and definitive secret, he nevertheless acts on the relative level in harmony with the perceptions of the beings to be trained.

Long, long ago, at a time more distant than a period of one hundred thousand measureless ages[20] multiplied by seven times the number of the grains of sand in the Ganges River, there was once, to the east of our world, a universal system called Excellent Source. In that place, there appeared a buddha named King of Thunderous Melody, and Manjushri, who at that time was a chakravartin, or universal monarch, by the name of Space, served and attended him and all his retinue with offerings of abundant excellence for a period of eighty-four thousand years. Now, as the gods had predicted, this universal monarch, together with his court, a countless myriad strong, came into the presence of the buddha and gave rise to bodhichitta, the mind of enlightenment. They became capable of bodhisattva deeds on a vast scale and, so the scriptures tell us, have now attained the state of perfect buddhahood.

And again, an incalculable number of measureless kalpas in the past, and at an inconceivable distance to the south of our present world system, farther away than three thousand buddhafields, there was a world called Equal. There Manjushri appeared for a period of forty thousand years in the form of a buddha called Foremost of the Naga Race. He brought to maturity seven hundred million beings through the vehicle of the bodhisattvas, eight hundred million beings through the vehicle of the shravakas, and ninety-six billion beings through the vehicle of the pratyekabuddhas. And in due course, after extending the shravaka sangha to an immense degree and bringing benefit to the world of gods and humankind, he passed beyond sorrow. And the scriptures tell us that his relics, increasing in quantity, were transformed into 360 million stupas, and that thanks to the offerings made to them, the Dharma endured for a period of one hundred thousand years.

At the present time, away to the north of the Field of Endurance,[21] which is our world, Manjushri appears as a buddha, the King of the Jeweled Mountain, the Essence of Joyful Aspiration. His universe is called Eternal Aspiration of Beauteous Joy, and there he sets forth the Dharma. His world is a place of happiness, of measureless life and splendor—where they do not even have words for suffering, where misfortunes like sickness and age are unknown, and where there is not even the mention of shravakas and pratyekabuddhas.

As for the future, let us imagine, for example, that the present three-thousandfold universe were reduced to atoms and that each atom represented a quantity of universes equal to the total number of these same atoms. Then if one were to proceed in the eastern direction for a distance equal to the universes represented by the sum of those atoms, and if one were to repeat the same operation in the ten directions, one could say that for a number of kalpas far greater than the number of the atoms of all those universes, Manjushri will enact the deeds of enlightenment.

And at long last [at the end of that immense lapse of time], there will be, in the southerly direction, a supreme pure field called the Utterly and Perfectly Pure Accumulation Free of All Defilement. Qualitatively, it will resemble Sukhavati, even though the latter would be utterly eclipsed thereby—a single drop of water on the tip of a hundredth part of a horsehair as compared with the ocean itself. And there it is that Manjushri will show himself as the perfect Buddha named All-Seeing. His life span will be inconceivable as will also be the life spans of the bodhisattvas in the sangha attending him. Such are the ways in which Manjushri reveals himself in the form of buddhas, past, present, and to come.

Moreover, from the moment that the buddhas and their bodhisattva heirs first generate the mind of enlightenment until they at last attain enlightenment, Manjushri manifests as the foremost of their bodhisattva sons, assisting them in their deeds of enlightenment and in their accomplishment of the path of the transcendent virtues ocean-vast. Furthermore, for beings as many as the immensity of space, he appears in the form of bodhisattvas, shravakas, and pratyekabuddhas, who train beings on the path. He manifests as ordinary human beings, or as birds and other animals—in short, as the diversified nirmanakaya, both animate and inanimate. In so doing, he works for the sake of beings to the very confines of space itself and in accordance with their needs. As we find in the secret tantra of Manjushri,

> I appear in various forms throughout the triple time.
> And in the age when all the Doctrine fails,
> The moment for my teachings to arise will come.
> Inasmuch as beings may be peaceful,
> I shall come in forms of utter peace.
> Inasmuch as beings may be wrathful,
> I shall come in forms of utter wrath.

And as it is said in the *Sutra of the Question of Susthitamati Devaputra*,[22]

> A wicked demon asked, "The sound of the countless myriads of names of the bhagavan buddhas is imperceptible to us, whereas the single name Manjushrikumarabhuta, Manjushri ever youthful, is quite different. When we hear the name Manjushri, we are

filled with terror and dread, thinking that death is upon us." And the Lord replied, "O Evil One! This is because Manjushri-kumarabhuta, Manjushri ever youthful, has brought beings without distinction to maturity and will bring them to maturity. The countless myriads of buddhas do not do this."

Again, in the *Description of the Excellence of Manjushri's Buddha-field*,[23] it is said:

> Compared with reciting the names of a hundred thousand myriad buddhas, to pronounce the name Manjushri-kumarabhuta gives rise to far greater merit. For in every kalpa, Manjushri accomplishes the benefit of beings—a thing that all those buddhas do not do.

These and other things are spoken of at length in the sutras and the tantras. Accordingly, if the tathagatas themselves praise the life story, profound and secret, of Manjushri and laud the illusory display of his enlightened deeds as something that exceeds even their own knowledge, it goes without saying that of all the bodhisattvas residing on the ten grounds and of all the beings in the three worlds, the gods and humans, the yogis, the shravakas and pratyekabuddhas, there is no one able to comprehend the enlightened actions of Manjushri. For in reference to this great lord, it is said in the *Tantra of Praise in the Form of Song*[24] that the wisdom body of all the tathagatas should be recognized as being Manjushri in very truth.

As it was said, therefore, he is never parted from the great non-conceptual wisdom of all the buddhas, the space-like dharmata, whereto nothing can be added and whence nothing can be taken. From this he is permanently inseparable, and therefore at all times he is beyond transition and change.

Nevertheless, the essential meaning of the story of his life— profound and secret as it is but couched in terms suitable to the ordinary perceptions of beings to be trained—is found in the later tantra the *Net of Illusory Manifestations of Manjushri*:[25]

> The body of Manjushri is both glorious and complete.
> His qualities are extraordinary, nondual, and all-pervading.
> Equally, throughout the triple time,
> He is revealed as sire of all the conquerors.
> He shows himself as dharmadhatu, as the Mother,
> As supreme among the bodhisattva children.

As this text reveals, Manjushri is, at first, the very object of the generation of the supreme mind of enlightenment of all the buddhas of the three times and the ten directions—the buddhas who are all the equal of the dharmadhatu. Subsequently, he is their helping friend in the practice of the path of the two accumulations. And finally, when they attain manifest enlightenment, he shows himself as the foremost of the bodhisattva children. He is therefore the one father who begets all the tathagatas.

Furthermore, he sets forth unnumbered ways of entry to the Dharma of the lesser and greater vehicles, in accordance with the character and aspiration of the three families of beings [shravakas, pratyekabuddhas, and bodhisattvas]. For this reason, and because of his boundless activity of bringing relief to beings in the place of enlightenment, he is the embodiment of the perfection of wisdom, the very mother who gives birth to the four kinds of noble beings [shravakas, pratyekabuddhas, bodhisattvas on the path of vision and above, and all the buddhas]. And wherever are established the lamps of the enlightened activities of the buddhas past, present, and to come, Manjushri, Gentle Glory, appears directly, in order to act for the benefit of all beings in the ten directions and in the three times.

He initiates discussions that reveal the subjects of the teachings profound and vast; he asks questions and gives counsel to others; and through his superior knowledge and marvelous way of life, he acts in the manner of the foremost of the buddhas' children. He upholds the treasure house of the Dharma and nurtures all those who remain to be trained. For reasons such as these, he is noble and supreme; he is the great hero, beauteous like the mandala of the full moon in the midst of a host of stars.

As it is said in the *Net of Illusory Manifestations of Manjushri*,

> Of all the buddhas, he is the great mind;
> He rests within the mind of all the buddhas.
> Of all the buddhas, he is the great body.
> Likewise, he is the speech of all the buddhas.

Accordingly, he is the sovereign of the wisdom body of all the buddhas in their infinity. Endowed with the major and minor marks, he is ever youthful, like the new sun in the moment of its rising, free of any trace of aging or decay. Showing himself in youthful form, he is at all times the embodiment of the illusory, space-pervading fabric of appearance and emptiness inseparable. As we find in the text just cited,

> The wisdom body of the Bhagavan,
> The Great Ushnisha, Lord of Words,
> The self-arising wisdom body,
> Manjushri Gentle Glory, wisdom-being.[26]

As the essence of the profound and vast teachings of the tathagatas and bodhisattvas, Manjushri is never sundered from the ineffable melody of Brahma, the union of sound and emptiness, or from the splendor of the infinity of sounds and languages of the animate and inanimate world. He is thus adorned with the names of King of Eloquence and Lion of Speech.

As it is said in the *Principal Realization of Manjushri*,[27]

> Manju, gentle, is the perfect speech of buddhas.
> He is different from the other tathagatas,
> Who therefore cannot know his power.

Likewise their children residing on the grounds,
Beyond this world and ten in number,
And also you, O Lord of gods,
Owing to the differences dividing you from him,
You cannot comprehend this perfect sage.

As the embodiment, free from attachment and impediment, of the twofold wisdom[28] possessed by the ocean of all victorious ones, he shows himself in the manner of the supreme wisdom being, never separate from immaculate wisdom and love.

As it is said in the later *Tantra of Praise in the Form of Song,*

Perfect vajra wisdom, mandala
Of the fabric of illusory display,
Manjushri is the vajra point
Residing neither in samsara nor nirvana.
Whenever one may settle in the ultimate expanse,
Free from any thought, we find him there.

In this way, and likewise in the teaching of the peerless Lion of the Shakyas, the fourth buddha to appear in this present Good Kalpa, Manjushri is praised as the foremost of the bodhisattva children.

In the *Root Tantra of Manjushri*[29] it is said,

Endowed with the wisdom body, at all times free of aging and decay, you range, Manjushri ever youthful, through every buddhafield, past, present, and to come and shed your light therein. And therefore also in the teaching of myself, the king of the Shakyas, you show yourself, Manjushri, as a bodhisattva and the best of humankind—and thus contrive the benefit of beings.

And as it is said in this and other texts, when the Buddha appeared in this world, [Manjushri] requested and upheld the ocean-like pitakas of the teachings of the sutras and the tantras, the essence vast and profound of the Dharma of the supreme vehicle. At the moment of his manifest enlightenment, he assumed the form of Yamantaka, king of wrathful deities, and crushed the race of demons. Through a wondrous display, and through actions skilled in means, all inconceivable, he benefited beings on the three levels of existence. By driving throughout the whole of space the chariot of the enlightened activities of the Conqueror, he is indeed mighty among the bodhisattvas, the children of the Buddha's mind.

Moreover from the time when the Sugata passed into nirvana until the end of this age of strife, Manjushri's activities for the sake of the Doctrine and beings continue and will continue in their unbroken course. Indeed, his blessing and his compassion are now more swift than ever.

> In the period of unbearable destruction,
> When the Doctrine of the Lion of the Shakyas,
> Our Protector, sinks into decline,
> 'Tis then that I will do my work.

And as it has been widely taught in these and other texts, the glorious and noble Lord Nagarjuna, the great charioteer of the Doctrine in the noble land of India, together with most of the other great masters, adornments of our world—Chandrakirti, Shantideva, the great bodhisattva abbot Shantarakshita, the master Manjushrimitra, the great pandita Vimalamitra, and so on—have all manifested as the playful display of the wisdom of Manjushri ever youthful. Guided by him, they have unmistakenly expounded the wisdom of the Conqueror, to the increase and propagation of the Dharma of learning and realization. Moreover in the capital city of Shambhala in the north, Manjushri appeared as the eighth sovereign, Manjushriyashas.[30] He brought together the holders of various yogic disciplines into a single family of the unsurpassed anuttaratantra of the supreme Vajrayana and composed the tantra in five chapters, which condensed the meaning of the root tantra of the primordial Buddha.

In the land of snows, in the time of the dharma king Songtsen Gampo, he appeared as Thonmi Sambhota, the first bilingual translator, then as the omniscient mahaguru Loden Chokse Tsal, then as the sovereign lord Trisong Deutsen, the charioteer of the Doctrine in Tibet, then as the great translator Vairotsanarakshita, and subsequently Nubchen Sangye Yeshe. In later times, he appeared as the fearless mahapandita Rongzom Chözang, then as Jamgön Sakya Pandita Kunga Tenpa'i Gyaltsen, and as the omniscient Longchen Rabjam, powerful and victorious. Later, he appeared as the lord, the great being Lozang Drakpa (Tsongkhapa), as Jamgön Lochen Tenpa'i Nyinche,[31] and so on. Indeed, most of the learned, nonsectarian masters of the old and new traditions—accomplished holders of the Doctrine, guided by the supreme deity (Manjushri), and not one without his empowering blessing—were all acknowledged as emanations of Manjushri, as their individual biographies make clear. And further in the future, it has been intimated in the prophecies of the Kalachakra scriptures that he will take the form of the ferocious Lhamin Tharche (Destroyer of Asuras), the wheel-brandishing Kalki of Shambhala, who will destroy the armies of the barbarians and will propagate the Dharma generally and most especially the teaching of the unsurpassed Vajrayana.

Moreover, all these beings, who are not separate from the wisdom play of the venerable Lord of Knowledge—all of them appearing in the past, present, and future—are acknowledged as emanations of the Guru of Orgyen,[32] the knower of the three times. The Lord Atisha [who was also an emanation of Manjushri] said that from Khenchen Bodhisattva (Shantarakshita) onward, and for as long as the buddhadharma lasts, all khenpos who have appeared and will appear in the vinaya lineage would be one with him in nature. The manifestations of the great bodhisattvas residing on the grounds of realization are indeed inconceivable. As it is said in the *Sublime Continuum*,[33]

> Wherefore in all the water vessels—
> Disciples to be trained—

The sun-like image of the Sugata
Will immediately arise.

Furthermore, the Lord Mipham himself was able, with the clear vision of the wisdom of a superior being, to see directly what was hidden, and he was able to reveal the manner of his previous births. In an earlier existence, he was the master Dothog Thelpa Dorje Gyaltsen, a yogi of the Secret Mantra who became the principal spiritual preceptor of China.

In order to put him to the test, the Chinese enclosed him in a box inside a stupa, which they kept sealed for one year, with no one being allowed to open it. When, after twelve months, they looked inside, they found the master exactly as he was when they left him. He told them that it seemed to him that no more than an instant had passed. The Chinese emperor and all his court immediately had faith in the yogi and showered him with honors. Consequently, when the master returned to Tibet, he was able to give great assistance to the yogis living there. Jamgön Jamyang Khyentse Wangpo himself said to Mipham Rinpoche that, thanks to his own clear-sighted wisdom, he too had seen that the yogi had indeed been one of Mipham's previous incarnations and that, at that time, he had explained to others the five texts of Maitreya one hundred times.

Moreover, when the all-seeing Khyentse Wangpo was Rigdzin Jigme Lingpa, Mipham was Tsangtö Chöje Trapukpa, a scholar highly accomplished in the tenet systems of both the sutras and the tantras but especially in the field of logic and epistemology. It is said that after hearing that the omniscient Jigme Lingpa's knowledge had simply burst forth without his needing to study, Tsangtö Chöje went to meet him in Chaksam Labrang at Palchen Chuwori, intending to test him and defeat him in debate. He became convinced, however, that Jigme Lingpa was completely free of ignorance and a master of immense stature in both learning and accomplishment. He became the greatest of his heart sons, and it was actually he who requested the composition of the *Treasury of Precious Qualities*[34] and who acted as the scribe for its great autocommentary *The Two Chariots*.[35] Furthermore, he hoisted the victory banner of practice for three years [in retreat] at the hermitage of Tsering Jong. He excelled in the three kinds of service pleasing to his master, and finally the minds of master and disciple mingled together. It was thanks to this auspicious connection that, in the present age, the two great lamas appeared again in the relationship of master and disciple. Jamgön Khyentse said repeatedly that Mipham's prowess in logic and epistemology had arisen through the power of habitual tendencies forged in the past.

Once, when the Lord Ajita, Mipham Rinpoche, was building a new hermitage at Karmo Taktsang, he pointed to the window for the skylight that he had just made with his own hands and remarked jokingly to Lama Ösel Rinpoche, his attendant, that, previously in India, he had been an extremely skillful carpenter, on account of which such tasks came easily to him.

Thanks to his clear vision born of wisdom free from obscuration, Mipham Rinpoche knew many of his wondrous preexistences. But because he constantly concealed such things and kept them secret, there exists no sure record of what he said about his previous lives. In this life in particular, through his unrivaled knowledge and astonishing intellectual prowess and assurance, he nurtured the precious Doctrine of the Conqueror through teaching, debate, and composition, and through elucidation, spiritual practice, and activities. Through the greatness of his genuine qualities of elimination and realization, such as his scholarly discernment, experiences, realizations, and perfect action, he was in no way different from the great charioteers of India. He wonderfully adorned this world of ours and even the realms of the gods. It is thus that, on the basis of the valid knowledge of direct perception, we know with certainty the causes that made him a noble and sublime bodhisattva. In this life, his qualities of elimination and realization were immaculate—and this is something I find even more amazing than the record of his many hundreds of incarnations in times gone by.

2

THE BIRTH OF A BODHISATTVA

Mipham Rinpoche had, from the very first, severed the tendrils of
the root of samsaric existence. Nevertheless, impelled by the aspirations he made and the bodhichitta he generated while on the
path of learning, the display of his emanations remains without
interruption for as long as space exists. This is the intrinsic nature
of the bodhisattvas, the offspring of the Conqueror.

This great being accordingly took birth in Dokham, the region
of four rivers and six ranges, in Drida Zalmo Gang—that is to say,
on the bank of the river Drida, which flows gently down from the
Zalmo range of mountains to the north of the great royal capital of
Derge. There, in the heart of a nomadic territory shaped like a jewel
of good fortune, there lies the beautiful and prosperous valley of
Ju, so named because it was the place where the race of the gods of
clear light came down to earth on a celestial rope (*'jus*). Successive
generations of learned and accomplished masters were born there,
all adorned with the qualities of the seed of their divine forefathers.

Among them, for example, was Pema Sangak Tendzin, who was
guided by the Lion-Faced Dakini, the mighty subduer of demons,
and who reached the kingdom of the accomplishment of union [of
awareness and emptiness]. There was also Pema Chöying Dorje, a
disciple of Machik Labdrön and a holder of the transmission of
Severance, the profound path that vanquishes the maras. There
were also numerous powerful practitioners of Mantra. Four were
like the pillars of the doctrine of the vajra essence of the Great
Secret; eight were like the adamantine beams of the celestial palace of the Great Vehicle; and twenty-four were like the lesser roof

beams: powerful yogis who displayed all the signs of having completed the profound path.

In that region of 'Ju, blessed as it was by successive generations of such masters, lay the district of Chukham, home to the clan of Achak Dru (one of the six main tribal groups in Tibet). One of its members had been the chief minister to Wang the Mongol khan and subsequently became a subject of King Tenpa Tsering, protector of the Dharma. He achieved certainty in the generation and perfection stages of several yidam deities. To that clan also belonged generations of tantrik yogis who acquired amazing skill and power in [the practice of] wrathful mantras. There were thirteen families of mantrikas on whose black yak-hair tents were emblazoned the symbols of the protector deities, a sign that they had subjugated and pressed into service the eight classes of spirits. As such they were an object of terror for all their enemies, and many of their descendants were endowed with strength and bravery.

One of these yogis was Anye Kali, Mipham Rinpoche's paternal uncle. He possessed an abundance of temporal and spiritual talents. He was a manifestly accomplished master of the glorious wisdom protector Ganapati and had such power that whenever people were touched by the light reflected from the mirror that he wore over his heart, they would fall senseless to the ground. Later, when Anye Kali died, his half brother, Anye Sangak, went to Kathok and made his way to the dwelling place of Drungchen Rinpoche, who was at that time in retreat, his door sealed with mud. There he made an offering of the experiences and realization that had arisen in his mind. Drungchen Rinpoche was extremely pleased by this. He exclaimed how happy he was that a truly hidden yogi of the caliber of Anye Sangak had arrived, and he agreed to see him. Anye Sangak offered to Drungchen Rinpoche the fragments of Anye Kali's bones and said that, during his life, his half brother had performed, among other things, many red rituals.[36] This being so, he asked Drungchen Rinpoche to think of him and bless his bones by blowing on them. Drungchen Rinpoche replied, "There is no need to guide the consciousness either for him or for me. In the past, when Guru Rinpoche granted us the empowerment of the most secret wrathful deity, both Anye Kali and I drank from the same nectar."

Once, when Anye Sangak was on his travels, he came upon some children playing. One of them, a boy, small and naked, stared up at him. He ran toward him and, placing Anye's foot on his head, cried out again and again, praying, "May I become just like you!" Ju Lama Anye Sangak looked down at him from his horse and said, "Well, I think it would be difficult for you to be quite like me, but if you work hard at your studies and training, it is certain that you will become an excellent person!" And with these words, he continued on his way. This was clearly a word of prophecy, for the child grew up to become a learned and accomplished monk by the name of Mang-ge Dorje Chang. These stories show that Anye Sangak was indeed a hidden vidyadhara and a mighty siddha.

Another master from that sacred region was Ju Lama Pema Dode. When he went on pilgrimage to Lhasa, he found that an outbreak of black pox had broken out in the province of Ü. The population of the country had almost been destroyed, when suddenly a woman's voice was heard resounding powerfully from the roof of the Potala palace, proclaiming that if the Khampa by name of Pema Dode were to distribute a remedy, it would be of great benefit. A search was organized and the lama was found. A medicine was prepared and distributed throughout the province, and the epidemic was arrested. From that moment on, apart from those whose life span and karma were exhausted, all who took the medicine were saved from death. Such were the great qualities of Pema Dode. As Mipham Rinpoche himself said,

> Another of the line of gods of clear light
> Was the supreme siddha Pema Dode,
> Gunanatha's peerless emanation.
> The wisdom form of hero Vajrapani
> Directly blessed this hidden yogi.
> The wisdom dakinis, the guardians of

Tsaritra and other sacred lands,
Predicted him in various declarations.
The deities of five and twenty mandalas
Have manifestly blessed him.
Within the nectar mandala,
The self-experience of awareness,
Everything he saw he could empower as remedies.
He dispelled the ills, the karmic fruits, of wandering beings.
All links with him were meaningful.
The proud and haughty spirits were his servants.

Mipham Rinpoche was thus the nephew of the previously mentioned Anye Kali, the hidden yogi who attained the level of vidyadhara with power over life. Mipham's father, Ju Gonpo Dargye, was a man of perfect disposition. He was kind and possessed all the qualities of a person belonging to the family of bodhisattvas. Mipham's mother was Singchung. Her father was foremost among the minor chiefs of Getse, an outlying district of Derge, and it was through her that Mipham belonged to the clan of Mukpo Dong, renowned for its power, courage, wealth, religious virtues, and the respect in which it was universally held. Perceiving these five favorable conditions, the lord Mipham freely chose to take birth in this family in the fire male horse year, which was the *parabhava*, or fortieth year, of the fourteenth *rabjung* (1846). He was born in the morning of the day in which the Ambrosial Drop [the moon] was in the mansion of *purvashaddha* and in a place called Chuiding Chung, an area watched over by the great *genyen* spirit Dagyal Dorje Phenchuk, a regional protector obedient to Guru Rinpoche.

These then were the circumstances of the birth of Mipham Rinpoche, who was himself, like the rising sun, adorned with marvelous marks and signs. Like a lotus afloat upon a great ocean, he was brought up and cared for according to the customs of his country. His paternal uncle, Wön Lama Drupchok Pema Dargye, crowned him with the name Mipham Gyatso (Unvanquished Ocean) just at the moment when a wonderful horse, a *Kyang*, was born.[37] Later, when his father's property was being divided into two portions, Mipham Rinpoche declared that the horse was his and that it should remain part of his inheritance and was not to be removed from it.

From his early childhood, all the youthful vigor of the excellent qualities of the family of the Great Vehicle ripened powerfully in him. For as the Regent Maitreya has said,

> Compassion, aspiration, patience,
> Conduct excellently virtuous—
> To have these qualities before they have been taught
> Reveals that one is of the lineage.

Indeed, Mipham Rinpoche possessed quite naturally an incomparable intelligence, and among many other qualities, he had faith, compassion, and a determination to leave samsara. He took the greatest delight in anything to do with the monastic life and with the study of texts. Whenever his family was traveling, he would sit in a box made of hide and, taking a stick in his hand, he would swirl and brandish it like Manjushri's sword. Quite beyond the way of ordinary children, he had no thought other than that of his yidam deity, Manjushri in peaceful and wrathful form, and of Gesar his protector.

Until all his first teeth were grown,[38] he possessed a clear, unforgetting memory [of his previous life]. Around the age of six or seven, he committed to memory the root text of the *Ascertainment of the Three Vows*[39] and received a detailed explanation of it from the venerable master Lama Drakpa Gyaltsen, a bodhisattva and the very embodiment of the three trainings.

After studying with his uncle and a Mongolian geshe the preliminaries of the black astrological tradition,[40] he acquired a comprehensive understanding of the entire subject. By the time he was ten years old, he was able to read and write fluently and had even composed some texts, which he wrote on slate tablets.

It was about that time, moreover, that the region of 'Ju was threatened by an army of about one thousand brigands. The [ten-year-old] Mipham had such doughty courage that without the slightest fear, he took his bow and arrow and marched straight into the middle of the horde. And such was his skill that at a distance of eighty paces, he was able to shatter a fragment of goat dung stuck on the tip of a needle!

Judicious in his judgments and true of heart, he became the object of universal praise. People used to say that, had he decided to found a family, he would have reached the summit of worldly positions.

3

Entering the Dharma

Following the general custom of the country, when Mipham Rinpoche reached the age of twelve, he entered Ju Mohor Sangak Shedrup Chöling, a branch monastery of the glorious Shechen Tennyi Dargye Ling. The latter was located in the great sacred place of Rangjung Sangwa'i Dorje (actually the pure field of Devikhota) and followed the dharma lineage of Ogmin Orgyen Mindroling, the source and wellspring of the most secret teachings. Mipham's monastery, where he lived as an ordinary monk, boasted an unbroken line of realized and accomplished masters. Those were indeed the days of sublime masters who never deviated from the constant practice of pure monastic conduct. It was as we find in the *Garland of Lives*,[41]

> Like light that follows on the heel of dawn,
> He followed in the footsteps of their perfect conduct.

From his earliest years, Mipham would reflect that if he were to squander a single day in meaningless activity, the little that had entered his understanding would be lost. This weighed heavily on his mind, and it was constantly in his thoughts that if only he were to meet a learned master, he would give himself utterly to study and reflection. And it was in such a fervent state of mind that, at the age of fifteen, he made his way to Dzogchen Monastery, in the company of a large contingent of his fellow countrymen.

They were granted an audience with Mingyur Namkha'i Dorje, the fourth Dzogchen Rinpoche, a powerfully accomplished master who had a complete realization of the four visions.[42] Most of the people in Mipham's party did no more than ask the lama for predictions about how long they would live and so on. After he had finished giving his replies, the master turned to Mipham, who till then had been silent.

"You," he said, "should complete the approach and accomplishment phases of the practice of the supreme wrathful deity, the main figure in the cycle of the *Gathering of Glorious Ones*.[43] The three worlds will be brought beneath your power, and you will subdue the three levels of existence. Your life will be a mixture of comfort and pain, and you will live for eighty years." He made many predictions in the same vein. As it turned out—his presence being needed elsewhere—Mipham did not live out his predicted life span. But the other prophecies of Dzogchen Rinpoche, who had an unobstructed vision of the three times, did indeed come to pass.

About that time, the king of Dharma and great emanated treasure discoverer Chokgyur Dechen Lingpa opened the door to a sacred land at Ziltrom.[44] And it happened that Mipham Rinpoche was making a circumambulation of the upper part of this place when he experienced a rain of *arura*, the best of medicines, and was able to fill the fold of his robe with it.

Nevertheless, it proved impossible for him to receive teachings and to study in that place and at that time. He consequently made his way to Meshö where he met a certain Lama Pema, who was from his own native region and was actually a disciple of Gyalse Shenphen Thaye. The lama gave him a letter for the omniscient master Khyentse Wangpo, who at that moment was living at Terlung, in the house of his father. When Mipham Rinpoche met him, he offered him the letter from Lama Pema and requested the ritual blessing for the sadhana called *Praise of Manjushri*[45] and the permission ritual for the practice of Manjushri, Lion of Speech,[46] together with some instructions on the Svarodaya.[47]

"For the Manjushri permission ritual," Khyentse Rinpoche replied, "you will need to stay for a few days. As for the Svarodaya, although I studied it when I was young, I have now forgotten it.

Generally speaking, when one accomplishes the supreme yidam deity, one acquires an extraordinary intellectual capacity. Without such accomplishment, how can one understand by hearing about things from someone else?"[48] With these words, he went on to bestow the permission to practice.

On his way home, Mipham visited Palpung Thubten Chökhor Ling, the great monastic center and one of the sources for the study of logic in the snowy land. There he met for the first time the great bodhisattva Khenpo Karma Tashi Özer. They immediately became fast friends, as close as father and son, and the khenpo predicted that in the future his mind and the mind of Mipham Rinpoche would mingle into one. From the great treasure of compassion Palpung Wöntrul, he received a detailed explanation of the four glorious medical tantras, the meaning of which he completely assimilated. From Khenchen Mangala (Karma Tashi Özer), Mipham borrowed an old, incomplete volume of the root text of the Svarodaya, which the khenchen had received from Jamgön Kongtrul Rinpoche himself. There was no one who could explain it to him, but he said that after praying repeatedly to Manjushri, he needed only to read the text to gain a full understanding of its words and meaning—and not only of the text itself but also of the pith instructions and the secret sealed teachings of the oral transmission lineage. In later life, Mipham Rinpoche was to compose a commentary on this very text.[49]

Returning to his homeland of Ju-Nyung, he took up residence in the hermitage of Chime Chokdrup Ling. There he spent sixteen months in retreat practicing the approach and accomplishment phases of the sadhana of Manjushri, Lion of Speech, enhanced with the preparation of consecrated pills. This practice belongs to the lineage, and is based on the oral instructions, of Dampa Sangye, the guide of supreme adepts. Many signs, common and particular, of ordinary and extraordinary accomplishment manifested.[50] Most especially, Mipham Rinpoche had a direct vision of Vajratikshna,[51] the treasure of intelligence and wisdom deity of all the conquerors. A ray of light shone from the deity's heart and

The hermitage of Chime Chokdrup Ling at Junyung. It was here that, in his late teens, Mipham had the vision of Manjushri that unleashed the power of his intelligence. Photo by Matthieu Ricard, used with permission.

melted into him, and from that moment onward, through a simple reading of the major or minor texts, of the sutras, tantras, or the various sciences, he was able to assimilate their contents with an overwhelming sun-like brilliance. He used to say that because he was unhindered in the three actions of exposition, debate, and composition, there was never any need for him to labor in studying and learning from other masters, and that this was thanks to the kindness of Manjushri.

When Mipham Rinpoche was seventeen, the nomads from the northern reaches, harassed by their enemies from Nyarong, fled to Golok. Mipham Rinpoche went there also and became famous for his expert mastery of astrological calculations. In his eighteenth year, he was accompanied by Gyurzang, his maternal uncle, on a pilgrimage to the central provinces of Ü and Tsang, the field of perfect thought and deed. There he spent a month at the great monastic center of Drok Riwo Ganden and visited widely the holy places in the south of Tibet. In particular, he went to Lhodrak Karchu, the most important of the great places blessed by Rangjung Pema Gyalpo, the self-arisen Lotus King (Guru Rinpoche). There his ordinary perceptions dissolved into the ultimate expanse, and all that he saw or did was experienced as the union of bliss and emptiness. And for several days, his body was filled with an intense sensation of warmth and bliss. Later, when speaking about that time and place, he would say to his assistant that his experience was certainly due to the blessing power of the region.

4

STUDY AND REFLECTION

It is said in the noble sutra *Source of the Three Jewels*,[52]

> Even if bodhisattvas have no desire to depend upon others, even if they have no desire to seek guidance from others, and even if they have no particular wish to gaze upon the faces of others, yet in order to enter the dharmadhatu, they must rely upon their virtuous friends and masters; they must understand them; they must reverence them with honor. To hear the teachings so profound, they must have a perfect attitude of inquiry.

So it was that, on returning from the Lhasa provinces, Mipham Rinpoche visited the vajradhara Lap Kyabgön, Wangchen Gargyi Wangchuk Gyerab Dorje,[53] who granted him the ritual permission to practice the venerable White Manjushri of the tradition of Pandita Mati, together with the reading transmission and practice instructions for the *Peerless Rain of Blessings*, a sadhana composed by Lap Kyabgön himself, as well as the entrustment of the life force of Sengchen Dorje Tsegyal according to the pure vision teachings of Lharik Dechen Rölpa'i Tsel.[54] Mipham later became a disciple of Lab Kyabgön's supreme spiritual son, the venerable Loter Wangpo, who cared for him with unusual tenderness and on one occasion made the following prediction: "Of the four of my disciples who bear the name Manjushri, you (Mipham) will be the most eminent. And if in later life you have the occasion to go to China, you will bring inconceivable benefit to beings, in terms of material wealth and of the Dharma itself."

It was at Loter Wangpo's hermitage, Pema Sangak Dechen Gakyil, that Mipham completed the approach and accomplishment phases of the practice of White Manjushri and of the most secret practice of Hayagriva. Following the empowerment and approach phase of Manjushri, he exhibited the sign of accomplishment as described in the sadhana, namely, the "bean-sprout test."[55] There were indeed many auspicious indications of his extraordinary connections with this practice. From that moment on, moreover, he propitiated as his chief protector Sengchen (Gesar), the king of warrior spirits,[56] and he composed many marvelous teachings, profound and vast, related to him.

From Jigme Chökyi Wangpo (Patrul Rinpoche), the very embodiment of Avalokita, noble and supreme, he received for a period of five days an oral explanation of the "Wisdom Chapter" of the *Way of the Bodhisattva*.[57] He completely assimilated all the profound and crucial points of the words and meaning, and he himself composed a marvelous commentarial exposition that nakedly reveals the profound and crucial points of the view and meditation of the teachings of the Vajra Essence of the Old Translation school.[58] He also received teachings on the texts to be read in the course of funeral ceremonies, together with the *Litany of Manjushri's Names*[59] and other texts.

Most especially, Mipham Rinpoche attended, with the three kinds of pleasing service,[60] the omniscient Jamyang Khyentse Wangpo, who was Manjushri in person and the charioteer of the entire Doctrine. The latter began by introducing Mipham to the practice of White Manjushri according to the tradition of Pandita Mati, and subsequently explained to him the many aspects of the common and uncommon teachings of earlier and more recent times. In particular, he bestowed on him various cycles of teaching from his secret treasury of the seven great transmissions[61]—for example, the *Adornment of the Middle Way*[62] received in a direct lineage from Shantarakshita, the two *Differentiations* of the regent

Maitreya,[63] the commentary on the root tantra of the *Net of Illusory Manifestations of Manjushri* by the great pandita Vimalamitra, the *Garland of Views*[64] by the master Padmasambhava, and so on. All these texts are like the life force of the Doctrine and yet their transmission lineage had become rare. Of the profound and secret tantras, their commentaries (the explanatory tantras), and the pith instructions of the Vajrayana of the Old and New Translation schools, Jamyang Khyentse Wangpo impartially bestowed the empowerments and guiding instructions that bring disciples to maturity and freedom, together with the reading transmissions and explanations, which act as their support. He bestowed on Mipham the pith instructions and the most crucial teachings for their implementation. With the greatest satisfaction, he granted him all the sublime teachings of his heart, profound and vast, as though he were filling a vessel to its very brim, leaving nothing aside. And in the midst of the supreme disciples that, like a starry constellation, thronged about Jamyang Khyentse Wangpo, Mipham was like the disk of the moon robed in the brilliance of its fullness. The master heaped upon his disciple words of uncommon praise and nurtured him at all times with deep affection. The vast expanse of their minds became inseparable.

From Jamgön Kongtrul Lodrö Thaye, a master whom the Buddha foretold as one who would bring together all the profound and secret teachings, Mipham Rinpoche received the transmission of various texts of the outer sciences: texts on language such as the *Grammar* of Chandragomin,[65] together with the great commentary on it by Situ Panchen, as well as the text of instructions for purifying mercury.[66] He received several transmissions of the New Translation schools, such as the great empowerment of the glorious and sacred primordial Buddha Kalachakra according to the Jonang tradition. Likewise, he received limitless extraordinary transmissions of teachings—maturing empowerments and liberating instructions—exemplified by the many profound teachings of the Nyingma school, such as the *Iron Scorpion* and the *Surrogate Iron Scorpion*, both practices of Manjushri, Lord of Life, and all nine volumes of the *Union of the Sugatas, the Eight-Mandala Cycle*, a treasure text of the master of Nyang.[67]

From Radha'i Lama, the vajra holder Tenzin Wangpo of the monastery of Gatö Benchen, he received maturing instructions relating to the profound path of the Six Yogas of Naropa together with the instructions for the yogic exercises.

From Shechen Rabjam Gyurme Kunzang Tenpa'i Nyima,[68] he received the short and extensive empowerments of the longevity practice of Ratnalingpa, the *Gathering of Secrets*.[69]

From Phenkhang Khen Rinpoche, Pelden Lodrö Gyaltsen, he received all the empowerments and transmissions relating to the nine deities of Vajrabhairava from the Sakya tradition.

From Dzogchen Khenpo Pema Benzar, he received numerous teachings, including an explanation of the root tantra of the *Net of Illusory Manifestations*.[70]

Gyarong Namtrul Kunzang Thekchok Dorje offered him the reading transmission of the several texts of the cycle called the Smelted Ore of Yamantaka.[71]

The great master Kilung Togden Tenpa'i Gyaltsen granted him the empowerment and instructions related to the Great Perfection text *Highest Wisdom*.[72]

From Lama Tampa Pelden, he received the reading transmission of the entire Kangyur, the precious translated word of the Conqueror, and from Seshul Geshe Lharampa, he received the *Treasury of Abhidharma*.[73]

From Lama Pema, he received the five texts of the Regent Maitreya, and from Loter Wangpo, the vajradhara of the Ngor tradition, he received the *Treasure of Valid Cognition*.[74]

The above is just an example of the teachings that Mipham Rinpoche received from many masters who were free of sectarian bias. He also studied the *Collected Tantras of the Nyingma School*;[75] the orally transmitted teachings, the concealed treasure teachings, and those transmitted in pure visions;[76] the *Scripture of Summarized Wisdom*, the *Net of Illusory Manifestations*, and the *Mind Teachings*;[77] the Heart-Essence teachings both ancient and new,[78] the earlier and the later collections of spiritual treasure teachings. He received so many other teachings that it was as if he had traversed the entire ocean of the Doctrine. Since we do not have the complete list of all the teachings belonging to the Old and New Translation schools that Mipham Rinpoche received and studied, it is impossible to record them here with certainty. Moreover, this is not just a case of producing a list of texts requested and received. As Panglo Lodrö Tenpa said,

> He studied all the texts in lives gone by.
> To understand them now was just an incidental game.

To be sure, throughout his previous lives beyond count, his most pure eyes of Dharma had gazed upon primordial wisdom free from stain and were made more lovely through the glory of an infallible memory and a perfect assurance and prowess through which he had assimilated the oceanic vastness of supreme and holy teaching, thereby attaining the eight great treasures of undaunted assurance. As we find in the *Vast Display*:[79]

> The treasure of an unforgetting memory; the treasure of intelligence, that is, an intelligence fully developed; the treasure of understanding through the assimilation of the sense of all the sutras; the treasure of dharani, the retention of all that has been heard; the treasure of assurance and prowess, the fact of satisfying all beings by dint of perfect explanation; the treasure of Dharma that comes through perfectly upholding the sacred Doctrine; the treasure of bodhichitta through not severing the lineage of the Three Jewels; the treasure of accomplishment through being able to accept the teaching on unborn [emptiness]. All these eight treasures were obtained.

Accordingly, it was only by way of an exemplar and in accordance with the common perceptions and capacities of the ordinary beings whom he had accepted as his disciples that Mipham Rinpoche constantly received teachings and guidance from the masters previously mentioned and from those who will be named later. But from the very beginning, he himself had absolutely no need to study and train in any of the texts of scripture and commentary, and his perfect grasp of their meaning was evident to everyone. So, for instance, on the basis of a single hearing of the reading transmission of the *Abridged Prajnaparamita* given by the incomparable master Juwön Jigme Dorje, Mipham delivered an explanation of the same text that lasted at least a month. And when he received the *Introduction to the Middle Way*[80] from Bumsar Geshe Ngawang Jungne, Mipham said to him that, apart from giving a reading transmission with an explanation, there was no need for the master to tire himself with a detailed commentary. When the geshe had given it, he asked for a demonstration of Mipham's understanding. The latter explained the entire text from start to finish in such a way that the geshe exclaimed, "I am the one with the title of geshe, but I have not even a fragment of the intelligence of this master!" He expressed his amazement in front of everyone and repeatedly scattered over Mipham the flowers of his praise.

Mipham Rinpoche merely listened to the reading transmission of the *Adornment of the Middle Way* and the two *Differentiations* given by the omniscient Manjughosha [Jamyang Khyentse Wangpo] and he then immediately expounded the profound and crucial points of the extraordinary sense and meaning of those texts, revealing in their naked truth all [the aspects] of the scripture and arguments of the view of the Great Madhyamaka of the supreme vehicle. Without the slightest impediment, he composed great commentaries, beautifully expressed, which rooted out from their very depths the darkness of false opinions. His great and fearless lion's roar of scripture and reasoning resounded in the midst of countless masters of logic of the highest caliber, so that they expressed, one and all, their complete astonishment. "He is," they said, "a sovereign of intellectual discernment. It is as if the supreme charioteers of India had once again appeared in our world!" And in the sight of everyone, these masters bowed to him with repeated and sincere praise.

While Mipham was at Dzongsar Tashi Lhatse, he chiefly read the works of Jamyang Khyentse Wangpo—together with the scriptures, their commentaries, the tantras, pith instructions, and so on. And when he reviewed the crucial points of numerous doxographical textbooks composed by other authors of India and also of the old and new schools of Tibet, the acuity, speed, and profundity of his intellectual acumen, both inborn and acquired, was utterly unrivaled, thanks to his mastery of the four perfect knowledges.[81] It was unnecessary for him to read all these texts in detail. It was enough for him simply to scan three or four sentences at the beginning, middle, and end. By such means, he was able to review at least nine volumes a day, declaring that he had assimilated without error or confusion all the crucial points of their words and meanings. It was thus that he reviewed the old and new editions of the Kangyur seven times. He said that when he had read just once the root sutra of the Vinaya, he found it slightly difficult to understand, but that by the time he had finished all thirteen volumes of the Vinaya, there was not a single word that he did not understand.

Once when Mipham Rinpoche was suffering from an illness that resulted in a blockage in his throat, he went to make circumambulations around the protector temple at the monastery of Dzing Namgyal. When he was cured, he borrowed twelve volumes of the Tengyur from the same monastery for his own consultation; and having perused them for three days, he returned them. Now his attendant, Lama Rigchog, was present and asked him if he had managed to assimilate them all—to which Mipham openly replied that while he had not memorized every word, he had nevertheless understood their meaning.

In particular, he held in his mind the meaning of the words of the entire *Collected Tantras of the Nyingma School*. In the course of a single month, he would always recite the entire collection from memory as if it were a prayer. He used to say that when he was making citations from the tantras, he did not need to search through the texts, for he knew precisely in which volume each verse was located. Thanks to his unfailing memory and his immaculate eyes of Dharma, free of obstruction and attachment,[82] he had a manifest knowledge of an incalculable infinity of teachings, the profound meaning of which he understood perfectly.

The Buddha said,

> The bhikshus or the scholars both
> Should test and scrutinize my word
> Like gold that's smelted, cut, refined
> And not assent to it through piety.

So it was that, boarding the ship of an astonishing critical discernment, Mipham set sail upon the great ocean of the sacred teachings—the pitakas of the greater and lesser vehicles of the Mighty Sage and the outer and inner tantras of the Mantrayana, together with the wisdom commentaries of the numerous accomplished scholars of both India and Tibet. He repeatedly examined the views and philosophical assertions of his own and other schools, assessing the crucial points of their profound wisdom, whether specific to themselves or held in common. With the certainty of valid knowledge based on scripture and reasoning, he investigated without confusion every faulty assertion arising from mistaken ideas or simply from a lack of understanding. Taking whatever did not contradict the wisdom intention of the Tathagata and constituted the stainless view and meditation of the authentic path, pleasing to the Conqueror, he distilled the essential richness of these precious and immaculate jewels. He accurately explained their crucial points profound and vast, and offered them as a heritage to those of his virtuous disciples who were fortunate to be blessed with the same analytical acumen. As he himself recorded,[83]

> In my young days, there were many excellent masters
> of both the old and new traditions. But apart from
> receiving the "Wisdom Chapter" of the *Way of the*

Bodhisattva from Patrul Rinpoche, who was foremost among learned bodhisattvas, I did not study very much. Instead, it was through the kindness of my teacher and my supreme yidam deity that later on, without the need for much toil, an understanding of the difficult points of the Doctrine naturally arose in my mind simply through a reading of the texts. When I was studying, I found that the books of the new schools were easy to understand, whereas the texts of the Old Translation school were more difficult. I thought, however, that this was only because of my incapacity, and I always nourished an attitude of thinking that great things were to be discovered in the profound texts of the vidyadhara lineage. I did not doubt it for a single instant, and it was thanks to this auspicious ci.cumstance that my understanding was able to ripen fully. When in later years I examined these texts, I was able to see that the complete range of the profound and crucial points of doctrine is to be found only in the doctrinal tradition deriving from the precious lineage of the old translations. And thanks to this, I reached a state of supreme certainty.

It was at that time, moreover, that my refuge lord, the vajradhara Khyentse Rinpoche, commanded me to compose textbooks for our own tradition. Therefore, in obedience to my teacher's wish, and as a way to train my own intelligence, I composed some texts on the cycles of sutra teachings, holding within my heart only the precious doctrine of the Conqueror. Nevertheless, because I stressed the assertions of the tradition to which I belong, slightly distinguishing it from other tenet systems, it was understood by [the upholders of] those same systems that I was refuting them. And in due course, a great many letters of refutation and debate arrived here from all directions. In truth, however, my writing was motivated simply by the desire to fulfill the wishes of my teacher and by the fact that, nowadays, the doctrine of the Nyingmapas has dwindled to no more than the painting of a butter lamp. Most of its adherents imitate the traditions of others, and rare indeed are those who even wonder about the key points of the teaching of their own school, or engage in intelligent reflection and ask what the position of its learned masters might be. And it was in view of this that I composed my texts, hoping to be of some small assistance. I never even dreamed of showing hostility toward the traditions of others or expressing partial attachment to my own. On that score, if those who possess the eye of wisdom now look on me directly, I have certainly nothing to be ashamed about. On the other hand, with regard to what I have written in reply to objections, I myself have not attained the status of a noble being and for this reason, it is as the saying goes, "Intellectual knowledge is contingent and thus indefinite. There is no certitude; the relative is wearisome." How therefore can I have an understanding of all the profound things that are to be known? And yet if even a person like me relies on what is tenable or otherwise according to the spotless teachings of the Sugata and the commentaries, the illuminating words of the great charioteers of India and Tibet, and if, as I say, someone like me examines and declares what is reasonable or otherwise, then it may happen that some slight benefit might incidentally accrue—even though of course there is no question of my actually being of positive help to others. If, on the other hand, through a failure to understand, or simply through my own mistakes, I misrepresent the scriptures and their profound commentaries, I would be closing the door to my own liberation and would be leading many others to the same fate, thereby contriving their permanent ruin. What greater fault could there be? Therefore, if I am refuted by

STUDY AND REFLECTION — 43

someone who possesses the eyes of Dharma, with perfect arguments based on scripture and reasoning, this
would indeed be like a medicine. It would be something
on which to rely, not something against which to retal-
iate with anger and attachment. With this sincerity of
mind, I have therefore indulged a little in disputation.

It was in this spirit, and with such candor and intellectual
confidence, that Mipham Rinpoche would speak to Gyaltsap
Rinpoche,[84] lord of Dharma, and other leading scholars of great
intelligence.

For innumerable lives in the past, Mipham had developed treasures of unforgetting memory and intellectual assurance, a prowess
as deep as the ocean and as vast as the sky. He had assimilated
and realized correctly the entire meaning of infinite teachings in
infinite buddhafields. He was a mighty treasure keeper of the profound secret of all the buddhas. It was said in reference to him,

> Thus from the vast expanses of awareness-emptiness,
> He opened wide the doors of eight great hidden treasures.[85]
> Learned in the supreme skillful means of
> Mantra, he who from the brave Manjushri's heart had been
> Well born, was by the Victor utterly empowered.
> *Éma!* By deeds through countless ages well performed
> And pleasing to the Conqueror,
> His supreme mind was ripened and replete
> With eight profound great treasures.
> Found nowhere but within himself,
> He had the strength to hold them.
> Whoever has the wisdom to rely on him
> Will enter through the door, so it is said,
> Of the wish-fulfilling treasure vast as space:
> The perfect qualities of the victorious ones.
> On such a person will the buddhas
> And their bodhisattva heirs bestow the key.

So it was that Mipham Rinpoche's intelligence and intellectual acumen were not different from those of the supreme ornaments that embellish the world, and of the eight accomplished vidyadharas—the great charioteers of the sutras and the tantras. He was able to clarify profound and subtle points of doctrine that lie beyond the grasp of anyone who is not on the level of noble beings.[86] As he himself said,

> The time and place are both inferior,
> And yet I have elucidated deep and subtle points
> Contained within the spotless words of the great charioteers,
> Not spoiling them with false distortions and opinions.[87]

Regarding the texts of the orally transmitted teachings, the treasure teachings, and the pith instructions, Mipham Rinpoche radiated a wonderful light of wisdom endowed with the four reliances, in a manner as all-embracing as space itself. According to his own profound understanding, he expressed the sublime meaning of the Victorious One and of the lineage of vidyadharas in several extraordinary and immaculate commentaries—tools for scholars of intelligence and superior discernment and a service to the teaching of the Conqueror. These texts were renowned not simply as the eloquent explanations of a scholar, the mere imitation and repetition of what had been said by others in the past. For Mipham grasped the perfect wisdom of the Conqueror, exactly as it is and without distortion, and expounded it correctly as he himself had realized it. He declared,

> Whoever may correctly enter
> The tradition that accomplishes as one
> The teachings of the two great charioteers
> Will reach the kingdom of the Dharma of the perfect Mahayana.
>
> If I were to repeat what others have affirmed,
> Accepting and rejecting as the case may be,

Indeed, I would win favor with the holders of such views.
Instead I ask all those who take exception to be patient
With this candid explanation of the Charioteer's perfect
text.[88]

These commentaries are by no means just superficial explanations of words that fail to penetrate the essence. For Mipham was able to reveal clearly and extensively all the secret key points crucial to the understanding of the profound and ultimate meaning of the teachings—as if he were placing something directly in the palm of your hand. Because he was settled in his own Nyingma tradition of the Old Translations as set forth by the omniscient masters Rongzom and Longchenpa, he was able to expound clearly the vast expanse of the wisdom of its specific doctrines without making the mistake of getting into disputatious controversy. The words and meanings of his writings are never unclear through falling into the extreme of excessive brevity. On the contrary, for those who had eyes to see, he illuminated, as though by the light of the sun, all the points that are difficult to understand. It is as Mipham himself declared,

> Many indeed are those who speak about their "Detailed
>   Explanations."
> Most rare are those who understand and savor the deep
>   meaning.
> If there are any who possess the supreme tongue—who
>   know what is yet more profound than the profound—
> Let them taste herein the supreme flavor of the meaning
>   most profound.[89]

In particular, it was with an unbiased and discerning candor and with the blade of validly established scripture and reasoning that Mipham could at a single stroke cut through all the conceptual nets of the philosophical positions of those who failed to grasp the meaning of the perfect view, or who had wrong opinions or doubts about it. And just like Manjushri's sword, all the essential points of Mipham's teachings were sharp and irresistible, clearly revealing the profound and unadulterated sense.

> What use is all this chattering of jumbled thought?
> The mind that holds the naked, deeper points of tenets,
> Which are like life itself, the root of all the faculties,
> Is like a swan that strains the milk from water.[90]

The supreme deity, the sunlight of the omniscience of all the buddhas, remained as the wisdom deity within the eternal knot of Mipham Rinpoche's heart. And it was thanks to this that his writings, replete with all their hidden subtleties, are not just investigatory reflections based on a reading of texts, or conclusions deriving from a merely intellectual understanding, as in the case with other scholars. On the contrary, through the blessings of his teacher and his yidam deity, his wisdom channels opened and his knowledge burst forth wonderfully from within. And it was thanks to this that the texts he composed, in possessing the extraordinary crucial points of the profound and vast teachings, are a matchless source of blessings—just like the works of the omniscient masters, father and son.[91]

> These valid arguments, direct, incontrovertible,
> Resound like thunder pleasing to Manjushri.
> The dreamy sleep that fails to differentiate the tenets—
> Is instantly dispelled on meeting them.[92]

> If one beholds these perfect explanations,
> Every doubt both great and small is banished.
> Intelligence and certainty are made brilliantly to shine,
> And a great treasury of prowess inexhaustible is found.

Many are the attestations of the excellence of Mipham's teachings and of his many miscellaneous compositions. It was easier to gain understanding through working on a single text for one month with Mipham Rinpoche than through studying hard for a whole year with someone else. And this, it was said, was the effect of Mipham's prayers and bodhichitta. Once, when he was giving an explanation of the *Tantra of the Wheel of Time*,[93] he remarked to Lama Ösel Rinpoche that all the monks in the assembly would in the future be born in Shambhala in the entourage of Raudra Chakrin,[94] the Fierce Holder of the Iron Wheel.

Indeed, when establishing the pure view of his own Nyingma school, he simultaneously, and by the use of scripture and reasoning, refuted the opinions of other tenets. He established the unique position of his own tradition and eliminated all objections to it. As it is said in the *King of Concentrations Sutra*,[95] "What does it mean to protect the Dharma? It means to demolish any attack against the Dharma through the application of what is in agreement with that Dharma." And in the *Commentary on the Root Downfalls*,[96] it is said that "to criticize other positions with the intention of dispelling inferior views and guiding those who profess them to a superior understanding is not a fault. Indeed, merit is greatly increased by such a practice." According to what is said here and elsewhere, to elucidate the meaning of the supreme vehicle, to protect the treasure house of the holy Dharma, and to dissipate the ineptitude of false understanding—all are necessary and of great importance.

Specifically, when at the behest of Jamyang Khyentse Wangpo, the true incarnation of the omniscient Longchenpa, Mipham Rinpoche edited the great commentary to the *Precious Treasury of Wish-Fulfilling Jewels*,[97] he composed numerous indispensable ancillary texts and gave related oral explanations. While doing so, he declared that, just as with the omniscient Jigme Lingpa and other masters of the past who had been guided by the supremely enlightened master Longchen Rabjam, it was in his case thanks to the reception of a slight portion of the blessing power of Longchenpa's representative, the All-Knowing Dharma Lord (Jamyang Khyentse Wangpo), that he (Mipham) had also been able to realize easily all the profound essential points of the Old Translation tradition. And so, he concluded, if he had to debate with a hundred geshes, he had, as the saying goes, enough of a stomach not to lose his belt! He also used to say that his extraordinary conviction in the view of the Vajrayana as presented in the Nyingma school had come to him from the excellent teaching of Longchenpa, the omniscient king of Dharma, as found in *The Treasury of Wish-Fulfilling Jewels*. He would say that because the profound blessing of the mind-to-mind transmission had entered his heart, a treasure of intellectual certainty had been released in perfect accordance with the writings of Longchenpa, endowed as they are with the four reliances.

Now when Mipham Rinpoche's treatises—the melodious lion's roar of his perfect explanations—came into the hands of scholars who abode within the ample reaches of sectarian bias, the advocates of the Geluk school (scholars of high caliber) produced numerous texts contesting the meaning of his compositions. And in Mipham's replies to them, the profound confidence of his intellectual prowess, like the color of the mountains touched by the golden light of the rising sun, and the loud laughter of his arguments, based on scripture and reasoning, served only to bring the controversy into focus and to render the intellectual discernment of the learned contestants even clearer. The great Geshe Khangmarwa Lozang Chöpel of Drepung praised him in statements such as this:

> In order to be of assistance to the doctrine of the Old
> Translations to which he belonged, this most holy being
> composed many remarkable treatises that displayed the
> threefold character of refutation, assertion, and elimi-
> nation of doubts, and were adorned with many points
> of scripture and reasoning. In this assertion of his own
> tradition, there emerged a few points that diverged from
> the assertions of other schools. When several scholars
> of the Geluk school composed one or two treatises that
> refuted him, this saintly scholar refuted them in return
> by means of a hundred arguments drawn from scrip-

ture and reasoning. It was like the fearless roar of a five-headed lion amid a herd of deer. Based on reasoning, his replies were actually very difficult to destroy; his refutations always hit home.

Likewise, Lozang Rabsel, a supreme scholar from Palri in the north,[98] a master of peerless intellectual discernment who belonged to the great tradition of the second buddha Lozang Drakpa,[99] corresponded on numerous occasions with the Lord Mipham, debating the positions and assertions of the traditions of the Old and New Translation schools. Eventually, their minds blended into one. Lozang Rabsel proclaimed,

> Powerful in his striving and discernment,
> A yogi [*kusali*] of great learning and experience,
> Who labored long in search of the deep meaning:
> My great confederate, master Mipham . . .

and

> To me, a poor man, hesitant and hungry
> For the words of the great treasure of the secrets vast and
>   deep,
> The master Mipham, through the herald of his words,
> Speaks here today in answer to the prompting of my letter.
> By threading thus a faultless garland of white lotuses,
> Let Mipham Jamyang, skilled in showing forth the essence
> Of the teachings vast and deep, be my brother
> In the unending mandala of infinite victorious ones.

In these and other words, he made the profound aspiration that Mipham and he should be reborn together in the same pure field and that by the sole strength of their spiritual discussions, they might become holders of the secret treasure of the Conqueror. In a later rejoinder in his debate with Mipham Rinpoche, he wrote,

In the golden mandala renowned as Kham,
Within the vast expanse replete with rich and massing clouds
    of Dharma,
There beats with pleasant sound the great drum of the gods.
How I rejoice in you, O King of Dharma of definitive
    meaning!
That I might from my heart confess my downfalls and my
    faults,
With sparks that burn away the straw of ordinary
    knowledge,
I spread a spotless scarf, white canopy of cloud, upon the sky
Above the mighty peak that is your form.

Subsequently, Lozang Rabsel said to his attendant, Loden Rigpa'i Wangchuk, that, apart from just as few differences of epoch and of expertise in the path of reasoning, there was not the slightest atom of difference in quality between the supreme scholar Mipham Namgyal of Derge in Dokham and the great being Tsongkhapa—whether in the skill, acuity, and speed of their superior knowledge of the hidden subtleties of the vast and deep teachings, or in all the words and meanings of well-turned exposition. "These lords of Dharma are manifestations of Venerable Manjushri, ever youthful," he would say—tuning again and again his flute of most sincere praise.

Later, the great Khenpo Lama Tashi Özer presented to Khangmar Geshe copies of the earlier and later "answers to refutation" composed by Mipham and said, "When you have completed your examination of the meaning of these texts, if you find that their author, this supreme scholar who expounds the wisdom-meaning delightful to the peerless Buddha, is truly renowned as a great charioteer—that he really is the Lion of Speech himself—I request you to compose a eulogy."[100] And the geshe himself replied that, in answer to the request, he would compose a eulogy on the supreme scholar Mipham Namgyal that would be brief but filled with meaning.

So, in Khangmar Geshe's words,

From smoke you know there's fire.
And from water birds, you know there's water
    near.
The measure of a bodhisattva
Is discerned through signs and qualities.

The powerful scholar Mipham Namgyal had, from a most tender age, lived a monastic life in the company of numerous fully qualified masters. He had studied much and reached the other shore of learning. Inwardly and to his heart's content, he had imbibed from that glorious treasury a precious store of qualities of manifest realization. He had moreover placed his lotus feet upon the heads of innumerable learned and accomplished masters, [accepting them as his disciples,] throughout the three provinces of Dokham, Ü, and Tsang.

Renowned therefore as a great master of all doctrines, he is known everywhere as *mipham nampar gyalwa*, "the unvanquished victor." In certain truth, he is indeed the illusory manifestation of the wisdom deity, Manjushri, the supreme son of the Conqueror—in relation to whom he is like the beams of sunlight that issue from the sun itself. And when one reflects on how he has appeared in the form of a spiritual teacher appropriate in kind to beings like ourselves in this time of the five degenerations, and when one recalls his extraordinary activities for the Buddha's Doctrine, it is as Jamgön Sakya Pandita said,

At the outset, they learn all that can be known.
They then give perfect expositions in the company of scholars.
Finally they strenuously meditate on all that has been learned.
This is how the buddhas act, past, present, and to come.

And this is precisely how Mipham Rinpoche has proceeded.

When Mipham engaged directly in debate, his adversaries would lay out their arguments in terms of evidential sign, thesis, and pervasion. He would respond without difficulty with the four kinds of replies. He demonstrated that the thesis was not established, forcing his opponents to accept unwanted consequences, and so on. In this way, he would inflict upon his attackers the threefold shame of being silenced, of having a vajra seal placed upon their lips, and of having their reputation damaged. And on many occasions, he justifiably sounded the victory drum of universal triumph. As a scholar of the first magnitude, he is worthy to be invited to take his seat upon the lion throne prepared for such masters as the glorious Dignaga and Dharmakirti, father and son. He has repeatedly engaged great scholars in debate. And especially, when scholars who had fallen into sectarian partiality (to say nothing of the unlearned) saw *The Path of Reasoning That Illuminates Suchness: An Answer to Objections*,[101] which was Mipham's answer to the great master Lozang Rabsel of Palri, what grounds did they have for objection? Scholars of integrity, on the other hand, having reached a state of perfectly clear conviction, could not but join their hands upon their hearts and exclaim that the great scholar of these degenerate times, renowned as Mipham Namgyal, was a unique ornament for the precious Doctrine of the Buddha in general and of the teaching of the Old Translation school in particular.

And Khangmar Geshe further remarked that Mipham Rinpoche was famous in all the great centers of learning in the eastern provinces of Tibet.

On the basis of scripture and reasoning, Mipham made several examinations and refutations of the positions held exclusively by the Old and New schools. And yet nowadays, people who consider themselves logical thinkers, without even fathoming the profound understanding of the view of their own tradition, fall into sectarian partiality and with brazen arrogance criticize the meaning excellently explained by the powerful thinkers of the past. Without even worrying about accumulating the evil karma of rejecting the Dharma, they shout their views like village folk, praising and blaming according to their likes and dislikes, like old dogs barking down an alley. It is hardly the debate of learned scholars.

To defeat the maras and the non-Buddhist extremists with the lion's roar of the Tathagata, after carefully distinguishing their tenet systems and determining as carefully as possible the views that they intend—this is what brings joy to the intelligent! It is by investigating the scriptures and their commentaries until the essential meaning of the Doctrine is found—like gold that is smelted, cut, and polished—that one accomplishes properly and without error the wisdom intention of the Buddha. By offering flowers of praise to all the tenet systems that are based on the realization of the definitive meaning, while at the same time clearing away discordant positions by pointing out their defects, Mipham Rinpoche did not propound some sort of obscure, esoteric message or interpretation fit for the ears of fools. In the presence of many powerful scholars, who were intelligent and learned, and who possessed the pure eyes of the Dharma, he would analyze again and again the different tenets in the light of the scriptures and with acute and conclusive reasoning. And with an infinitely deep assurance, he would fearlessly proclaim his position without fear or hesitation, like the loud drum of a victorious hero.

It was for this reason that the best scholars endowed with candor and integrity considered the writings of the peerless Jamgön Mipham to be on a par with the traditions of the great charioteers, the supreme ornaments of the world, of both India and Tibet, and they honored them as an elixir for the mind.

Mipham Rinpoche once visited Patrul Rinpoche, Jigme Chökyi Wangpo, the king of scholars and of ordained adepts of Tibet in the region of upper Dza. He said to him, "When I was young and although my intelligence had yet to ripen, nevertheless because of the weighty injunction of vajradhara Kyabje Khyentse Wangpo, I composed commentaries on the 'Wisdom Chapter' of the *Way of the Bodhisattva* and other texts. Are they worthy of confidence?" And so saying, he offered to Patrul a pill of Manjushri consecrated by the practice of Khyentse Wangpo and a pill of Vajrasattva coming from a treasure revealed by Chokgyur Lingpa. Patrul said to Mipham, "Wisdom did not manifest in me when I was young, so there is little hope that it will do so now, even if I do take the Manjushri pill! On the other hand, I should take the Vajrasattva pill because my samaya is weak." And with these words he ate it. "Regarding the treatises that you composed," he continued, "it is as the saying goes, 'the quality of ghee is determined by fire; the quality of a teaching is determined by a teacher.' Now, Japa Dongak is here, and he is learned in the teachings of the New Translation school. You must debate with him on the basis of the crucial points of the view of your commentary on the 'Wisdom Chapter' of the *Way of the Bodhisattva*. I will be the witness."[102]

The debate with Dongak took place as Patrul Rinpoche requested and lasted for many days. On the basis of how the contestants stated their positions, the common folk who were present were unable to tell who was winning and who was losing. When Lama Rigdzin Thekchok asked who was victorious, the Dharma Lord Patrul Rinpoche replied, "I can't decide one way or the other, but anyway, as the worldly saying goes, 'A son is not praised by his father but by his enemy; a daughter is not praised by her mother but by the neighborhood.' Some of Dongak's monks told me that before the debate started, Lama Mipham prayed before the statue of Manjushri that he used as his meditative support. They said that they had clearly seen a ray of light coming from the heart of the statue and melting into the heart of Lama Mipham. I think the meaning of this is clear."

Patrul Rinpoche then remarked, "Dongak had composed a commentary on the words 'The Great Perfection teachings are the general form (the perfect expression) of primordial wisdom.' Some people understood him to be refuting this claim, others that he was demonstrating its truth. So now let the two of you debate." The contest was duly held and was brought to an end when Patrul Rinpoche said, "In their learning and understanding of the sutra teachings, these two masters are equal. In the tantra teachings, however—in this debate about meaning of the ground, path, and fruit—their capacity is very different. Thanks to his superior and more profound manner of appealing to scripture and reasoning, Mipham is the winner."

Every crucial point was debated, and, at the end, Japa Dongak was reduced to silence. He acknowledged his mistakes and praised Mipham for his victory in learning. The Dharma Lord Patrul Rinpoche also applauded Mipham and, comparing his inexhaustible intelligence with that of Bodhisattva Manjushri, he placed around his neck a white scarf decorated with the symbols of long life as a sign of utmost admiration and praise.

Sölpön Lama Pema once asked Patrul Rinpoche, "Between Lama Mipham and yourself, who is the more learned?" "On the level of the sutras," said Patrul, "we are about the same. On the level of the tantras, however, there is a very slight difference. Mipham is more learned."

Khenchen Pema Benzar Pönlop, who was a sovereign of learning in the profound and secret tantras, once remarked that, in the power of his wisdom, the qualities of his realization, and his extraordinary mastery of scripture and reasoning, Mipham Rinpoche was in no way different from the Omniscient King of Dharma (Longchenpa), the one and only charioteer of the teaching of the Vajra Essence of luminosity (the Great Perfection). His knowledge, so Pema Benzar said, was born from the depths of his being.

Now although many accomplished scholars in former times had wished to make editorial corrections to the *White Lotus*, the auto-commentary to the *Precious Treasury of Wish-Fulfilling Jewels*, no one had done so. It had been left untouched, just as it was. And so, [like Jamyang Khyentse Wangpo before him] Pema Benzar earnestly requested Mipham Rinpoche to perform the task. "For," as he once said in conversation, "the mind is liberated through learning, and this is certainly the case with Lama Mipham. When he was young, I thought there was something wild about him, but now his mind is peaceful and tamed, smooth like a well-buttered soup! He is filled with great devotion, and he is completely in harmony with the Dharma." He said this with tears in his eyes, his hands at this heart.[103]

When Mipham was editing the *White Lotus* commentary just mentioned, he asked Jamyang Khyentse, the omniscient sovereign of the doctrine of the Great Secret, "With regard to what is manifestly incorrect and what is missing, is it all right to make additions in the form of appendixes?" Khyentse Rinpoche responded by praising him, saying that in so doing he would be rendering a great service to the Doctrine. And he repeated several times that whatever Mipham added as a means of rectifying what was omitted, this did not in any way detract from the diamond words and special profound blessing power of the omniscient Lord of Speech. And with this in mind, he instructed Mipham to insert them into the text.

Khyentse Rinpoche also encouraged Mipham Rinpoche to compose a general overview of *Dispelling the Darkness in the Ten Directions*,[104] Longchenpa's commentary on the *Guhyagarbha Tantra*. And also, in the hearing of other scholars [such as Khenpo Shenga], he said that, in all the world at that time, there was no one as learned as Lama Mipham and that if he were to describe his previous existences and the grandeur of his excellent qualities, he could fill a volume as big as the *Prajnaparamita*. "But if I did so," he added, "Lama Mipham would not be pleased!" Khyentse Rinpoche would repeatedly say that at that time Lama Mipham was the one who had achieved confidence in the two stages of the practice of Yamantaka and that he was accordingly a vidyadhara who had attained the level of accomplishment.

Jamgön Kongtrul Rinpoche praised Mipham as the sovereign lord of the profound and secret tantras, saying that he was endowed with an inconceivable prowess therein and was like Vajrapani himself, the Lord of Secrets. He had himself received numerous teachings from Mipham and included them in his *Collection of Precious Treasure Teachings*.[105]

So it is that, in all their profundity and hidden subtlety, the teachings of the omniscient Jampa'i Dorje [Mipham] are established outwardly as philosophical tenets; inwardly, they bring together all the crucial points of practice; and secretly, they possess a flavor of blessing that never fades. They are no different from the great, renowned treatises composed in India and Tibet, endowed as these were with the three kinds of valid cognition.

As for the way in which he preserved the precious teaching of the Conqueror in general and especially the doctrine of the three yogas of the inner tantras of the Great Secret—cherishing them like his heart, his eyes, his life itself—Mipham himself declared,

> I do not utter praises to congratulate myself.
> Yet in the sky of my own mind
> The sun of excellent discernment shines resplendent.
> Let the wise therefore behold it in my writings.

Khenpo Kunzang Pelden, a powerful scholar in this age of strife, once said, "Regarding the perfect explanations of the omniscient Mipham, one should first examine them in depth. Then one should study and reflect upon the treatises of other masters. It is then that one may see directly for oneself the difference between them. It is like comparing the light of day with the dark of night."

For those of honest mind, Mipham Rinpoche's intellectual assurance—that which was innately his and that which he himself cultivated—is like thunder, the melody of the drum of spring, which is sweet in the hearing of the peacock. It is a matter of direct perception, and there is no need for someone like me to point it out. And this is not all. In order to guide his disciples—ordinary or extraordinary as the case may be—he lavished upon them his greater and lesser teachings, with all their subtlety, as well as the Tripitaka taught by the Buddha skilled in means, the six great classes of tantra, and so on. Starting from minor activities—even showing people how to make cross-threaded talismans to attract worldly happiness—he would go right up to the pith instructions for gaining the [minor] accomplishment of the four activities of pacifying, increasing, magnetizing, and wrathful enforcement, as well as the treatises that reveal the extraordinarily profound crucial points of the sutras and the tantras. As though opening up the treasure house of a universal monarch, he thus provided them with a complete range of all that was necessary. Calling him "omniscient" was not at all like giving an honorific title to some limited thinker who was engaged merely in the path of scholarship.

Thanks to the unbounded flowering of the thousand-petaled lotus of his all-seeing wisdom, this chief of bodhisattva heroes manifested an inconceivable illusory display of marvelous activity, bestowing on beings the instructions suited to their disposition and aspirations.

> Through the kindness of my teacher Manjughosha,
> Whatever subject I am studying
> There it is laid out before me.
> The moon of my intelligence
> Shines fair thereon, seconded
> By the light of perfect attitude

and,

> Only father, shining with the brilliance of the rising sun,
> Protect the youthful lotus of my mind!
> Never let me be discouraged

By the range of things to know,
Extending to the edges of existence vast as space,
Nor by the time it takes to know them.

This is the kind of thing that Mipham Rinpoche would say. And those who possessed great wealth of knowledge could see that, in this age of dregs, the quality of kindness and the pure exploit of opening wide the path pleasing to the buddhas and bodhisattvas of the three times were to be found solely in Mipham Rinpoche.

Jamyang Lodrö Gyatso[106] of Shechen (daystar of the teaching of the ultimate secret), Lama Ösel Rinpoche (Mipham Rinpoche's heart son and assistant), and Kunzang Pelden (that is, Khenpo Kunpel, a great and powerful holder of the Tripitaka) repeatedly made collections of his writings, great and small. And it was thanks to the kindness of such great beings as Dharmasara Jigdrel Situ Panchen, the fifth Dzogchen Tulku Thupten Chökyi Dorje, and Jamyang Chökyi Lodrö (who was the personification of the enlightened activity of Jamyang Khyentse Wangpo)—masters who held nothing but the Doctrine in their exalted hearts—that Mipham's complete works were printed from blocks in the kingdom of Dome Deshi Gechu (Derge). Likewise it is thanks to the kindness of both Shechen Gyaltsap Rinpoche Jamyang Lodrö Gyatso, the charioteer of the doctrine of the Great Secret, and Lama Ösel, Mipham's personal assistant and heart son, that we possess the complete reading transmission of the works of the great vajradhara himself, which they received either directly from him or in the presence of his relics when no direct oral transmission was extant. Later, Mipham Rinpoche, in his wisdom body, transmitted to both of them the blessing power of the ultimate lineage, thereby granting them the transmission of all his writings.

It is thus that the complete oral transmission of the collection of Mipham Rinpoche's works remains intact and was passed without interruption to Khyentse Trinle Röltse, to Jamgön Yangtrul Pema Drime Legpa'i Lodrö, to Sangye Nyentrul, as well as to my humble self. Regarding the explanatory tradition, it is thanks to the kindness of the great Khenpo Kunzang Pelden, sun of speech, and others—all the heart sons of Mipham—that this intellectual feast for intelligent minds is being propagated. The upholders of the Dharma of transmission and realization who appeared in later times have thus been able to study these teachings and to reflect and meditate on them, fathoming to their depth the excellent explanations left to them as a legacy by the Venerable King of Dharma. Preserving without error the activity of explanation and propagation, they became the representatives of the kindness of our only father, Mawa'i Nyima Shönnu, Mipham Rinpoche, the youthful sun of speech. And to be worthy to serve this doctrine inherited from our father, and with a high intention as white as the roots of the lotus flower, I in my lowliness place my hands at my heart and repeatedly make one-pointed prayer.

5

PRACTICE

In this degenerate age, those who have some slight training in the field of intellectual study make no effort at all in the practice that brings such knowledge into experience. Then again, there are some who, boasting of the little practice that they have done, regard any conventional learning, be it elementary or advanced, as something to be avoided like a thorn in their eye. In general, Mipham Rinpoche was at all times gripped by a determination to leave samsara forever. His mind was constantly imbued with a sense of impermanence, and whenever there was something to be done on the morrow, he would say, "If I am not dead, I will do it." Whatever suffering fell upon him, great or small, even the slightest aches and pains, he would say that it had come to him as the fruit of past karma.

Certainly, he took no pleasure at all in distraction and dissipating pastimes. He would say repeatedly that, given the condition of the teachings and the behavior of beings, influenced as they were by the climate of the present period of the last five hundred years, it had become difficult for anyone, including himself, to accomplish any extensive benefit for the Doctrine and beings. And, he would go on to say, how perfect and meaningful it would be, in these increasingly disheartening times, when life is short and hindrances many, if everyone were able, in this life and the lives to come, to practice perfectly in solitude for the sake of self and others. In the *Sutra of the Lion's Roar of Love*,[107] it is said,

> O Kashyapa, if a bodhisattva were to fill the entire universe with flowers, perfumes, aromatic powders, and

> incense and were to offer it in worship to the tathagatas
> three times by day and three times by night for a hun-
> dred thousand years, such a bodhisattva would generate
> less merit than another who, in fear and dread of the dis-
> tracting talk of mundane occupations—and indeed in
> terror of the entire three worlds—took but seven steps
> in the direction of a solitary retreat with the clear wish
> to be of benefit to beings.

As this text implies, the need for solitary practice is crucial in
many ways. Most especially, the principal way of all the accomplished ones, the vidyadharas of the Secret Mantra of the Nyingma
school, has always consisted in secret yogic discipline pursued in
solitude. By such means, they have assiduously traversed all the
grounds and paths of the inner tantras of the Vajrayana and have
reached the kingdom of the vidyadharas, becoming beautiful
with the radiance of enlightened action whereby the two aims are
achieved. Consequently, this way of the Nyingmapa is eminently
superior to every other teaching tradition.

The second buddha, the master Padmasambhava himself, arising
in the form of Dorje Trolö, placed under oath without exception all
the gods and spirits of phenomenal existence and entrusted them
with the guardianship of the teachings of the profound treasures.
He blessed and empowered the land of Tibet as a great and sacred
place of the Vajrayana, the source of prosperity and happiness—
especially the thirteen places that bear the name of *taktshang*, or
"tiger's nest."[108] Of these, the one in the east of Dokham, the solitary place called Meshö Karmo Taktsang, was where the regent
of the lake-born vajradhara—that is, Pema Ösel Dongak Lingpa
(Jamyang Khyentse Wangpo)—had his retreat cave known as Dule
Namgyal.

It was also at Karmo Taktsang that Mipham combined the
practice of his own supreme yidam deity (Manjushri, lord of all
families of peaceful deities) as explained in the tantras with the
summary expositions found in the Kama, Terma, and Pure Vision

The hermitage at Meshö Karmo Taktsang in Dokham, Mipham's principal residence from the age of thirty until his death. Photo by Matthieu Ricard, used with permission.

teachings—which are especially sublime owing to the many profound key points of their pith instructions. This he devised as the practice of peaceful Manjushri according to the tantra [or Mahayoga] system.[109] It was also at Karmo Taktsang that he composed the sadhana of Yamantaka called *The Secret Moon*,[110] which unites the traditions of Padmasambhava and Nubchen Sangye Yeshe and is like the quintessence of the teaching of the three inner tantras of the Great Secret, the Vajrayana. These practices laid great emphasis on the approach phase of the sadhanas.

In addition to this, Mipham Rinpoche practiced the approach and accomplishment stages of the following sadhanas:

- the Yamantaka practice entitled *The Smelted Ore*[111]
- *Red Kimkang*[112]
- various repelling rituals[113]
- the most secret practice of Hayagriva based on the texts of three treasure revealers[114]
- the *Black Horse with a Mane of Iron* of the sovereign Nyangrel Nyima Özer[115]
- the *Glorious Vishuddha, Wisdom of the Rulu Secret*[116]
- the *Glorious Vajrakumara*, elucidated according to the (Mahayoga) tantra[117]
- the *Lord of Secrets, Subjugator of All Arrogant Spirits*[118]
- the *Ferocious Mantra of Rishi Lokatri*[119]
- the *Black Lady of Wrath*, also a terma of Nyangrel Nyima Özer[120]

In particular, in the course of one year, during which he maintained a vow of silence, he recited the long mantra of Yamantaka, Lord of Life,[121] a total of fifty million times.

Mipham lived at Karmo Taktsang for thirteen years, and, in all that time, he took tea no more than twice a day. Apart from a brief period of repose in the evening, he devoted his time one-pointedly to the approach- and accomplishment-stage practices. Since the location was of geomantic importance, he lived for six months at the hermitage of Yangwen Pema Deden, which had been rebuilt by his attendant Lama Ösel Rinpoche and some other disciples from Gonjo. While there, Mipham Rinpoche made a six-month retreat, also in silence, in which he practiced the elaborate approach and accomplishment phases of the peaceful and wrathful deities from the *Union of the Sugatas, the Eight-Mandala Cycle.*

In his own native region of 'Ju, he spent a year at Chime Chokdrup Ling, his retreat house, in the course of which he spent six months practicing the approach and accomplishment phases of the long-life practice known as the *Gathering of Secrets,*[122] one of the four gathering cycles (Tib. *'dus pa*) of the profound treasures of Ratna Lingpa. During the remaining six months, he practiced the approach and accomplishment phases of *Red Manjushri, Increaser of Life and Wealth.*[123]

At Chöjung Yangteng, the retreat place at Chamdo Dzongo, Mipham performed the recitation practice of the glorious Kalachakra and at Gothi Tashi Pelbar Ling, the retreat place of the Dilgo family in Denkhok, he performed the sadhanas of Kalachakra and Consort[124] and of White Saraswati.[125] Each of these recitation retreats lasted one hundred days.

At other unspecified places and times, Mipham Rinpoche also performed the following sadhanas:

- extracting the Essence of Manjushri,[126] called the *Luminous Pith Instruction*
- the daily practice of *Orange Manjushri Who Accomplishes All Activities Called Sherab Yeshe*[127]
- *Immaculate Sky, an Instruction for Liberation from Bondage* based on *Manjushri, Vajra of Supreme Generosity*[128]
- the verse sadhana of *Manjushri, Vajra of Supreme Generosity*
- *Sadhana of the Dharani of Manjushri*[129]
- the secret practice of the *Sharp Vajra of Manjushri*[130]
- *Sadhana of Manjushri of Great Bliss*[131]
- *Sadhana of Manjushri's Syllable DHIH*[132]
- the two sections of the approach phase of the *Single Syllable A of Manjushri*[133]

- *Yamantaka, Black Butcher of Enemies*[134]
- *Manjushri Nagaraksha's Diamond Blade*[135]
- the daily practice of *Kingmar, the Essence of Yama*[136]
- the sadhana that condenses three ferocious deities entitled *Boiling Metal*[137]
- the daily practice for the long-life practice *Union of Secrets*[138]
- *The Wrathful King Shikhinra's Dissipation of Evil Spells*[139]
- *The Wrathful Deity Bhumkurkuta of the Lord of Nyang*[140]
- *The Wrathful Daka Bhumkurkuta of Guru Chöwang*[141]
- various sadhanas of *Glorious Vajrasattva*

Concerning the cycle of meditation and recitation of *Most Profound Single Syllable*,[142] Mipham Rinpoche practiced a set of teachings related to the creative power of awareness, as follows:

- *Orange Manjushri*
- *White Manjushri*
- *Prajnaparamita*
- *Sadhana of Manjushri's Seed-Syllable DHIH*[143]
- *Precious Harvest*[144]
- *Sadhana of Manjushri's Syllable MU*[145]
- *White Vairochana*[146]
- *Lord of the World*[147]
- *The One Who Rests in the Nature of the Mind*[148]
- *Amitayus*
- *Vajrapani*
- *Akashagarbha*
- *Kshitigarbha*
- *Vajra Fist*[149]
- *Amoghasiddhi*
- *Kurukulle*
- *Saraswati of the Vajra Family*
- *Vasudhara*
- *Mahadeva of the Male Class* (of Protectors)

- *Ekadzati of the Female Class* (of Protectors) together with Vasudhara
- *Pandaravasini*
- *The Master Surrounded by Four Dakinis*[150]
- *Quintessential Amrita of Manjushri*[151]
- *Manjushri of Great Bliss*[152]
- *Guru Yoga of Rigdzin Garab Dorje*
- *Secret Practice Sealed by Hung of the Eight Mandalas*[153]
- *Sadhana of the Ruby-Colored Vajradharma*[154]
- *Sadhana of Hayagriva in Two Sections*[155]
- *Sadhana of Manjushri's Vajra Life*[156]
- *Manjushri Nagaraksha*[157]

He also practiced other sadhanas belonging to the Nyingma tradition such as:

- *Sadhana of the Dakiraja*[158]
- *Sadhana of Hayagriva, the Spontaneous Accomplishment of Activities*[159]
- *Red Samvara*[160]
- *Sadhana of Mahadeva, the Garland of Rubies*[161]

To these were added certain sadhanas linked with the eight great bodhisattvas: Akashagarbha, Maitreya, Kshitigarbha, Sarvanivaranavishkambhin, Avalokita, Vajrapani, Samantabhadra, and Manjushri. To these were added practices of

- *Prajnaparamita*
- *The Great Peacock*[162]
- *The Goddess of the Victory Banner*[163]
- *Mahapratisara, Goddess of Spells*[164]
- *White Parasol*[165]
- *Yellow Jambhala*[166]
- *The Longer and Shorter Sadhanas of Vasudhara*[167]
- *The Blazing Ushnisha*[168]
- *Devaguru*[169]

These were followed by practices of other deities figuring in the *Scripture of Summarized Wisdom*[170] as found in the long oral kama lineage.

Mipham Rinpoche also performed the following practices, accumulating the number of recitations of the mantra specified in the texts:

- *Akshobhya* according to the tradition of Atisha[171]
- *White Tara* according to the Sanskrit text of Ngawang Drakpa
- *The Five Great Knowledge Goddesses, Bestowers of Fearlessness*[172]
- *The Three Queens of Knowledge (Buddhalochana, Pandara-vasini, and Mamaki)*[173]
- *Orange Manjushri, the Only Hero*, according to the Sakya tradition[174]
- *The Wheel of Manjushri's Wisdom called Jnanachakra*[175]
- *Manjushri, Lord of Speech, called Prajnachakra*[176]
- *Powerful Manjushri, Anangavajra*[177]
- *Secret Sadhana of Red Saraswati Called Jnanadarsha*[178]
- *Avalokita, the Hope-Fulfilling Lion's Roar*[179]
- *Meditation and Recitation of Avalokita Called the Four and a Half Syllables*[180]
- *Wrathful Mahabala*[181]
- *The Great Mother Mukhale*[182]
- *Long and Short Meditation and Recitation of Samayavajra*[183]
- *Self-Visualization of Vajrapani in Two Parts*[184]
- *Akshobhya*
- *Hayagriva*
- *Black Manjushri, Subduer of the Nyen Spirits*[185]
- *Two-Armed Vajrabhairava*[186]
- *Bhairava of the Ra Tradition*[187]
- *Kalachakra with Coemergent Consort*[188]
- *Red Yamantaka*[189]
- *Chakrasamvara*[190]
- *Hevajra with Coemergent Consort*[191]

Even in the case of sadhanas where the required number of recited mantras was not specified, Mipham Rinpoche would complete a minimum of three hundred thousand recitations of the root mantra for each practice without exception.

As far as concerns his root yidam deity, he performed in sequence the approach and accomplishment phases of the peaceful and wrathful forms of Manjushri, not once but repeatedly. Moreover, he would recite each of the different hundred-syllable mantras that sever the continuum of karmic obscuration one hundred thousand times together with their completing recitation. And to this he added the recitation of the dharani of dependent arising, which he recited thirteen hundred thousand times at Demchok Podrang, his retreat place in Tragu.

In short, there was not a single cycle of Mipham's writings or pith instructions that was not grounded in practices that gave rise to signs of accomplishment. This was indeed a marvelous thing completely beyond the reach of ordinary understanding—especially when one considers that none of his recitations were performed in a state of distraction, whether of tongue or eye. At the age of thirty, he took up residence at Karmo Taktsang and from then until his death, apart from a few days going here and there, he spent most of his time in retreat according to a strict regime of regular sessions and a determined number of mantra recitations.

With regard to these endeavors, for the samaya substances appropriate to the practice, for the supports suitable to accomplishment of the deity on which he was relying, and finally for the pith instructions on how to perfect [the four] activities, and so on, he referred to the hidden indications of the tantras, their commentaries, and the practice instructions belonging to the vidyadhara lineage. And it is evident from the lists of supports and substances required for each practice that he completed all these sadhanas in meticulous detail—even with regard to the way of sitting—as stated in the texts, without defect or mistake.

Mipham Rinpoche had not a mustard seed's worth of care for this life, for profane activities and the vain pretensions associated with the eight worldly concerns. Indeed, as he was living in various solitary places, his needs were few. His way of life was confined to that of a hidden yogi free of all activity—which in this day and age is a great and sublime marvel. Later, when his qualities of elimination and realization began by their own power to show themselves, the drum of his good reputation began to resound loudly in the realm of the gods and other reaches of the world. Accordingly, the great and noble came from all directions—from Ü, Tsang, and Khams—to bow down before the lotus of his feet. On such occasions, however, he rarely spoke to them, and even when he did, it was only on matters of the greatest importance. For never, to the slightest degree, did he indulge in useless talk.

In many of the scriptures, the Buddha has spoken repeatedly of the evils that accrue from the misuse of religious offerings and of the mischiefs that flow from wrong livelihood. Therefore when these visitors made material offerings as an expression of their faith, Mipham Rinpoche never considered that they were for his use. He used to say, moreover, that in these degenerate times, the attachment of beings to their wealth and possessions increased year by year. "Nowadays," he said, "the obscurations deriving from ill-gotten goods are ten times stronger than they were when I was young. And now, at this later time, especially because of the uninterrupted torment of my illness, I do not make any great accumulations of merit through the building of supports for offering [stupas, statues, and so on.] Therefore, I really have no need of religious offerings; nor is there any reason for me to use them casually." So saying, he never under any circumstances accepted any kind of offering made through faith in the form of gifts, large or small. Apart from the food and material indispensable for retreat in solitude, he never hoarded a single sesame seed in the way of material possessions.

Throughout his life, spiritual practice alone was the root and nerve of his entire existence. He brought to perfection the great power of the wisdom of the superior dharmakaya: the inseparability of the purity and equality of all phenomena in both samsara and nirvana. All appearance and activity were for him an infinite display of the mandala of the illusory net of great bliss. It was thus that he followed the perfect path of the four vidyadharas to its very end and discovered the secret treasure of supreme and ordinary accomplishments. In the earlier part of his life, he practiced the six vajra yogas as presented in the tradition of Naropa, the accomplished adept of the perfection stage of the fivefold class of the anuttaratantra. Later he implemented the yoga of the six-branch practice of the glorious Kalachakra, which is the essential sap of the nondual tantras of Vajrasattva. By such means, he brought to perfection the yoga of the channels, winds, and essence-drops of the self-arisen city of the vajra aggregate[192]—perfecting in an instant the grounds and paths of the Vajrayana. He therefore became the sovereign *heruka*, the lord of the great mandala that consists in the perfection of the seven qualities of union resulting from mastery of the supremely unchanging wisdom that is emptiness supreme in all its aspects conjoined with coemergent bliss.[193]

As a result of the blessings gained through reading the volumes of the precious collection of the Nyingma tantras, the realization of the wisdom of the ultimate lineage awakened in his mind. Thanks to this, and through following the teachings of the Great Perfection, he brought to complete fulfillment the equality of awareness and emptiness, the state of openness and freedom of the ground of both samsara and nirvana, and the great virtuosity of the four visions of spontaneous luminosity.

Consequently, the three kayas arose in his own direct experience and he actualized enlightenment endowed with the six special features within the expanse of the wisdom of the primordial lord, the ultimate Manjushri, the lamp of self-arisen wisdom. Endowed with the wisdom body, he is the great and universal sire of all the buddhas and the charioteer of the vajra essence of luminosity of the supreme vehicle.

Through the extremely feeble merit of his contemporaries, the prosperity of the world and its inhabitants was in a state of decay and the strength of the Dharma much diminished. But through his inconceivable bodhichitta, Mipham Rinpoche protected the beings of his time from the sufferings that were the result of their karma. And he accumulated merit in many ways. For example, following the promise he made in the presence of Kyabgön Gyerab Dorje,[194] who was one of his most important teachers, he offered one hundred thousand lamps and an equal number of offerings of incense and food as well as many hundred thousand flower and mandala offerings. He made five thousand circumambulations around the protector temple of Dzing Namgyal and the same number equally around the temple of a hundred thousand buddhas at Kathok Dorjeden. At the retreat center of Shechen Monastery, while circumambulating the mani wall[195] erected by the great siddha Sherab Yarphel,[196] he recited one hundred thousand times the abridged *Litany of Manjushri's Names*, a terma of Guru Chökyi Wangchuk. Every month without fail, he made feast offerings on the tenth day of the waxing and the waning moon. Every day he made offerings to the dharma protectors, and on the twenty-ninth of the lunar month, he would offer the *Torma of Venomous Molten Bronze*. Moreover, on the fifteenth day of every month, as well as every Tuesday without fail, he would even recite the offering to Saraswati from the volume of mantras and pith instructions on how to brighten one's intelligence. This is just a sample of Mipham Rinpoche's spiritual discipline and is meant to show how he performed continually and unfailingly an endless series of practices of purification and accumulation of merit.

At the end of each year, during the month when tantra practitioners perform ceremonies of repulsion, Mipham would devote seven days to the ritual of the exorcism torma taken from the *Union of the Sugatas, the Eight-Mandala Cycle*.

There was a prophecy uttered by the venerable Manjushrikumarabhuta himself to the effect that if Mipham Rinpoche were to erect a statue of the Buddha surrounded by images of the eight close sons, this would be of supreme and general benefit for the teaching of the Conqueror. Moreover, exhorted by the words and writings of his precious teacher, Lama Ösel constructed an image of Manjushri that was later to serve as the receptacle for the omniscient Mipham's relics. At the retreat center at Chamdo Dzongo, Mipham completely restored and reconsecrated the protector temple dedicated to Ekadzati, Rahula, and Vajrasadhu, which had been constructed in a geomantically significant site during the time of Minling Lochen.[197] He also had new printing blocks carved of the sadhana of White Manjushri composed by Kyabgön Wangchen Gyerab Dorje; of the *Litany of Manjushri's Names*, which had been translated during the early period; and of the *Jeweled Garland, the Myriad Names of the Buddhas and Bodhisattvas*,[198] which he himself composed. He likewise published the *Prajnaparamita-sutra* in one hundred and fifty lines and the *Abridged Kalachakra Tantra* together with his great commentary on it in two volumes.

In addition, he performed many wonderful activities as a means of accumulating merit and purifying defilements. He offered the money and materials necessary for the publication of a bilingual grammar, the great commentary on poetics, his own commentary on the *Ornament of the Mahayana Sutras*,[199] and so on. Indeed, as the *Ornament* itself declares,

> In order to complete the two accumulations,
> Those whose minds are full of faith
> Offer to the buddhas raiment and so forth—
> In real and in imagined ways.

> The offering of one who made the aspiration
> That the coming of the Buddha should be beneficial,
> In a manner free from thoughts of the three spheres,
> Is indeed a perfect offering to the Buddha.[200]

It is also said in the *Noble Sutra of the Engagement of Maitreya*,[201]

> Although for many a myriad ages,
> A discourse could be made upon these merits,
> Such a lapse of time would never be sufficient
> For a discourse on their fruits.

Of course, there is absolutely no need to speak of the merits generated by Mipham Rinpoche's activities—which had so many objectives, whether in immediate or in ultimate terms.

6

A Hidden Life

Generally speaking, the sphere of the profound qualities of elimination and realization, the inconceivable secret of the body, speech, and mind of an enlightened being, is beyond the grasp even of bodhisattvas who directly behold the truth of the dharmata on the noble path. This being so, there is no need to speak of the comprehension of ordinary beings. As it is said in the later tantra of the *Net of Illusory Manifestations of Manjushri*,

> Emptiness exceeds the grasp of ordinary minds.
> It is present of itself.
> It is the wealth of everything, beyond adoption and
>   rejection.
> If one rests within this nature, inconceivable Manjushri,
> Not dwelling on him, with no other thoughts,
> One will, in quality, become his equal.

One may appreciate the truth of these words from what was said earlier, albeit briefly.

Even so, it is said in the *Garland of Lives*,

> Through his merit's strength,
> He was of manifest nobility.
> He possessed a bright intelligence
> As was clearly seen though signs—
> Just as fire may be detected through the sign of smoke.

Great and supremely noble bodhisattvas may be assessed through the outer evidence of their words and deeds. They can be known through many signs, direct and indirect, that indicate that they are completely different from ordinary childish beings. Through the accurate perception of even small qualities of elimination and realization, fortunate beings can gain a partial understanding of their superior excellence in the same way that, by tasting a single drop of seawater, one can understand the taste of the entire ocean.

It is said on the basis of trustworthy report that when at Karmo Taktsang, Mipham Rinpoche was absorbed in the concentration of boundless love, and when he reflected on the sufferings of beings in the hell realms, he fell into such a state of grief that he could not eat and he would say that he needed to relax his mind [by meditating] on the empty nature of the dharmata. At Lab Dzutrul Puk, when he was absorbed in the approach phase of the practice of White Manjushri according to the Mati tradition, he would concentrate on the garland of the mantra turning at such speed that the entire environment would seem to him to be revolving like a chariot wheel. The rough perception of ordinary appearance would cease and he would pass his time in a state of concentration as described in the texts. When this happened, he would say that it was "probably just through the blessings of his teacher."

Once, as he was offering circumambulations at the Tara temple at Longtang, he said that Tara appeared to him directly and gave him a prediction. On another occasion, he recalled that once, when he had been in retreat for many years, he had remained in the one-pointed concentration of the generation and perfection stages just as the texts describe such that he never recited a single mala of mantra with a distracted mind.

On another occasion, when Mipham was visiting Jamyang Khyentse Wangpo, the latter asked him, "How do you practice while you are in retreat?"

"When I am engaged in intellectual study," came the reply, "I pursue my investigations to their conclusion. On the other hand, since I feel I have to accomplish the generation stage while in retreat for the approach recitation of the yidam deity, I practice with great care."

"It is difficult to do all that," said Jamyang Khyentse Wangpo. "But didn't the Omniscient One (Longchenpa) say that one should simply stay where one is without doing anything? Personally, that's how I practice, and I never saw the so-called face of the mind as something with a white and rosy skin! All the same," he said with a peal of laughter, "I could die now, and I wouldn't have the slightest anxiety." Mipham Rinpoche considered this to be a direct instruction from his teacher.

On the other hand, he thought that through his intense practice of the generation stage, he had—of the five levels of meditative experience—reached that of *habituation*, which is like the peaceful flowing of a river.[202] And he thought too that through his practice of calm abiding, he had probably achieved by then a one-pointedly focused mind.[203]

"Still," he said, "if now I have achieved a state of calm abiding, I have had deep insight already for a long time—since I was a child."

We may deduce from his words that through the power of the awakening of his innate and acquired intelligence, the ultimate nature was manifest to him from the beginning [of his life] and that he thus enjoyed the simultaneous occurrence of realization and freedom, the complete possession of the power of awareness.

At Karmo Taktsang during his practice of the approach and perfection stages of Manjushri Yamantaka, he said that whether in waking life, meditative experience, or dreams, all the signs explained in the texts manifested perfectly without a single exception. [He said too that,] in the evening of the eighth day of his approach recitation of the deities of the *Eight Mandalas*, he saw in reality, in the sky before him, the great mandala, completely perfect, of the worldly *mamos*, the heruka Shimukale surrounded by countless millions of dakinis. And in front of this great multitude, he saw Pelden Lhamo Remati,[204] our only mother, in the demeanor of a servant, who with dancing gestures was making prostrations. Whereupon, Mipham Rinpoche said, he sang the prayer of offering to Remati composed by Rigdü Drakpotsel, the accomplished master of Repkong, together with certain additions composed by himself.

It was about that time also that, early one morning, when his assistant, the precious Lama Ösel brought him his tea, Mipham Rinpoche said,

"A dakini has just been here. She sang the Seven-Line Prayer to such a delightful melody. Didn't you hear her?'

"I did not," said Lama Ösel.

"You must be joking!" Mipham Rinpoche replied. "It's the reason I composed this guru yoga practice based on the Seven-Line Prayer. If you recite it, it will be very good for you!" And he gave it to him with an explanation on how he should practice it.

During the course of his life, precious Lama Ösel recited the Seven-Line Prayer thirteen hundred thousand times, as a result of which several marvelous signs of accomplishment appeared. And it was thanks also to his repeated requests that we now have the *White Lotus*, Mipham Rinpoche's commentary on this same prayer.[205]

Once, during the ritual of the paper effigy that follows the throwing of the torma in the practice of *Manjushri, Lord of Longevity*, Mipham Rinpoche fired the rifle himself, and the effigy surrounded by grass and brushwood burst into flames. And again, when he arranged the sadhana of the *Union of the Sugatas, the Eight-Mandala Cycle* and precious Lama Ösel was making a copy of it, there was a sudden fire in Mipham's room.[206]

At Karmo Taktsang, during the long-life ceremony for Lama Pema, after Mipham Rinpoche had for four days performed the obstacle-repelling ritual of Black Hayagriva taken from the Nyangter, the rock that had been the target of the torma-throwing ritual was wreathed in fire and smoke, and the following day it was found that it had crumbled to dust and had been blown away.

On another occasion, he went to the top of a cliff in the same region in order to select a geomantically suitable location for a new retreat center and to subdue the land. Mipham Rinpoche suddenly made as if to fall from the top of the cliff, which was as high as a three- or four-story building. Lama Ösel hurried down in a state of panic, only to find Mipham sitting comfortably cross-legged without the slightest injury.

Once when the princess of Derge had fallen ill, Mipham Rinpoche performed a ceremony for the ransoming of her life energy. As soon as he concentrated on the sheep effigy, it turned in the correct direction of its own accord. This was witnessed by everyone present.

When the region of Meshö was devastated by a serious drought, Mipham Rinpoche went, at the behest of the queen mother of Derge, to the Ser-ngul Turquoise Lake in order to perform a rain-making ceremony. By the time he had finished the ritual (which can now be found in his collected writings), the precipitation was so great and the tops of the nearby mountains were covered with so much snow that travel was difficult.

On another occasion, at the request of Jamyang Khyentse Wangpo, and with the financial support of the queen mother of Derge and Palpung Situ Choktrul, Mipham Rinpoche performed the pill-making ritual belonging to the sadhana of Manjushri, Lion of Speech. As a manifest sign of successful accomplishment, the pills increased in such quantity that the whole mandala was completely covered with them.

Once, when Mipham Rinpoche was living in the little forest at Rudam at Yangwen Pema Samten Ling, a great snowfall occurred through the mischief of *gyalpo* spirits. He subjugated them, tormenting them for seven days by means of mantra and concentration and by striking them with a club—an attribute of Yamantaka, the yidam that he was then practicing. Mipham later declared that no gyalpo or gongpo spirits would be able to come within a league of where the club was kept.

When he performed the approach-phase recitation of the longevity practice of the *Gathering of Secrets*,[207] the nectar in the ritual vase and the *amrita* and *rakta* [on his shrine] overflowed and the top of the mandala shone with a shimmering light. It was on this occasion that Mipham Rinpoche told the fourth Shechen Rabjam, who was visiting at the time, "I have been practicing this sadhana of longevity continuously for a whole year. The long-life drink is the same as it was when I set it down on the shrine. Since it neither went sour in the summer nor froze in the winter, this is a sure sign that the deity has been accomplished." And when, at the time of taking the accomplishment, both master and disciple distributed the substances of long life, the people who received them, including the king and officials [of Derge], all lived to their full span of life.

Subsequently, Mipham Rinpoche advised Thupten Chökyi Dorje, the supreme tulku of Dzogchen Monastery, that for the latter's long life and the increase of his activities, he should make the great thousandfold offering according to the longevity practice of the *Gathering of Secrets*. So Dzogchen Rinpoche prepared a great and elaborate offering at the monastery of Rudam Dzogchen Gön. Mipham directed his mind to it while the precious Lama Ösel went there to preside over the ceremony. Many excellent signs appeared: the amrita and rakta began to boil and for seven days nectar dripped from the offering torma.

At another time, when the general fortune of the important families of Junyungma was declining, Mipham made an invocation, conjuring the dharma protectors to guard them against the inroads of brigands and enemies and to bring improvement to their fortunes. In a dream, he clearly saw Bernak, the protector of Dru Gade, astride a black horse and with a spear in his hand. He gathered from above the region of Junyungma [what looked like] a black yak-hair cloth and threw it far away. Subsequently the situation of the Ju clan improved and its general fortune strengthened— although, as Mipham Rinpoche remarked, no one knew that this had been thanks to him.

Once when he was staying at the monastery of Drupgyu in Gatö, two foreigners arrived in the area. Just before they arrived in the place where he was staying, a great deal of snow fell and they were struck with snow blindness. The high road was not very far from the house, but they got lost and had to take another road. They were mounted on mules, which took fright and bolted as soon as they saw Mipham Rinpoche's dwelling in the distance, and their saddlebags filled with many samples of earth, water, and so on were scattered and their contents lost.[208] Later, when Mipham was traveling to Tridu, he stopped on the way and made camp. Many vultures landed close by and for the rest of the day followed him wherever he went. Some stayed there the whole night and flew away the next morning.

Once, when he performed ceremonies of lustration and offering at Gatö Tago in the presence of relics of Buddha Shakyamuni, these same relics multiplied on the spot.

On another occasion, when Mipham Rinpoche was staying in the retreat place at Gatö Trangu, a large battalion of Chinese soldiers passed along the valley road at the foot of the mountain. As soon as they came within the vicinity of the retreat place, however, the shaft of their standard shattered and the horse of the Chinese commander suddenly lay down on the road and refused to move.

Again when Mipham was in Chamdo, the venerable Lama Ösel was greatly worried by the commotion made by the Chinese army there. But Mipham said to him, "The Fierce Holder of the Iron Wheel (king of Shambhala) will be able to destroy the barbarians; and since I will be one of his greatest captains, what damage can this present army do to us? Everything will be fine!"

At that time, on the day when Mipham Rinpoche began his great commentary on the glorious *Kalachakra Tantra* entitled *The Light of the Adamantine Sun*,[209] he made offerings and recited prayers in front of a thangka of White Tara that the Vajradhara Khyentse Wangpo had given to him. And at that moment, the prayer for Mipham's long life that was written on the back of the thangka and that celebrated his names in relation to the four great reasons [explained later][210] was heard to resound all by itself.

"If," he said, "a hermitage were built according to geomantic principles in the mountain solitude in Denyul Dilgo, it will be of some slight benefit to the Dharma King and his realm of Derge." And indeed, in all the places of that region that he visited, Mipham saw and identified many self-appearing six-syllable mantras and footprints of the dakinis together with many wondrous signs.

Once, in order to pray for the happiness of Tibet and in order to create the circumstances whereby the essence of the earth might be restored, Mipham Rinpoche went to the bank of the river Drichu, rich in gold, where he offered a vast quantity of precious substances—grains, silk, medicine for the nagas, and amrita that liberates through taste. He attached some ribbons to the neck of an arrow, which he then threw into the middle of the water. The arrow lodged upright in the water as if it had been thrust into the ground and remained there, its ribbons fluttering in the wind. Mipham Rinpoche then walked slowly back up the riverbank, reciting many prayers and aspirations for good fortune. And as he did so—and this was seen by everyone present—the arrow, with its ribbons as though spread out over the water, moved of its own accord back toward the bank.

Again, while he was making a geomantic assessment in the center of the sacred site of Gothi, he began with the ground-taming ceremony and performed the ritual dance. At that moment, many vultures swooped down from the sky and stood by with their wings opened. Many such extraordinary signs occurred.

Mipham Rinpoche used to say that, in general, whenever he embarked on the composition of a text, a ray of light would come from the heart of the statue he had of Manjushri, his yidam deity, the support for his practice. The light would sink into his heart and without the slightest impediment, he would write down whatever arose spontaneously in his mind. Sometimes from the end of the ray of light coming from Manjushri's heart he would see the glittering form of the letters of which the texts would be composed. In the case of some of them, for example, the prayer *Unchanging Good Fortune*,[211] the statue would come to life as Manjushri, who would recite the prayer himself. On such occasions, Manjushri would give Mipham Rinpoche many prophetic messages. Precious Lama Ösel said that this was something he heard directly with his own ears.

This image of Manjushri moreover had come naturally into Mipham's possession once when he had gone to Dzagyal and in a particularly auspicious circumstance. And since that moment, he had constantly taken it as the support for his practice and had it with him at all times. All his achievements in teaching, debate, and composition, he said, arose through the blessing power of this image. He prized it above all things, regarding it as in no way different from Manjushri himself. At a later time, after Mipham's death, and according to the wishes expressed in his testament, this sublime image was kept in the temple of Kshitigarbha at Shechen Tennyi Dargye Ling. It was placed in the heart of a statue of Manjushri, which precious Lama Ösel, lord of Dharma, had himself made. When he placed it there, a copious shower of amrita fell. This statue was of an incomparable splendor and numinous power. My primordial lord, Shechen Gyaltsap Rinpoche, the heart son of Mipham Rinpoche, recounted how, when he wanted to put in order the *Trilogy of the Uncontrived Mind*,[212] he at first encountered some difficulties in the organization of the texts. He therefore made many offerings and fervent prayers before the statue containing Mipham relics, and as a result, an unmistaken wisdom was born in his mind so that he was able to complete his task.

Many other stories were told about that statue. Mipham Rinpoche said that when he was performing the visualization and recitation of the deities in his meditative practices as mentioned earlier, it was as though the statue became indistinguishable from the main figure in the mandalas. And it was through its blessing power that the creative force of his awareness would be stirred and the wisdom channels would open in such a way that many texts of sadhanas and praises would burst out from the expanse of his wisdom.

Once when Kyabje Shechen Gyaltsap Rinpoche was urging him to compose an explanation of the *Eight Great Mandalas*, Mipham replied, "Of course, this is something anyone might do if it were simply a matter of writing something on the basis of intellectual reflection. But no benefit comes from this kind of thing. Thanks to the compassion of my teacher and my yidam deity, something sometimes arises naturally in my thoughts, and without having to make many corrections, I just write it down without any effort. It just happens, and when it does, it is quite easy and very beneficial. For this reason, we must bide our time. You should pray to your teacher and yidam deity, and exhort the dharma protectors to perform their entrusted work." This is what Mipham Rinpoche actually said. Moreover, it was the same even in the case of the omniscient Jamgön Khyentse Rinpoche (Jamyang Khyentse Wangpo). Whatever he exhorted Mipham to compose, the latter would reply that, until he received the blessing of his yidam deity and until some extraordinary need presented itself, it was difficult [i.e., undesirable] simply to compose on his own account. And to some disciples who had faith in him, he once said in so many words that if he were to write simply on the basis of scholarly expertise, he could produce as many books as the Kangyur and Tengyur combined. There would be no end to them, and yet they would be of no great profit. On the other hand, he said that it was definitely and only because the blessing power had come down on him, and because there was a special purpose, that the kind of texts he had written so far had been composed. And it was for that reason that the fortunate could place their trust in them.

It was his usual habit to keep a lamp lit after nightfall and to have a quantity of paper close by him. For it would often happen that he needed to compose something during the night. Once, when the great Khenpo Lama Mangala repeatedly pressed him to compose an extensive commentary on the *Litany of Manjushri's Names*, Mipham replied that it was not appropriate for him to compose it at that time. For, he said, it would prove to be the very last of his writings. And weighing up his words, we may well understand that it would not be something that he would compose simply on his own account. Indeed, at the moment of his death, he remarked that whereas it had turned out that a separate commentary on the *Litany* had not been written, all the important points could be found in the great commentary on the *Kalachakra Tantra*.

As Mipham Rinpoche himself said,

> Deriving from the lotus of the heart
> Of Loden Chokse Tsal Manjushri,
> A jeweled treasure of profound and supreme Dharma
> Has burst forth from the ocean of my mind.

This and other statements placed at the end of the majority of his works show clearly that Mipham Rinpoche's works—like the cycle of texts on the *Heart-Essence*[213] and the seven treasures of Longchenpa, the omniscient king of Dharma—were, quite certainly, mind treasures that were made to look like treatises. Moreover, it would seem that in several of his writings, Mipham included the symbolic script of the dakinis.

When he was composing some texts on the *Abridged Kalachakra Tantra*, together with certain other writings, important obstacles arose and his health was seriously impaired. Later when he was explaining the tantra, he said that, for some time previously, it had been his wish to compose a commentary on the secret meaning of that scripture but that the right time had not yet arrived. By then, he said, the burden of his illness weighed him down and his strength was unequal to the task of exegesis and elaboration, correcting, and so on. It is clear from this that in order to break the seal of the teachings, the time and all the various circumstances had to be right. Moreover, when his compositions were compiled into a single collection, it was done in a way quite unlike the collected works of other scholars renowned for their learning and accomplishment—that is, with the texts classified according to subject matter. By contrast, Mipham Rinpoche arranged the texts in the order in which they arose in his mind and according to other quite particular criteria and intentions. This is something I heard directly from Mipham's assistant, the precious Lama Ösel. And also in the case of the category of sadhanas, he would never even show the text to others before he had himself completed the approach-stage recitation. He said that the cycles of practice texts that he composed had all been written for himself—for his own practice of the phases of approach and accomplishment—and to that extent, they had fulfilled their purpose. He would say that they were of no use to others and that there was no point in having hopes and fears in their regard. There is a profound point of doctrine to be understood here. In general terms, it is as Aryashura[214] has said,

> Those who studied much are without pride.
> The truly rich are without avarice.
> Those retreating in the forests are content with what they
>   have.
> This quality is their supreme adornment.

Mipham Rinpoche would say that he had not the slightest good quality. Moreover, as it is said in the *Deliberate Utterances*,[215]

> As mules are by their wombs destroyed[216]
> And reeds and plantain trees
> Laid waste by bearing fruit,
> Likewise are vulgar men destroyed by honors.

Accordingly, he would say that from his childhood to the present time he had never felt even a mustard seed's worth of pride in thinking that he possessed this or that good quality. He did not even have the pride of thinking of himself as a practitioner on the path but would always refer to himself as an ordinary person and would take a low seat. He would say that nowadays almost no one had extraordinary qualities of elimination and realization. When one has some slight qualities, he said, if one allows them to appear, it becomes unacceptable to people of this degenerate age. They cannot stand to hear about them, with the result that it becomes nothing more than the source of obstacles. For this reason, he would say that to be humble and secretive was the best way to behave. Accordingly, Mipham Rinpoche hid his realization of the profound and secret path like a lamp inside a vessel. Nevertheless, the real situation was as Shantideva described:

> Whenever I desire to gaze on him
> Or put to him the slightest question,
> May I behold with unobstructed sight
> My own protector Manjughosha.

So it was that whenever it was necessary for him to grasp some important point—something profound and difficult to understand in the meaning of the sutras and tantras—a direct understanding of it would arise through receiving the blessing of his teacher and yidam deity. On one occasion in his early youth, when he was studying the *Commentary on Valid Cognition*,[217] he experienced some difficulty in grasping the words and meaning. He prayed repeatedly to Manjushri, and that same night, Jamgön Sakya Pandita appeared to him in a dream—with his nose slightly bent at the tip and wearing the pale-blue robes of the accomplished panditas of India. "Have you understood the *Commentary on Valid Cognition*?" he asked. "I have read it and thought about it," said Mipham, "but it is hard to grasp." "But what difficulty is there in understanding logic?" Sakya Pandita asked. "It's just a matter of refutation and proof!" And with that, he took the volume of the *Commentary* in his hand and divided it into two. He then gave the two parts to Mipham, saying, "Now put them together again." As soon as Mipham had done so, the book turned into a sword and it seemed to him that all objects of knowledge suddenly appeared vividly and distinctly before him. He waved the sword once and felt that he had understood them all in a single moment and without impediment. From that moment on, he said, he had a perfect grasp of the entire text.

There exists a copy of a prophetic text written in Mipham Rinpoche's hand, which says,

On an excellent moment of the third day of the eleventh month of the fire monkey year, the day of the second planet (Tuesday) and the nineteenth star, in this auspicious conjunction of star and planet, there occurred a sudden prophecy of Padmaraja,[218] the all-creating king Manjushri endowed with boundless life.

> The support for your life is inseparable from the
>   vajra,
> Mount Sumeru, the mountain
> Naturally arisen in the northwest,
> With its hermitage of white-crystal.
> The wish-fulfilling trees down in the valley
> Are the Jambu Vriksha trees.
> The vase is the unvanquished lake that never
>   warms.
> Unassailable and everlasting are the stupa, sun
>   and moon.
> The skull cup liquor is Lake Kokonor and the
>   Dzachu River.
> These eleven items are the support of your life.
> As long as you remain at Yumar,
> This supreme connection will remain and should
>   be prized.
> Free from obstacles, you may live for eighty years.
> This was written in the morning of the day just
>   mentioned.
> *Mangalam*

Another prophecy declares,

> You who turn the wheel of blissful Dharma
> Fulfill all needs and wishes like a precious treasure.
> Like a lotus growing in the mud, you are not stained
> By defects of samsara.

You are a vajradhara who have understood
The sense of the five wisdoms.
Your glorious deeds secure the benefit
Of both yourself and others.
Your sixty-eighth will open.[219] Virtue.

The meaning of this is clear to everyone.

Once he said jokingly to the vajra-holding Lord of Refuge Shechen Gyaltsap Rinpoche, "If one is a Nyingmapa, one ought to be able to show some sign that one has been able to accomplish the generation and perfection stages. What kind of power do you have? Speaking for myself, if one day I had to kill many people— but for my fear of the karmic consequences—I could do it!" And he added cheerfully, "In general, those who have extraordinary powers—that is, people who have gained confidence in the performance of wrathful activities—are like [a fence of] iron mountains that protect the teachings." It was thus that he indicated that he himself had achieved such a state of perfect certainty.

And at another time, when he was young, he went with Jamgön Kongtrul Rinpoche to the region of Nyak where they trained in the refinement of precious substances. On their way home, after crossing the Le pass, in the area below the glacier, they encountered some brigands from Golok. It was Guri and his band. Guri shot at them three times but without wounding them. Some years later, when Mipham Rinpoche went to Dzagyal Gön, he bumped into Guri again.

"You once treated me with great disrespect," he said, "and we did not meet again since then. But now that we have, I could take you to court and demand reparation for disrespect and outrage to a teacher of religion. I shall not do so, however. But just to show you that I have the support of the Three Jewels, in three months time, you will receive a definite sign from the dharma protectors."

Three months later, Mipham Rinpoche was at Dzogchen Monastery where he performed the ritual conjuration of the *Magic*

Monkey Skull. That same day, several bad signs occurred for Guri's house. His little son, who was about five or six years old, was chased by three crows that pecked him on the head. Beside himself with fear, Guri immediately regretted and confessed his crimes. It was only after some time, however, that Mipham Rinpoche accepted his confession—and subsequently took loving care of him on several occasions.

In the same vein, when someone went mad, it was only necessary to tie around their necks a talisman of the *taduma* scorpion knot blessed by Mipham Rinpoche and their madness would be cured. A scrap of paper with a single letter written on it by Mipham Rinpoche, or a tiny fragment of his clothing, was enough to grant protection from any kind of weapon. When people who had faith in him asked for his advice on important matters, he would tell them that he had no clairvoyant knowledge of hidden things. And then, in the way that ordinary worldly people would do, he would say something like, "I think it might be good if you did such and such a thing."

He never gave the slightest indication that he possessed prophetic insight into arcane matters. But whatever advice he gave in the form of exemplary stories to his cherished students, telling them what to do and what not to do, things would invariably turn out as he had said. He once remarked that when he was young, a state of clarity would sometimes arise in his mind and he would know whether a sick person was going to live or die and could tell without any confusion what joys and sorrows would occur in that person's life.

Later, just before he died, he wrote the following song:

> *Kye Ho*!
> Easy it is to understand
> One's own karmic appearances.
> If now I linger for a little while,
> Disturbing states of mind and waves of pain,
> An ocean of delusion, I shall cross.

In six months and a half, my voyage will be over.
So many times I've thought that I was mad or dying.
And yet, at last, through light of the compassion
Of Padma, Manjushri, and Arya Tara,
And of all the other buddhas of the ten directions,
I shall reach the plain of no-more fear,
And will be welcomed to a place of happiness.
The thought of illness—"this strong malady"
Will naturally subside.
The madness at the time of thinking
"I am mad" will also cease.
And in the moment of intense disorder
There will be an end of torment.
Then the radiance of awareness
Will resound with eightfold laughter,
And gradually the blissful state
Of fearless space will show itself.
In meditation, dreams, and in the waking state,
Many blissful signs will come to pass.
King Gesar now and Warrior Werma will rejoice and smile,
Their peals of laughter sounding far and wide.
Now I have no fear. For if with thoughts of the three roots
I'm able to be carefree and relaxed, what harm can come?
If everything in my experience is purified,
All that appears arises as illusion.
This death that's now upon me
Is just the playful work of wind and mind.
For a time and through the power of karma,
There will be no signs or indications,
But afterward experiences will blaze,
A play of bliss and clarity—
And then accomplishment of mighty Padma—
Ha! I shall attain
On the fourteenth in the second month
In the year of the water mouse. Virtue!

Many similar texts appear in Mipham Rinpoche's writings, which indicate [his clairvoyance]—whether directly or indirectly. However, I could not include them all here. By and large, he declared that between the ages of twenty and thirty, his clairvoyance was unobstructed. And although he worked many extraordinary miracles [at that time], I have been unable to record them in writing according to a strict and clear order. Moreover, because Mipham Rinpoche subsequently adopted a mode of conduct that was secret and hidden, there is not much evidence in his later life attesting to this aspect of his character. In any case, as a means to ascertaining that he was the great daystar of the definitive and ultimate secret, the wisdom of all the buddhas, simply to talk according to our common perceptions about a great being such as this—whether in terms of the deities that he beheld or the minor miracles that he worked—is to do only what is liable to lead childish beings astray. Nevertheless, in order to plant the seeds of wondrous admiration [in the reader's mind], I have described a few events that were ratified by what certain devoted beings had seen and heard.

7

ACTIVITIES FOR THE
DOCTRINE AND BEINGS

Although, from the beginning, Mipham was utterly free from the shackles of samsaric existence, yet thanks to his great compassion and without thinking for a single instant of his own interests, he was unwaveringly concerned for the benefit of others. He truly was like the Bodhisattva Manjushri, ever youthful. So it was that every action performed in the life of this holy being, even to the blinking of his eyes or the extension and contraction of his limbs, occurred with no purpose other than the benefit of wanderers. Like the four great elements in both their nature and function, he was the ground and sustenance of [beings in] both samsara and nirvana. With him, it was as the *Lives of the Bodhisattvas*[220] describes:

> The moon has joy, the sun has utter clarity,
> While fire has heat and wind has swiftness as their nature.
> Compassion's joy, concern for others' welfare
> Is the inborn nature of great beings.

It is especially true that, tormented by the unbearable defects of karma and defilement, the sentient beings of this final period of five hundred years are all engulfed in the great ocean of suffering. Because of this, even the light of the precious teaching of the Conqueror is disfigured—polluted by those who are wayward, destitute of realization, and of mistaken understanding. Even though some possess a few of the immaculate qualities of the Dharma of realization and transmission, they are like the flowers of autumn, soon to fade. Yet the Buddha, our Teacher, nourished an attitude of love toward the beings to be trained of these evil times, who live for but a hundred years, and he took them to himself. Likewise also, the great hero Manjushri, his hair bound up in five tresses, willed to show himself in the display of a great and fearless *mahapandita*. And so it was that, once again, there blossomed forth a banquet of virtue. For it was then that Mipham Rinpoche appeared as the sole and incomparable charioteer of the Dharma of the Conqueror, displaying unassailable knowledge, unshakable compassion, and prodigious qualities in every field.

It was for this reason that, on a day marked by the conjunction of Jupiter and the constellation of victory, and other wondrous outward, inner, and secret signs of auspicious interdependence, Mipham's extraordinary root guru, Jamyang Khyentse Wangpo, Pema Dongak Lingpa—the lamp of the entire Doctrine, the lord of beings to be trained in all the three dimensions of existence, and king of all learned and accomplished masters—placed upon an altar volumes of the most profound teachings of buddhadharma and of all the different fields of knowledge, together with their ancillary topics. In front of them, he arranged many offerings on a vast scale and a throne contrived of thick brocaded cushions all piled up. He then requested Jamgön Mipham to take his seat on it and proceeded to bestow on him the ritual permission of Manjushri, Lion of Eloquence. He addressed him, saying, "I commit to you the totality of the teachings of these ancient and most perfect vehicles of sutra and mantra, the precious Dharma of the victorious ones. By means of explanation, disputation, and composition, and indeed all the twelve methods of scholarship, I entreat you to defend unceasingly and to the very end of existence, throughout the reaches of the world, the precious lamp of the teachings, that it may never disappear."

So it was that Jamyang Khyentse Wangpo invested Mipham Rinpoche as the most particular son of his heart and as the sovereign upholder of the teaching of the ultimate lineage, empowering him as a lord of the Dharma of definitive meaning. He then offered him an especially fine scroll-painting of Tara entitled the Immortal Wish-Fulfilling Wheel, on the back of which he had inscribed the following words:

> *Om Swasti Jayantu!*
> May the fame of him who understands aright
> The wisdom of the Lord Unvanquished—
> Who like Manjughosha knows all that may be known,
> And who like Dharmakirti is victorious—
> Pervade and fill our sea-appareled world!

And to these words he added "This was written by Khyentse Wangpo, the disciple pleasing to his master Manjughosha. *Siddhi Rastu.*"

In elucidating the qualities of elimination and realization on the noble path, and in elucidating the ocean-like activities of the Bodhisattva—the meaning of the pitakas of the Buddha's words in all their vastness—Mipham Rinpoche was like the regent of the Buddha, the mighty bodhisattva of the tenth ground, the Unvanquished Lord (Maitreya).

In the wisdom and knowledge whereby he perfectly discerned the secret crucial points of the profound view of the Great Madhyamaka of the supreme vehicle, the view of emptiness endowed with the three doors of perfect liberation, he was in reality the venerable and ever-youthful Manjushri.

Moreover, he clearly distinguished the earlier and later tenet systems associated with these [two bodhisattvas].[221] And by using scriptural authority and reasoning to eliminate mistakes and uphold the correct understanding thereof, he explained the crucial meaning of the profound and vast views. Mipham Rinpoche was a fearless lion of speech who could not be worsted by evil forces and other antagonists. He possessed a treasure of unassailable knowledge and intellectual assurance—to such a degree that he was indeed the brother and equal of the great pandita Dharmakirti.

So it was that the sweet and justified fame of his excellent qualities reached to the far shore of the world-enclosing ocean, and his
sovereign power of enlightened activity, a nectar-like medicine for
both the Doctrine and beings, adorns this world and suffuses it
with glory.

For the four great reasons just mentioned, Jamyang Khyentse
Wangpo bestowed upon him the sublime name Mipham Jamyang
Namgyal Gyatso, which means Invincible Manjushri, Ocean of
Victory. On that same occasion, he offered him the representa-
tions of the three vajras,[222] blazing with splendor and charged with
blessings. In order to show Mipham's ascendancy over an ocean
of panditas and siddhas, Jamyang Khyentse Wangpo presented
him with the pandita's hat that he himself had always worn as an
emblem of the limitless collections of teaching that he held, and in
so doing he enthroned Mipham Rinpoche and covered him with
the highest praise.

The supreme scholar Vasubandhu said,

> The teaching of our Teacher has two aspects.
> It consists of scripture and of realization.
> It alone should be upheld;
> It should be promulgated and accomplished.

Accordingly, Jamgön Mipham—this master, this great treasure of
knowledge, this lord of learning and accomplishment—realized
that, as Vasubandhu said, the essence of what people call "Buddhism" consists in nothing other than the scriptural tradition and
the realization thereof. He brought to utter perfection the qualities
of learning, reflection, and meditation in all the major and minor
sciences, common and uncommon—as well as the glorious ocean
of teachings of the sutras and the tantras. He devoted the activities of his entire life to the Doctrine, on account of which he sits
majestically and fearlessly on the lion throne of a dharma king, the
sovereign of the three worlds.

Some of the ways in which he nurtured the study of the Dharma of scriptural transmission, the meditation on the Dharma of realization, and an impeccable activity unmixed with the eight worldly concerns have already been mentioned above. Most especially, however, Mipham Rinpoche believed that the view, meditation, and conduct of the Vajra Essence of luminosity according to the Old Translation school[223] had been spoiled and compromised through the academic study of tenets and fabricated ideas. In consequence, he thought that the entirely self-sufficient teaching of the stainless tradition of Rongzom and Longchenpa, the two omniscient masters, father and son, had dwindled to no more than the painting of a butter lamp. And since the third omniscient master, Jamyang Khyentse Wangpo, repeatedly requested him with his vajra speech, Mipham proclaimed, with a powerful and fearless lion's roar, the true and definitive meaning of all the well-turned treatises of India and Tibet.

The glorious Sakya Pandita said that one should instruct with reasoning and appeal to scripture. Accordingly, Mipham would take as his basis citations that fully expressed the innermost meaning of the sutras, tantras, and treatises. He would perfectly determine their sense by means of numerous, profound, sharp, and extremely cogent arguments based on logic and the power of factual truth. All that he had understood for himself, he expounded with the greatest kindness to those who had the fortune to be his students. And he would do so by means of essential instructions, thanks to which the texts themselves became for them like teachings and guidance suited to them personally. Thus he would open the eyes of their unstained intelligence so that they too could correctly grasp the sense of the perfect view and doctrine of their own tradition. As a means to removing the darkness of erroneous ideas and theories and rendering the Buddha's teaching as pure as gold smelted in the fire, he taught and propagated all manner of major and minor texts, of earlier and later times, together with the commentaries on their meaning.

He taught chiefly in the monastery of Tashi Lhatse at Dzongsar. On one occasion, he expounded the *Norbu Ketaka*, his commentary on the "Wisdom Chapter" of the *Way of the Bodhisattva* to Khenpo Pema and a group of intelligent disciples. And it was also to this same Lama Pema, the great Nyingmapa, and to Khewang Dorje Rabten and six other disciples (all ordained and learned in the scriptures) that, over a period of twenty-one days, he expounded for the first time his great commentary on the *Ornament of the Middle Way* entitled *A Teaching to Delight My Master Manjughosha*. For as many as a hundred days, he explained the root verses, autocommentary, and supplementary texts of the *Precious Treasury of Wish-Fulfilling Jewels* of the Omniscient King of Dharma to the supreme incarnation of Dodrupchen, the great scholar and master of reasoning [Tenpa'i Nyima]; to Siddhi, exponent of scripture and reasoning; and to Rigdzin Thekchok and several other intelligent and learned masters. For a period of three months and three weeks, he expounded the *Treasure of Light*, his elegant exposition and great commentary on the *Commentary on Valid Cognition*, to the most learned and accomplished Tulku Jampel Jigme Rigpa'i Raltri; to Lhaksam Gyaltsen, learned in the five sciences; to master Jamyang Lekpa'i Lodrö; and so on, a group of logicians whose number equaled the components of the noble path.[224]

On one occasion at the college of Dzogchen Shri Simha, Mipham Rinpoche gave an explanation of the *Introduction to the Middle Way* to eight khenpos of great intelligence. To Amdo Gurong Tulku, a master of marvelous intellect, as well as to the most learned Lama Jamdrak and others, he gave an explanatory guide to the *Tantra of Glorious and Total Victory*.[225] On one occasion, he gave an explanatory guide to the *Treasury of Abhidharma* to seven learned scholars. To Rigdzin Tsewang Drakpa, the son of the great tertön Chokgyur Lingpa, to the Dzogchen Kusho, the venerable tulku of Gemang, and to other important holders of the Vajra Essence teachings of the Old Translation school, he gave, over a period of eight days, the *Essence of Luminosity*,[226] his overview of *Dispelling the Darkness in the Ten Directions*,[227] the great commentary of the omniscient Lord of Speech (Longchenpa), which itself explains in the form of extraordinarily profound pith instructions the *Illusory Net, the Womb of Secrets*,[228] the root of the eighteen great tantras.

On another occasion, after concluding a long period of approach and accomplishment practice at Karmo Taktsang, he bestowed to a group of more that ten scholars in Thubten Chökhar Ling at Palpung an extensive and extremely detailed explanation of the four medical tantras, together with certain practical and essential instructions drawn from his own experience. Many of these students were to become excellent doctors.

Mipham Rinpoche was later invited to Kathok Dorjeden—that replica of the central land of Magadha—where he gave to the omniscient Situ Panchen Dharmasara, Tulku Melong of Dorje Drak, and other sublime beings detailed explanations on the *Abridged Prajnaparamita*, the *Sublime Continuum*, the *Ornament of Clear Realization*,[229] the two *Differentiations*, the *Ornament of the Mahayana Sutras*, the *Essence of Luminosity* (his overview of the *Guhyagarbha Tantra*), and his commentary on the *Eight Great Mandalas*.

Later, Mipham Rinpoche went to Lundrup Teng in Derge. There, he gave to the king, the precious Ngawang Jampel, himself a great scholar, as well as to the great vajradhara Samten Lodrö, supreme abbot of the Lhundrup Teng Monastery, and to the learned master Jamyang Khyenrab Thaye and others a complete exposition of the five texts of Maitreya together with an explanation of *The Ornament for Rulers: A Treatise on Royal Governance*.[230]

On five occasions in the course of his life, Mipham Rinpoche gave the transmission of the *Gateway to Erudition*,[231] his excellent compendium of the profound and vast aspects of the Tripitaka. He expounded it once in the hermitage of Rudam Nakchung to the great khenpo and bodhisattva Karma Tashi Özer (chief of learned elders), to his highly accomplished heart son Sherab Ösel, to the great yogi Kunga Pelden, and to others. He transmitted it once to Shechen Gyaltsap Rinpoche, the daystar of the Old Translation teachings, and to his disciples. He transmitted it once at the retreat center of Drakar Gyatö to a group of fifty disciples, among whom were Zango Jedrung Tulku and Khenchen Kunzang Pelden, master of the pitakas. He transmitted it once at the monastery of Gönzik, in particular to Shapdrung Rinpoche, and finally in the retreat place of Gatö Trangu, he bestowed it on Palpung Situ Pema Wangchuk and his disciples.

For a period of forty-two days in the retreat center of Denyul Gothi, he expounded the *Light of the Adamantine Sun*,[232] his great commentary on the king of tantras, the *Glorious and Supreme Primordial Buddha*,[233] to a group of about twenty-one disciples, among whom were Mipham's assistant lama Chöying Ösel, the supreme Jedrung tulku, the vajradhara Tendzin Chögyal, and Benchen Sangye Nyentrul.

We can be certain that Mipham Rinpoche bestowed all the transmissions just mentioned. However, since we do not possess a complete list of all the other texts, major or minor, that he may have taught, there is some uncertainty regarding the full range of the transmissions that he gave. However, in addition to the list just supplied, he also gave instructions on the preliminary practices and trainings of the mind[234]—over a period of at least six years at Karmo Taktsang to Konchok Wangdar, Rigdzin, and five other disciples from Gonjo, and over a period of four years to Jamyang and some other disciples from the local area. These teachings he bestowed in the form of maturing instructions coordinated with the practice itself; and many of his students achieved decisive experience in the main practice of the Great Perfection.

Toward the end of his life, owing to the decline of the Doctrine and the merit of beings generally, Mipham Rinpoche was afflicted without reprieve by an extremely serious illness. He was able to devote himself only to the essential practice, and he no longer gave extensive teachings on the great texts.

Both in his earlier and later life, the disciples linked to him through empowerment and the transmission of teachings were, to be sure, too numerous to count. But to certain of his disciples, who were to become the principal holders of his tradition, Jampa'i Dorje Jikdrel Mipham Namgyal, as its sovereign master, entrusted the teachings of the ultimate lineage. These disciples became, so to speak, the regents of the kingdom of the essence of the supreme vehicle. Those of whom we can be certain are listed as follows:

- Jamyang Lodrö Gyatso'i Drayang, the crown jewel of the learned and accomplished monks of Shechen in Dokham
- Tulku Jigme Tenpa'i Nyima of Dodrupchen, a leading and incomparable scholar
- Kathok Situ Panchen Orgyen Chökyi Gyatso, the fearless lion of speech
- Wangchuk Ösel Jalü Dorje (Lama Ösel), who by completing the three kinds of service pleasing to the master, became a powerful yogi who brought to perfection the realization of the vast expanse
- The fifth Dzogchen Rinpoche, Thupten Chökyi Dorje
- Gemang Kyabgön Choktrul
- The fifth Shechen Rabjam
- Payul Gyatrul
- Karma Yangsi Choktrul
- Mura Choktrul Pema Dechen Zangpo
- Gemang Wöntrul Tendzin Norbu
- Tertön Lerab Lingpa
- Shakya Shri, the sovereign yogi who accomplished the state of union
- Drodul Pawo Dorje, the Bhutanese yogi of the heart of the supreme vehicle
- The great siddha Lama Dampa Dongak
- Jedrung of Ling
- Dzogchen Khenpo Sonam Chöpel
- Gemang Yönten Gyatso, upholder of the Tripitaka, a learned master steadfast in the discipline
- Kunga Pelden, who had a direct realization of the ultimate nature of the Great Vehicle

· Vajradhara Kunzang Pelden
· Rigdzin Tsewang Drakpa and Tsewang Norbu, sons of Tertön Chokgyur Lingpa
· Gurong Tulku of Amdo

These were all the lineage holders of the teachings of our Nyingma school.

Among Mipham Rinpoche's disciples belonging to the Kagyu lineage were the following:

· Palpung Situ Choktrul
· Palpung Wöngen Rinpoche
· Khenchen Mangal Remi
· Je Lama Jamyang Drakpa Rinpoche
· Surmang Drung Rinpoche, Karma Chökyi Nyinje
· Roldor Tertrul
· Lama Tashi Chöpel, the great scholar
· Sangye Nyentrul

The Sakyapa disciples of Mipham Rinpoche included:

· Jamyang Loter Wangpo, lord of the tantras of the Great Secret
· Khenchen Lama Samten Lodrö
· Jamyang Kyenrab Thaye

Among his Gelukpa disciples, we must mention Palri Rabsel, Khangmar Geshe, and so on, foremost among the scholars of the northern region.[235] They scattered over Mipham Rinpoche the flowers of their praise, and their devoted faith was no different from that of his immediate disciples, who had directly imbibed the nectar of his teachings. The Shiwalha and Phakpalha lamas from Chamdo[236] sent several of their most talented students to study the Svarodaya[237] and to receive the essential instructions in grammar from Mipham Rinpoche, whom they held in unequaled respect and esteem.

Moreover, many of the contemporaries of Jampe Dorje Lodrö Thaye [Mipham]—great beings and upholders of the nonsectarian tradition, masters of logic, and powerful yogis who realized the state of union—partook of a great feast of Dharma by studying his explanation of the *Commentary on Valid Cognition* as well as his commentary on the *Eight Great Mandalas*, the sealed and secret teachings on the practice of the approach phase of Yamantaka, and so on. For Mipham Rinpoche did indeed possess the boundless adamantine intelligence of Manjushri—as Jamgön [Kongtrul] Lodrö Thaye, king of Dharma, declared:

> *Om Swasti*
> Glorious and gentle wisdom deity, encompassing the
>   dharmadhatu,
> However numerous are beings, there you are to guide them.
> Supreme Lord of Speech possessed of twofold knowledge,
> Glorious lama, may you live and prosper for a hundred
>   kalpas.

Jamgön Kongtrul composed many such verses for Mipham Rinpoche's long life and heaped upon him the blossoms of his praises. He proclaimed him Mahapandita Mipham Gyatso and declared that he possessed great realization—to such an extent that, on the basis of all such statements, we too may have an inkling that this was indeed so. Of all the people high and low—the king of Derge, his son, his brother, and his queen, together with his courtiers great and small, the royal administration of the region, and the ministers, military leaders, and astrologers of the whole of Tibet—there was not one who did not bow in respect before Mipham Rinpoche's venerable feet.

Once when he was young, he spent an entire day expatiating on the sense of just one stanza of the eulogy in his *Sword of Wisdom*,[238] much to the wonderment of all his learned listeners. When the vajradhara Jamyang Khyentse Wangpo heard about this, he said to him, "This exposition of yours is very extensive, but in this degenerate age there is no one able to retain such detail. What is the point of going to so much trouble only to tire yourself? Like you, when I was young, I too had a powerful intelligence and knowledge. Now, however, I don't have a scrap of it left! If instead of making such detailed expositions that are beyond the retention of ordinary people you were to compose a treatise or a commentary, your exhausting efforts would have some point to them, and they would be of much greater benefit to your fortunate readers."

When Mipham Rinpoche expounded the *Commentary on Valid Cognition*, he did so in an unhindered manner, without holding anything back and without hesitating over the meaning of the words. His exposition was clear and easy to understand, like a flowing stream, like the melody of Brahma. Most of his disciples were utterly delighted. They would stay throughout the teaching, their eyes fixed untiringly upon the countenance of their master. And when they came to consider each of his words and reflect upon their meaning, their astonishment was like nothing they had ever experienced.

One of Mipham's direct disciples, the retreat director Könchok of Gonjo, once offered his realization to Wön Tendzin Norbu, the nephew of Gemang Gyalse Rinpoche (Gyalse Shenphen Thaye). At the same time, he requested some instructions on the *Highest Wisdom*.[239] Tendzin Norbu was extremely pleased and said to the many lamas and tulkus who were attending the monastic college that, in the case of someone with the level of realization of Könchok, a direct disciple of Mipham Rinpoche, it made no difference whether he received guidance or not. He said that Könchok was someone who had received the blessings of a teacher who had complete realization of the ultimate lineage. And he repeated this approbation on numerous occasions.

Once when the great accomplished siddha Shakya Shri was a young man, he went to Dzongsar to pay a visit to the omniscient Jamyang Khyentse. On his way, he passed by Karmo Taktsang in order to see Mipham Rinpoche, coming into his presence just as he was granting the empowerment of the creative power of awareness associated with the wisdom deity Manjushri—using the very statue that was the support for his practice. As Shakya Shri reported to Lama Ösel Rinpoche, the foremost of Mipham's disciples, it was thanks to this that he was able to progress in his meditative experiences and realization, going on to actualize the exhaustion of phenomena in the state of awareness and emptiness. In return, Ösel Rinpoche described to Shakya Shri, himself a master of the highest attainment, how realization had arisen in his own mind as he was practicing. On a later occasion, Shakya Shri, king of yogis, spoke about this to the students in his encampment. He told them that although they had spent their whole lives endeavoring in the practice, they were nowhere near the level of realization achieved by Ösel Rinpoche, the attendant who had offered the three kinds of pleasing service to the vajradhara Mipham, Manjughosha in person. Such, he said, was the character and excellence of a "suitable vessel," a disciple who had perfectly followed an authentic master. And he sent his main disciples to offer their realization to both master and disciple: to Mipham Rinpoche and Lama Ösel.

On a later occasion, Shechen Gyaltsap Rinpoche also praised Lama Ösel, saying that, at that time, his realization was unequaled in the entire region of Dokham. In fact, Mipham had several other heart sons directly or indirectly connected with him, who became holders of his lineage and were endowed with incomparable qualities of learning, discipline, kindness, and accomplishment.

Gemang Wön Rinpoche, Orgyen Tendzin Norbu, considered the *Precious Treasury of Wish-Fulfilling Jewels* by Longchenpa, the omniscient lord of Dharma, as the life force of the view and practice of the Vajrayana of the Old Translation school; and he once thought of expounding it. Nevertheless, even though his disciples pressed him to do so, he did not dare, considering that the exposition of the text by someone as lowly as himself would incur the punishment of the dakinis and wisdom protectors. Nevertheless, his many disciples were insistent in their request and asked how it could possibly be inappropriate. Now Mipham Rinpoche had told Wön Rinpoche that there had been many inaccuracies in the older editions of the *Treasury of Wish-Fulfilling Jewels* but that he himself had completely corrected them. This being so, he said to Wön Rinpoche that he should explain it later and that, thanks to the blessing power of the root text and its commentary—and also because he had entrusted them to the protection of the dakinis and dharma protectors—the teaching would be free of obstacles. And just as he had said, on the many occasions in later times that Wön Rinpoche and other disciples of the lineage expounded these texts, there were never any untoward circumstances.

By contrast, whenever Gemang Khenpo Yönten Gyatso, lord of the treasure house of the glorious Dharma of transmission and realization, started to explain the king of tantras, the *Guhyagarbha*, obstacles (all of them serious) would invariably occur. When he reported this to Mipham Rinpoche, the latter told him that if he first spent ten days giving a condensed explanation and instruction, followed by a more detailed exposition, no obstacles would arise. And from that moment till the present, Khenchen Yönten Gyatso and the teachers in his lineage have adopted this procedure with the result that until now, both master and all his disciples have encountered no further difficulties—as can be seen from the many disciples who have truly upheld this method of explanation.

To be sure, from the very first, Mipham Rinpoche was a king of the profound and secret teachings. As a result, even in this age of strife, dominated by the five kinds of degeneration, he was at all times like a *ketaka*, a sublime purifying jewel, plunged into the sea.[240] He accomplished the benefit of the Doctrine and beings effortlessly and on a great scale without mixing it with the vacuous clamor of the eight worldly concerns.

As it is written in the sutras,

> Those who at this time,
> When holy Dharma tends to its decline,
> Uphold both day and night
> The teachings of the Lord of all the world

Are far more noble in their merit
Than those who venerate the buddhas
Thousand or ten thousandfold
For ages equaling the sands in Ganga's stream.

And in the *General Scripture of Summarized Wisdom*[241] we find,

Those who, having understood, expound
The secret essence of the Conqueror
Are supreme among the mighty ones—
The object of the three worlds' adulation.

And,

Those who hold the secret of the Vajra Essence
Are the ones astride the horse that draws the chariot.
No others are their equal in the task.
And even their dismounting stone
Victorious buddhas venerate above their heads.

Indeed numerous texts to this effect are to be found in many of the sutras and tantras.

8

The Final Deed

Seeing that the hour was at hand for the good fortune of another pure field,[242] Mipham Rinpoche, the sun of enlightened action, who had brought supreme refreshment to the Doctrine and beings in this age of dregs, left his retreat in the first month of the water mouse year (1912). He was sixty-seven years old.

On the eighteenth day of the same month, he appeared to be upset by the arrival of some troublesome visitors and, as a result, drew up his last will and testament quite suddenly as follows:

Namo Manjushri jnanasatvaya
In Joy Made Manifest and other pure realms,
I will grow mighty in the ocean-vast activities
Of all the children of the Conqueror;
And for as long as space exists,
I promise to maintain an attitude of great compassion
For wandering beings as numerous as the sky is vast.
Tormented by my karma in this age of dregs,
I have taught the Dharma;
And through seventeen human years until this day,
I suffered dreadful illness in my inner channels,
Enduring bitter pain without reprieve.
Yet in this world I have remained,
Supported by this cage, this body of illusion.
Now, with a joyful mind, I come to die
And set in writing these my final words.
Yet now, as death arrives, what is there to declare?

Ah no, say nothing more!
A dying man is mute and swiftly gone.

Beginning with these words, his testament went on to give a rough description of what was to be done after his departure. Finally, he wrote that he no longer wished to remain in this illusory body tormented by disease, and with words expressing his eagerness to be gone, he concluded,

May everyone be happy and find freedom.
May the teachings of the Conqueror increase and flourish.
May all those linked with me be born in pure fields,
And may there be good fortune everywhere and always.

Mipham Rinpoche wrote all this and concealed it in the heart of a statue of one of the dharma protectors. Also, with the poem cited earlier, which begins "*Kye Ho*! Easy it is to understand one's own karmic appearances,"[243] he drew up his final testament in the course of the second month and left it on the table in front of his seat. During the second month also, he gave Lama Ösel instructions on what should be done after his death and recited the dharani of Akshobhya two hundred thousand times. On the tenth day of the third month, he went see Lama Ösel and said,

You and I, master and disciple, first met each other at Karmo Taktsang in the eleventh month of the year of the pig (1877). You repeatedly expressed a profound and decisive aspiration with the result that, until now, we have remained continually together. And since that time, there has not been a single act, a single step, that you have made in my service that I have not sealed by dedicating it as a cause for your enlightenment. All the difficulties and all the fatigue that you have endured have been meaningful. All the roots of virtue, great and small, represented by the practice of the approach and accomplishment phases [of the generation stage] and the composition of my treatises, without forgetting any of them from one day to another, we have accomplished together. Three times every day we have dedicated them for the benefit of the Doctrine and of beings. When I accomplished the approach and accomplishment of my yidam deity, you also accomplished the practice at the same time. We performed the practice together—as one, without any difference between us—in the manner of a group practice. I have received manifest signs from my yidam deity that whatever aspirations you have made will certainly come to pass. In the future, you will be like the venerable Manjushri himself. This is certain, and I am not saying it just to comfort you. So be happy!

If you are still uncertain or have questions about the practice, you should ask them now, today. For I do not think that I shall be here for very long. Nevertheless, you and I, master and disciple, from now until enlightenment, will never be parted.

These were Mipham Rinpoche's own words. And again he said,

You repeatedly implore me to remain as a source of benefit for the Doctrine and beings. And yet it is not because of the great fatigue I feel owing to the decline of this illusory body's youthful strength that I have no desire to stay. It is because the present times and this illness of mine are such that even if I did stay, it would hardly be for the good either of myself or of others. You therefore should perform your practice in mountain solitudes, bringing it into your experience as much as you can. You can practice on your own independently.

As for me, when I have abandoned this illusory body, tormented as it is by karma, I will have to go to a pure realm of my choosing. And there, at every moment my qualities will progress and, thanks to my clairvoyance and my boundless powers of vision, I will bless you. I will never forget you. Pray to me again and again; for now you have no need of any other teacher. We will meet each other constantly—in life, in death, and in the bardo state. In the pure fields of the ten directions, we will be together just as in this present life.

With these and other words, Mipham Rinpoche told Lama Ösel many marvelous things that he had never said before.

Because it was an auspicious day, there being a particularly favorable conjunction with the constellation of Victory, Lama Ösel asked Mipham Rinpoche to give an explanation of the Seven-Line Prayer addressed to Guru Rinpoche. At once he gave a complete instruction and went on to say,

> In general, for the practice or recitation of the texts that I have composed, it makes no difference whether you have received a transmission and instruction or not. I grant you the blessing for the simultaneous ripening and liberation of such practices. But since this text [the commentary on the Seven-Line Prayer] is one of my chief compositions, and since you have a great yearning for it, it is very good indeed that I should give you this instruction. For three years still, you should keep this teaching sealed. Practice it yourself without explaining it to others or propagating it. Afterward, you should share it with those who keep their samaya.

He then made several circumambulations around his hermitage. On the eighteenth day of the fourth month, Khenpo Kunpel[244] arrived, bringing with him the volumes of the Kalachakra cycle that had been printed at Kathok.

It was then that Mipham Rinpoche made the following remarks to Lama Ösel, lord of Dharma:

Generally, these days, if one speaks the truth, no one listens. If one tells a lie, everyone takes it for the truth. It is for this reason that I have never said before what I am about to tell you now quite openly. I am not an ordinary being. You can be certain that I am an emanation of Manjushri and have taken birth through the power of my bodhisattva aspirations. The intense sufferings that I have endured in my present physical form are but the residues of karma. Generally, it was through the evil conditions of this present age and through the power of great obstacles that, even though I am a powerful bodhisattva, I have had to take the support of the polluted aggregate of this illusory body, on account of which it has been difficult to avoid the ripened effects of karma. Impelled by the generation of bodhichitta while in this body, the result of the prayers that I have made will be that every being who simply hears my name will finally become like venerable Manjushri, ever youthful. Many signs have arisen confirming the manifest accomplishment of these words of truth. Now it is no longer necessary to experience the obscuring effects of karma. For you and the rest of my disciples who will explain this tantra after me, your present connections with me are very important. And so, starting from today, I shall confer on Khenpo Kunpel the explanatory transmission of the great commentary on the Kalachakra. Generally, it is indicated quite clearly in the text that this explanation of the tantra should last at least ten days, but now, because of an astrological configuration occurring this month, I shall complete it in eight days, finishing on the twenty-fifth. The carving of the woodblocks was left unfinished, and it may be that some of the letters are unclear. However, I have the power of blessing and I will give my blessing so that no defect will occur in the transmission to both of you.

On another occasion Mipham Rinpoche said,

> I am a great bodhisattva who donned a vast armor-like determination to liberate beings until none are left throughout the whole of space. In this present body, I should have been able to bring great benefit to beings and the Doctrine generally, but especially to the teaching of the tantras of the Old Translation school. But the merit of the Nyingmapas is meager, and thus they are assailed by great and harmful obstacles. Because of several crucial interconnected circumstances, there have been, at this late stage of my life, many hindrances and evil circumstances, including the suffering caused by the illness that torments my illusory body. Consequently, not even the thought [of performing such beneficial activities] has arisen in my mind. Yet certain commentaries and explanations have been composed. I had wanted to write a detailed and comprehensive exposition of the general meaning of Madhyamaka, but the occasion never arrived. Now, however, it does not much matter whether it was written or not.[245] If I had been able to complete the *Trilogy of the Uncontrived Mind*,[246] it would have brought life to the whole of the buddhadharma and would certainly have been extremely useful. But I have been unable to complete it in this life. Now is the end-time, and the destruction of the sacred Doctrine draws on apace. My mind is filled with such sorrow that I shall not take rebirth. If in the past I had been born at the time of the two brothers of Mindroling,[247] I would certainly have been able to bring greater benefit to the Doctrine and beings. But in these evil days at the very end of the age of strife, beings are wild and unruly, and their merit is small. Seeing that this is so, I have done what I could to help the teaching, chiefly through the profound practice of the approach

and accomplishment phases together with the stage of
activation [recitation] of many of my yidam deities. If
I do indeed take birth again, it will be in the body of
one who, on the basis of previous training, will be able
to attain the fruit at once and not as one who must tra-
verse all the stages of the path. But now I must leave this
world; I must go to other pure realms.

So saying, he continued as he had written in his testament.
Beginning on the twenty-second or twenty-third day of the month,
he announced that he was in a state of physical bliss, free from any
of the pain that had afflicted his illusory body. Day and night he
remained in the state of the vision of the full unfolding of the kayas
and wisdoms. He said to Lama Ösel, his attendant,

Ösel, it serves no purpose to grieve in the manner of
ordinary worldly people. But you and I have been such
friends for so long that now, as I suddenly leave you, it is
possible that you might feel great sadness. But your pain
will not last long.[248]

His explanation of the tantra was completed on the twenty-fifth
day of the month and he said,

I would have preferred to die quickly in a lonely place far
from the gaze of ordinary beings. Yet it seems it will not
be so. Tell all those who wish to see me in the moment
of my death to come.

He made prayers of aspiration and blessed all those who came
into his presence, promising to keep them in his compassion until
they attained enlightenment. Ditrul[249] and others implored him to
prolong his life and asked him—if he were to pass away and if his
incarnation did not to appear—to what buddhafield he would go.
"It is certain that I shall not remain," he said decisively, "and an

incarnation will not appear. For I am going to the pure realm of Shambhala in the north."

That same day, Lama Ösel Rinpoche sent letters posthaste to Shechen, Dzogchen, and other monasteries. Despite the prayers of Khenchen Yönten Gyatso, Khenchen Kunpel, and Lama Ösel, Mipham Rinpoche maintained his previous resolve to depart. He said that there was no further cause for him to remain in this world but that, on account of the auspicious connection,[250] he would stay a little longer. Although he had given up extending his life, he nevertheless blessed it so as to remain until the twenty-ninth day of the month of Saga.[251] Sometimes he would say that the entire sky was filled with syllables. On one occasion, he wrote the symbolic script of the dakinis on a scrap of paper and numbers from one to sixteen and he laughingly remarked to Lama Ösel that with eyes open or closed, he could write without difficulty[252] with either his right or his left hand—for it was indeed the case that he could write with both hands—after which, he ate some curd. From the afternoon of the twenty-fifth day, however, he spoke no more. With his eyes wide open, he gazed into the sky. Thus he remained, his countenance shining with splendor. On the twenty-ninth day, which was a Friday, when the moon was in the mansion of Rohini, he sat up with his legs loosely crossed, with one hand in the mudra of meditation and the other in the mudra of teaching. As the sun set, he became absorbed in the inner expanse of primordial luminosity. It was on that same day that his heart son, Gyaltsap Rinpoche, arrived.

On the eleventh day of the waxing moon of the fifth month—in order to urge Mipham Rinpoche to arise from the expanse of the youthful vase body, the dharmakaya of inner luminosity beyond the ordinary mind, in the form of the spontaneously present sambhogakaya, the primordial wisdom of outwardly radiating luminosity, and to display its naturally manifesting and space-pervading lamp—Gyaltsap Rinpoche, Dzogchen Rinpoche, and others bathed Mipham Rinpoche's precious form in lustral waters consecrated during the practices of Bhumkurkuta and Vajravidarana[253]

The hermitage of the Dilgo family at Gothi, which Mipham visited several times and where he died. It was here that, a few days after his birth, Dilgo Khyentse Rinpoche was brought by his mother to receive Mipham's blessing. Photo by Matthieu Ricard, used with permission.

and anointed it with fragrant substances.[254] In the various centers of his body, they wrote syllables in refined gold and set in place the customary printed mandalas that liberate through contact. They wrapped the body in a clean white cloth, and while constantly reciting mantras for the dispelling of obscurations, they packed it all around with sand. They set the body in position, placing a crown on the head and dorje and bell in the hands.

The two great khenpos, holders of the vows and the teachings of the Tripitaka, together with the sovereign master Gyaltsap Rinpoche, the venerable lamas Ösel, Sangye Nyentrul, and others—all the masters gathered there—were entrusted with the entirety of Mipham Rinpoche's writings and repeatedly took the transmission empowerment from the books themselves.[255] On an auspicious day, in accordance with the instructions given by Mipham in his testament, Gyaltsap Rinpoche, the two khenpos, and other masters and disciples performed the cremation of the wish-fulfilling jewel that was his body according to the *Heart Practice of Glorious Vajra-sattva*.[256] Canopies of rainbow light filled the sky and a powerful rumbling resounded continually. The earth shook throughout the whole region of Denyul, much to the amazement of its inhabitants. In the cremation stupa were found undamaged the heart, tongue, and eyes—dark blue and as hard and indestructible as diamond. There were other relics past imagining, such as a perfect image of Yamantaka, and all around were garlands of pearl-like relics. They are now lodged in the heart of the story-high statue of Manjushri at Shechen that had been built to receive them. Moreover, in the monasteries of Kathok Dorjeden, Dzagyal Gön, and Gothi Tashi Pelbar Ling—all the upper and lower monastic colleges, and dharma centers great and small—they made statues chiefly of Vajrasattva and Manjushri, large and small, to house the relics of Mipham Rinpoche. Funerary rituals of the old and new traditions and from both the Kama and Terma collections were performed.

According to the terms of Mipham Rinpoche's testament, all his writings and teachings were entrusted to Shechen Gyaltsap Rinpoche, while the supports for the dharma protectors that Mipham Rinpoche used in his daily prayers were given to Dzogchen Choktrul Rinpoche. In fact, all the accoutrements that he had used in his meditation—the statues, instruments of blessing, and articles for practice—and all the materials and substances that had been offered in gift—in other words, all Mipham Rinpoche's personal possessions—were offered to holders of the teachings, until there was nothing left and without anything being lost, even down to the last needle and thread. And Lama Ösel Rinpoche—a yogi who had himself attained the summit of the vehicle of the Great Secret—ensured that all the commemorative ceremonies were performed on a grand scale to mark the death of the master whom he had always served so perfectly in the three ways.

One day at dawn, about a hundred days after Mipham Rinpoche's departure, Lama Ösel had a vision of him while he was standing in front of the reliquary of the venerable Namkha Legpa, an emanation of Vajrapani. Mipham Rinpoche was just as he was in life, with his rather long nose and his pandita's hat. In that instant, all ordinary appearances melted away into ultimate space, and Mipham gave to Lama Ösel a volume that he composed then and there in a single instant. As Lama Ösel looked at it, all the letters turned into shimmering rainbow light so that it was hard for his eyes to focus on them. Afterward, however, as he made an effort to read them, he clearly discerned the words *jalü dorje* (vajra rainbow body). Mipham Rinpoche then transmitted to him numerous secret prophetic messages, and, as he was finishing, he looked fiercely and made the mudra of threatening at his heart. Three times the words *jalü dorje* resounded loudly, followed by the exclamation *Pet!* Mipham then melted away into space, and the minds of the two masters mingled inseparably together.

All Mipham Rinpoche's faithful and devoted disciples of pure samaya received advice and blessings from him—either directly in the waking state or in the form of meditative experiences or dreams. This was attested to by many marvelous and inspiring stories. Previously, Lama Ösel, the personification of unequaled wisdom and kindness, had specifically offered Mipham Rinpoche the necessary sheets of paper and with many prayers requested him to write down his outer, inner, and secret life stories. And this he did, producing an entire volume. Later, however, not long before his death, when Lama Ösel[257] was giving an explanation of the *Kalachakra Tantra* to Khenpo Kunpel, Mipham Rinpoche himself took the volume and burned it saying, "There is absolutely no need for things like this."

Extraordinary matters, profound and secret, are not, to be sure, objects suitable for common folk—and accounts of astonishing and wonderful happenings do not normally figure in expositions of the teachings. In my own opinion, however, accounts that are free of exaggeration or skepticism and that are based on trustworthy reports of what was seen or heard may become, for fortunate disciples, something on which to rely as a means of nourishing their devotion and faith.

O do not sleep within the peaceful sky,
The vast expanse of dharmadhatu,
Perfect wisdom of victorious ones.
Appear, through your compassion, close to us,
A teacher of both gods and humankind—
Arising as a virtuous friend (so hard to find in any age),
A gem that ornaments sublime, completely secret Doctrine.

In just a single step your supreme mind encompasses
All things that can be known.
Through illusory appearances a hundredfold—
Your feats of memory and mind's assurance—
Compose for us, until the ending of this age of dregs,
Effective discourses that guard
The dharma kingdom of the supreme vehicle.

Through the beating of your wings,
The stages of creation and perfection,
You have traversed the vajra grounds and paths,
And with your tuneful cry, the secret treasure
Of the final lineage, you have rejoiced the hearts
Of happy mountain folk and poured down on the plain
The jewels of Dharma of the threefold vehicle.

With garlands brilliant with a hundred lights
Of wisdom equal to the vast extent of space,
You extirpate the murky brambles of our ignorance.
Your power of speech cuts through the savage tangle
Of false words. The wonder of the ocean of your lives
Surpasses all imagination.

The lute of Brahma's melody,
Invoking through the triple time
Victorious conquerors in realms unbounded,
Sings your praises in a never-ending music

That encompasses the vast expanses of the Secret.
So sweetly does it fall upon on the ears amid the multitude
Of buddhas and their bodhisattva heirs.

Upon that thread of purest gold,
The mind endowed with faith,
The wondrous pearls, your qualities of excellence,
Are threaded as a garland by the fingers of devotion.
The freedom that derives from seeing,
Hearing, thinking of you is, of these, the finest jewel.

Upon the ocean of my faith a hundredfold,
Which lies beneath the hundred beams,
The sunlight of your greatness,
The nighttime lily with its anthers—my ten fingers—closed
Is rivaled by the dancing lotuses of universal joy
In the repeated rituals of devout prostration.
With an undistracted mind
And with a hundred tuneful melodies unhindered,
This song, a cloud of offering of true speech—
With all the wondrous sounds of Saraswati's mouth—
I offer in a manner fit to fill the vast expanses of the dharmadhatu.

Directly, indirectly, through delusion and false views,
All my sins and downfalls regarding the three secrets
Of the venerable teacher and the line of his disciples—
Along with all my other obscurations—I confess without reserve.

Treasury of excellence and virtue,
Worldly and beyond the world,
The merest part of which suffices to relieve
The sorrows of samsara and nirvana—
This is your life and liberation, hard to fathom.
The vast expanses of the heavens
I encompass with the white and smiling clouds of my rejoicing.

Arising from the secret treasure of your mind,
Completely free of all discursive thought,
Everywhere and always is your teaching suited
To the character and aspirations of all who might be trained.
It is a moving chariot of effortless enlightened deeds.
In all my lives, I pray to be conveyed therein.

Uncompounded, space pervading, vajra of the sky,
Flawless, empty yet appearing,
You who have the strength of youth,
I pray that in the vast expanse of supreme peace
You will remain at all times constant,
Never parting for as long as there are beings.

That the good accumulations, waters of ambrosia,
Completely free from poison of conceptual partiality,
Of the ocean of all mind-possessing beings in the triple time—
That they might lead them to the supreme fruit
Beyond samsara and nirvana,
I, a servant, pledge to you this virtue—
To you, the one and only sire of all the buddhas.

Throughout the garland of our lives,
And through the nectar that delights all-knowing buddhas
And is never parted from the anthers of our hearts,
May I and all the line of parent beings linked with me
Fulfill your wishes, teacher, gentle Lord.

Like you, O Manjughosha, Sharpened Vajra,
Perfecting in your one and only person all the host of deeds
And perfect qualities of all the conquerors,
Striving for the benefit of beings and the Doctrine
For as long as space endures,
O may we never wander from the path
So pleasing to yourself, our only father.

May the banquet of your teachings and your perfect writings
Constantly remain within the vessel of our hearts.
I pray that the unfailing strength of your intelligence,
The roaring of the lion of omniscience,
Bestow on us the feast of Dharma of definitive meaning.

May your unrivaled blessing that bestows all one could wish
Shine bright upon the tips of the triumphant ensigns
Of a faith a hundredfold—
Throughout phenomenal existence
May it banish all decay.
And like the cow of plenty, may it satisfy
All wishes for contentment.

May the three times be adorned
By new appearances and perfect signs that spread throughout
The vast expanses of the teachings of the supreme vehicle.
Thereby may we behold the perfect fortune
Of an ending to the troubles of this final age.

The master and lord of mandalas, Jamyang Khyentse Chökyi
Lodrö, the very embodiment of the enlightened activity of the
venerable mirror of primordial wisdom, the omniscient Jamyang
Khyentse Wangpo—the excellent and glorious lion of speech, the
sun of knowledge attained through scripture and reasoning, the
ocean of the intelligence of gentle and melodious Manjushri—told
me that it would be good if I composed a biography of the omniscient Jamgön Mipham, lord of Dharma, according to the reminiscences of the sublime lama who had been his personal attendant. I
took to heart his request, which was seconded on numerous occasions by the insistent demand of Jedrung Tulku, Kyabje Karma
Chökyi Nyinje, whose compassion and qualities of elimination
and realization have brought benefit to the Doctrine and beings of
the nonsectarian tradition.

So it is that, thanks to the fortunate circumstances provided by the written accounts of oral reminiscences taken down by my elder brother Shedrup Tendzin, who had an undivided devotion for the Vajradhara himself, and enjoined by the command of my teacher, the lord of the mandala, I took as my basis, without change or alteration, the words of the adamantine being Ösel Jalü Dorje, the precious lama of threefold kindness, who for thirty-seven years attended and followed, as his very shadow, the venerable Lama Mipham, that fearless, all-seeing charioteer of the Doctrine. To his account, I have made various additions taken from the writings of the Lord Mipham himself, and from other authentic sources, working them into a single book.

This task was performed by one who in all his aspirations has been sustained by the inexpressible kindness of that primordial lord of the definitive teachings, the dust of whose feet he has reverently placed upon the crown of his head—by one who was indeed the last and least of the vajra disciples to whom Jampel Gewa'i Shenyen Tsangse Gyepa'i Dorje, the omniscient master of surpassing love (Mipham Rinpoche), gave his first name, Tashi Peljor.[258] The work was completed on the twenty-ninth day of the waning moon of Saga of the female wood hare year, the thirteenth year of the six-teenth rabjung cycle (1939), when the author was in his thirtieth year.[259] It was the last day of the ceremonies held to mark the anni-versary of the day when the omniscient and accomplished bodhi-sattva Jamgön Mipham displayed the dissolution of the major and minor marks of his enlightenment in the expanse of inner lumi-nosity of primordial wisdom. The text was offered for the perusal of the glorious protector Jamyang Khyentse Chökyi Lodrö, who corrected it and supplemented it with additional details.

May it be the cause whereby the author, together with the entire multitude of beings who fill the whole of space, attain in the life-time of this very body the splendor exemplified by the life story, profound and vast, of the incomparable Sun of Speech—the one and only wisdom form of all victorious buddhas without end.

Virtue, virtue, virtue!

A Selection of
Jamgön Mipham's Writings

A carving of Manjushri made by Mipham Rinpoche himself, originally kept in the hermitage at Junyung. Photo by Matthieu Ricard, used with permission.

SELECTIONS ON MADHYAMAKA

MIPHAM'S NONSECTARIAN ATTITUDE, FROM MIPHAM'S ANSWER TO DRAKAR TULKU

There are, generally speaking, some slight differences in the manner of exposition adopted by the learned masters of Tibet of the earlier and later traditions.[260] Speaking for myself, I was, in this present life, born into the Old Translation school, and because I have imbibed the nectar-like instructions from the mouths of the great holders of its teachings, I feel an intense devotion to its doctrine and those who uphold it.

For this reason, and grounding myself chiefly in the essential principle that consists simply of not being possessed by an evil and destructive spirit—the wrong attitude of denigrating profound and sacred traditions—I composed a short explanation of our scriptural teachings, following in the footsteps of the holy masters of the past.

It seemed to me moreover that if, in that explanation, I had not alluded briefly to the different assertions of our own and other schools and to the ways in which their respective positions are upheld, the view and realization of the holy beings of the past (the sphere of profound primordial wisdom that is hard to grasp) would not be even vaguely understood. And I thought that those who are addicted to merely verbal disputation (the sphere of the ordinary intellect) would once again speak ill of the earlier tradition, being ignorant of its arguments. For they have cast away the unbroken transmission of the profound, essential instructions of the lineage of the learned and accomplished masters of India and Tibet; they reject the texts that explain the untarnished view thereof and hold in contempt the supreme and holy beings who upheld them. Seeing this, and wishing to be of assistance, I had no choice but to raise my voice, and I spoke generally of a few essential points—keeping my remarks to a strict minimum, despite the fact that there was a great deal to say.

The reason for this is that, for my own part, I have an equal and impartial respect for all the excellent teachings of the holy masters of both our own and other schools. Nevertheless, given the various divergent positions that may be adopted, points that differ from others incidentally arise as one speaks about one's own tradition. But however may be the assertions of the wise and accomplished masters of other schools, I have cultivated the attitude of thinking that they were made according to need and were meaningful for the training of their disciples.

I consider it an unacceptable fault to nourish the wrong attitude of angrily denigrating others, and I believe that it serves no purpose to speak about what one does not oneself find meaningful. And yet one only has to say something that diverges from the position of others, and the majority of people nowadays cling strongly and aggressively to their own side. They have no sense of impartiality. The readers of both the old and new traditions spend years squabbling over verbal formulations, squeezing every syllable of the words. Few are those who understand the profound key points correctly, whereas the ignorant majority think to themselves, "The teachings of Tsongkhapa and other great masters are being attacked even by this nonentity," and they are full of indignation. For this reason, and because those who grasp the crucial points are few, I did not say much.

Now in the snowy land of Tibet, the great and venerable lord Tsongkhapa was unrivaled in his activities for the sake of the Buddha's teaching. And with regard to his writings, which are clear and excellently composed, I do indeed feel the greatest respect and gratitude. Nevertheless, there are still some differences between his position and the view of the supreme and holy masters of the earlier tradition; and it is the responsibility of those who uphold that same tradition to treasure its teachings, establishing them by scripture and reasoning. This is the usual practice of all who expound tenet systems. Therefore, if others get angry when the upholders of the earlier tradition make statements to that end, they are simply making an exhibition of their own shortcomings. Conversely, when, in response to our refutation of diverging positions, the upholders of the teachings of later masters reply correctly with arguments based on scripture and reasoning, if we, the holders of the earlier tradition, react with anger, we too are at fault. For whatever is propounded by our own or other schools must be examined to see whether it accords accurately with scripture and is supported by reasoning based on objective fact. It is wrong to proceed simply on the basis of attachment to one's own side.

Trepo Drakar Tulku, Lozang Pelden Tendzin, from glorious Drepung, the great center of Dharma, who is renowned for his clear intelligence, has composed an exposition of the profound crucial points of Madhyamaka entitled *A Pleasurable Discourse for Those of Clear Understanding*. It is a lucid exposition of his own tradition and was sent to me as a refutation. When it arrived, not only was I not displeased to receive it, I was as thrilled as a peacock at the sound of summer thunder. When people have embraced the tradition through which they enter the door of the Dharma, they naturally object to whatever is said against it. Such is the good and noble practice of sons who follow in the footsteps of their fathers.

GREAT EMPTINESS, FREEDOM FROM ONTOLOGICAL EXTREMES, FROM MIPHAM'S COMMENTARY ON THE "WISDOM CHAPTER"

Now regarding the ultimate truth, an emptiness that is just a nonimplicative negation (*med dgag*): the understanding that phenomena are without origin and without abiding (the simple denial, in other words, that they come into being, that they remain in being, and so on) is no more than a point of entry into Great Emptiness, the freedom from all four ontological extremes. It is therefore referred to as the "figurative ultimate" (*rnam grangs pa'i don dam*) or "concordant ultimate" (*mthun pa'i don dam*). As it is written in the *Madhyamakalankara*,

> Since with the ultimate it is attuned,
> It is referred to as the ultimate.[261]

Because from beginningless time, beings are accustomed to cling to phenomena as really existent things, they have no occasion to engender the primordial wisdom that is beyond all four ontological extremes. This is why it is at first necessary to cultivate the kind of wisdom that is a mental factor able to understand clearly that, on the ultimate level, all phenomena are simply without existence. Accordingly, all the texts of the Svatantrikas say that, when the sutras and shastras refute form and so on as being nonexistent, the nonexistence in question is simply the contrary of true existence and is referred to as the figurative ultimate. But it is *not* said that the ultimate nature of phenomena is simply nonexistence. As the *Madhyamakalankara* says,

> Production and the rest have no reality.
> Thus nonproduction and the rest are equally impossible.[262]

The *Two Truths* says the same thing,

> Clearly, in the ultimate, there is no refutation.

When the path is being established on a provisional basis, however, although phenomena are without origin on the ultimate level, it is impossible to refute their appearance on the relative level as things that do originate. Relatively, phenomena do have characteristics, and they are established by the kind of valid cognition that investigates conventional existence. Ultimately, however, such phenomena are not established as existing in the way that they appear, which is why the rider "on the ultimate level" is always added as a qualification of phenomena that are refuted. It is therefore said [by the Svatantrikas] that phenomena do not exist on the ultimate level but are "unfailing" on the relative level. It is thus that each of the two truths is posited quite correctly on its own level; and, from the point of view of beginners, this is a far easier way to proceed.[263] As Master Bhavaviveka has said,

> Those who spurn the ladders of conventionality
> And try to scale the pinnacles,
> The roofs and gables of the palace
> Of the ultimate, are not to be accounted wise!

On the other hand, to say, with regard to their *ultimate condition*, that phenomena exist relatively but do not exist ultimately—in other words, to separate the two characteristics of existence and nonexistence each on its own side—is incorrect. Whatever appears (form and so on) *is empty*; whatever is empty *appears* (as form and so on). Therefore, for as long as the dharmadhatu, the *union of appearance and emptiness*, free from the thirty-two misconceptions, is not realized, this is not yet the authentic *prajnaparamita*.

This is why, from the very beginning, the glorious Chandrakirti, Shantideva, and others place emphasis on primordial wisdom, self-knowing awareness, free from the four ontological extremes. Through the refutation of "existence according to characteristics" on the relative level, the holding of the two truths as separate is also eliminated; and appearance and emptiness are united. By means of the view that goes right to the mode of being of the ultimate truth, wherein no assertions are made, all positions, whether of existence or nonexistence, are demolished by means of consequential arguments. On account of which, Chandrakirti, Shantideva, and those like them came to be known as "Prasangikas" or "consequentialists."

The distinction between Prasangikas and Svatantrikas was an

entirely Tibetan invention, devised by masters like the supreme scholar Butön and others. It was certainly not used in India. As far as the understanding of the ultimate meaning is concerned, there is no difference at all between the Prasangikas and Svatantrikas. They do, however, diverge in their methods of textual exegesis. This can be seen in Chandrakirti's refutation of Bhavaviveka's saying that in the commentary of Buddhapalita there was the fault of failing to add the rider "on the ultimate level" to the object of refutation. With regard to the key points of the ultimate view, there is, however, no difference at all between the great founders of the Prasangika and Svatantrika approaches. They diverge only in the way that they emphasize and explain either the figurative, or approximate, ultimate truth or the nonfigurative, actual, ultimate truth. I have discussed all this at some length in my explanation of the *Madhyamakalankara*, which the reader is invited to consult.

In the present, Prasangika context,[264] therefore, emphasis is placed on the great Madhyamaka itself, the union of appearance and emptiness beyond all conceptual elaboration. And it should be understood that, for this reason, no distinction is made here between the figurative ultimate and the nonfigurative ultimate.

Some say that the primordial wisdom of the Aryas constitutes the authentic nonfigurative ultimate, the freedom from conceptual elaboration, whereas all meditations on emptiness on the part of ordinary beings are meditations on the concordant (figurative) ultimate, which is no more than a nonimplicative negation. In the present context, when emptiness is being referred to, the refutation of form and so on is exclusively a nonimplicative negation. Indeed, if it were otherwise (if the refutation were being made in terms of an implicative negation), then, even though phenomena were refuted, the end result would be a clinging to really existent things, on which account, an implicative negation is not fitting as the meaning of emptiness. All the same, while phenomena are refuted in the manner of a nonimplicative negation, these same phenomena nevertheless continue to appear unfailingly by virtue of interdependence. In other words, their appearance and emptiness coincide. One must therefore overcome one's way of thinking about things exclusively in terms of assertion or denial. As it is said,

> Instead, to grasp the emptiness of things
> And still depend upon the karmic law of cause and fruit—
> It's this that is more wonderful than wonderful,
> More marvelous than marvelous![265]

And likewise we find in the *Panchakrama*,

> When voidness and appearance both
> Are seen as each the aspect of the other,
> They blend together perfectly
> And thus are said to be united.

The Two Kinds of Ultimate and the Equal Status of the Svatantrikas and Prasangikas, from Mipham's Commentary on the *Madhyamakalankara*

Now, within this [Madhyamaka] tradition, some [the Prasangikas] do not analyze conventional phenomena. They affirm them simply as they appear empirically in the common consensus. Others [the Svatantrikas] do examine phenomena and assert them in the manner of the Sautrantikas and other substantialists. But in the *Madhyamakalankara*, conventional phenomena are posited in accordance with the Chittamatra view, and thus this text inaugurates, for the first time, the tradition of Yogachara-Madhyamaka.

When examined with conventional reasoning, this way of positing the relative truth is found to correspond to what, in the final analysis, is the case on the conventional level. . . . In this context, it must be realized that the two kinds of valid reasoning, conventional and ultimate, have different spheres of application. Now, the best way of positing the conventional is that of the Chittamatrins, which as a method is extremely felicitous. . . .

When we consider the conventional in this way, we are not asking whether phenomena exist as mental projections on the ultimate level. We are instead using conventional valid reasoning to assess phenomena that merely, and incontrovertibly, appear. It is like when someone is asked whether the appearances experienced in dreams are the mind or whether they exist separate from the mind. A sensible investigator will conclude that they are simply the mind experiencing itself and that they cannot exist outside the mind. We speak in a similar vein. However, some people muddle the two kinds of reasoning. They think that to affirm a tenet that investigates conventional phenomena is incompatible with the Prasangika stance, which is to accept phenomena as they are, without analysis, according to the general consensus. It must be said, however, that in the context of pramana, or valid cognition, applied on the relative level, it is quite acceptable to say that phenomena exist according to their characteristics or that they are established by valid cognition and so forth. The important thing, however, is to distinguish (that is, not to confuse) the kind of valid cognition used in the assessment. For if conventional phenomena were assessed from the standpoint of ultimate valid cognition, they would not be even slightly established thereby. They would be just like darkness that disappears in a bright light. On the other hand, if the assessment is made from the point of view of conventional valid cognition, phenomena are, on this level, established ineluctably and undeniably. Therefore, however much conventional reasoning may be used to examine phenomena in accordance with their mode of appearance, this investigation will never become an examination on the ultimate level. . . . In brief, no Madhyamika (whether Prasangika or Svatantrika) refutes things as they are commonly perceived. On the other hand, no Madhyamika asserts an entity that is truly and intrinsically existent. As a matter of emphasis and according to the degree of realization of the way the two truths are united, there are different ways of establishing the ultimate. But it is inappropriate to assign a high or low position to a tenet system simply on the basis of how it explains the relative. . . .

In short, from the ultimate standpoint, the indivisibility of the two truths (as realized in meditative equipoise by primordial wisdom beyond thought and word), there is no need to make any distinction between the two truths. Phenomena are primordially beyond any thesis that affirms or negates their existence, nonexistence, both, or neither. This is similar to the way certain questions were answered by [the Buddha's] silence. Since the ultimate level is beyond all conventionalities, expressions, formulations, and conceptual constructs, and since it is the very equality of all things, it is beyond all assertion. But in postmeditation, according to the appearing mode of phenomena, which *is* an object of word and thought, one reflects on the phenomena of the ground, path, and fruit. Moreover, if there is a need to explain them also to others, one cannot but engage in the refutation or establishment of things, by correctly distinguishing and using the two types of valid reasoning. It should not be thought therefore that the Svatantrika approach differs greatly from that of the Prasangikas. Svatantrikas are different in the way they talk about conventionalities, but they also establish through reasoning the ultimate view of both Nagarjuna and Asanga as being indivisible.

If one understands the matter thus, all the different disputes of Tibetan scholarship, on whether conventional phenomena are established by valid cognition or not, resolve themselves quite naturally. The criticism made by certain people to the effect that the scholars of the earlier period mistook the genuine Prasangika view, and that they failed to understand correctly the view of Nagarjuna and his son [Aryadeva], is likewise naturally dissipated. . . .

. . . The path in which the conventional and the ultimate truths are united, without any assertion of their being either identical or different, constitutes the great vehicle. An individual who adopts this approach can be properly called a practitioner of the Mahayana, and in such a case, the name is being used correctly.

As a first step, at the stage of study and reflection, the two truths are combined in a manner whereby production on the conventional level and nonproduction on the ultimate level are the objects of words and concepts. In terms of this pairing, the ultimate level is called the figurative ultimate because, on the one hand, it is contrasted with existence on the relative level and because, on the other hand, it belongs to the ultimate side of things and is counted as the ultimate. Within the context of the two truths, it is the counterpart of the relative and is simply an avenue of approach that is in harmony with the nonfigurative ultimate.[266] For if one meditates on it, it has the power to destroy one's powerful clinging to the reality of things, which has been built up by force of habit from time without beginning. It should be understood, moreover, that it is only in terms of this figurative ultimate that statements like "There is no production" are made. And the philosophical investigations implied by such statements, however perfect and far-reaching they may be, are only a means of bringing certainty in the postmeditation period. As far as concerns the authentic ultimate mode of things, however, "nonproduction" (formulated in contrast with "production") is no more than a conceptual reflection (*rnam rtog gi gzugs brnyan*) constructed through the mental exclusion of "production." For the nonfigurative ultimate is beyond all conceptual constructs such as existence or nonexistence, production or nonproduction, and so on. It is not the domain of thought and language; it is what the Aryas see with the utterly stainless primordial wisdom of meditative equipoise. This is the unsurpassable nonfigurative ultimate. From this standpoint, the Svatantrikas make no assertion either. Now, since the figurative ultimate comes close to the nonfigurative ultimate and is in harmony with it, it is counted as "ultimate," being also referred to as the concordant ultimate (*mthun pa'i don dam*).

Those who, through practice associated with the view of the concordant ultimate, thus attain the experience of the nonfigurative ultimate truth may be called either Prasangikas or Svatantrikas depending on the way they make or do not make assertions in the postmeditation period. But one should know that in terms of their realization, there is no difference between them. They are

both in possession of the wisdom of the Aryas. This is very important and will be explained further when the purpose of this text is
expounded.

What is the cause of the wisdom experienced by the Aryas in
meditative equipoise? It is the complete assimilation of the correct
understanding of the two truths. There is absolutely no alternative
to this. Only two sticks together can be used to make a fire; one
stick by itself is useless. In the same way, if the two approaches
are not evenly united, the certainty of the state free from the conceptual constructs of the four ontological extremes can never be
achieved. . . .

Therefore, according to the tradition of the great charioteer
Shantarakshita, the wisdom fire that comes from uniting the two
spotless ways of valid reasoning, which investigate the relative
and the ultimate, can burn up all the tinder wood of dualistically
appearing knowledge objects, leaving nothing behind. As a result,
one will remain in the evenness of the dharmadhatu beyond all
conceptual extremes. When two sticks of wood are rubbed together
and fire is kindled, the sticks themselves are also consumed. In the
same way, the wisdom fire kindled when the two truths are truly
united also consumes the apprehension of, and clinging to, the two
truths as being two separate things, so that one remains in the perfect freedom from all ontological extremes: the dharmadhatu in
which appearance and emptiness are indivisible.

Conventional Phenomena Are Mind
Only, from Mipham's Commentary on the
Madhyamakalankara

The way of describing the two truths . . . is not the preserve of only
one tradition. It is the great path of the Mahayana in general. For
while all phenomena are empty of intrinsic existence, their mere
appearance on the conventional level is said to have no cause other
than the mind alone. The *Lankavatara-sutra* says,

> From time without beginning mental imprints in the mind
>   appear as objects,
> They are like reflections in a looking glass.
> But if one sees them as they are, in all their purity,
> One finds that there are no external things.

This shows that there are no extramental objects. All such things
are but the mind.

> The personal continuum and the aggregates,
> Causation and the atoms likewise,
> Prakriti, the creator God:
> All are fancies that the mind alone constructs.

The second quotation shows that there is no creator outside the
mind. This beginningless existence, composed of various phenomena, has not arisen by itself, uncaused. Neither is it brought about
by extraneous causes, the passage of time, or the combination of
infinitesimal particles, through God, *purusha*, and so forth. It has
arisen through the power of one's own mind, and to speak in this
way is none other than the teaching of the entire Mahayana. The
venerable Chandrakirti has likewise said,

> The vast array of sentient life,
> The varied universe containing it, is formed by mind.
> The Buddha said that wandering beings are from karma
>   born.
> Dispense with mind and karma is no more.[267]

To say that the world of appearances does not arise from the
mind necessarily implies the belief that it is caused by something
else. And since this involves the assertion that beings are bound in
samsara or delivered from it through causes other than their own
minds, it will doubtless cause one to fall into non-Buddhist tenet
systems. It is therefore established step by step that if there is no

external creator and no external world, extramental objects are but the mind's self-experience. Thus this assertion that conventionalities are "mind only" exists in all the Mahayana schools.

Why is it then that the glorious Chandrakirti and others do not posit the conventional level in this way? As was explained above, when he establishes the ultimate in itself, which accords with the field of wisdom of Aryas while they are in meditative equipoise, it is sufficient for him to refer to, as objects of assessment, the phenomena of samsara and nirvana as they appear and are experienced on the empirical level, without analyzing or examining them. Since from the beginning these phenomena are beyond the four conceptual extremes, it is not necessary for him to enter into a close philosophical investigation of the way phenomena appear on the conventional level. When one assesses appearances with words and concepts, one may, for instance, say that phenomena exist or that they do not exist, that phenomena are or are not the mind. But however one may assert them, they do not exist in that way on the ultimate level. Therefore, with the consequences of the Prasangika reasoning, which investigates the ultimate, Chandrakirti is merely refuting the incorrect ideas of the opponents. And given that Chandrakirti's own stance is free from all conceptual references, how could he assert a theory of his own? He does not. In this way, he can refute, without needing to separate the two truths, whatever assertions are made concerning existence and nonexistence. In the present Svatantrika context [of Shantarakshita's *Madhyamakalankara*], since the two truths are assessed with reasoning specific to each of them, nothing can be refuted or established without distinguishing these same two truths. But in Chandrakirti's tradition, assessment is made using the valid reasoning that investigates the ultimate nature of the two truths united—the actual nonfigurative ultimate. As Chandrakirti quotes from a scripture in his autocommentary to the *Madhyamakavatara*: "On the ultimate level, O monks, there are no two truths. This ultimate truth is one."

Thus the honorable Chandrakirti emphasizes and establishes the nonfigurative ultimate from the very beginning. He does not refute mere appearances, for these are the very basis for investigation into the ultimate; they are the means and gateway to it. He therefore accepts them as a basis for debate and establishes them as being beyond all conceptual extremes. Then, in the postmeditation period, he establishes his own position and refutes those of his opponents concerning the path and result in accordance with the way they are assessed by the two kinds of reasoning. And thus even Chandrakirti makes assertions on the conventional level, and these cannot be invalidated. He asserts conventional phenomena as mere appearances or simply as dependent arisings. If, with regard to these mere appearances, an investigation is made using conventional reasoning, Chandrakirti [and the Prasangikas generally] do not deny the manner in which samsara and nirvana are produced through the forward and backward progression of the twelve interdependent links of existence. Phenomena are shown to arise dependently through the power of the pure or impure mind. And this clearly expresses the tenet of Mind Only.

FREEDOM FROM THE FOUR CONCEPTUAL EXTREMES, FROM MIPHAM'S COMMENTARY ON THE *MADHYAMAKALANKARA*

Freedom from the four conceptual extremes arises in a person's mind in the following manner. In the case of a beginner who penetrates it step by step, perfect and stainless reasoning first eliminates the "conceived object," that is, the misconception that all compounded or uncompounded phenomena really exist. Reasoning then refutes the conceived objects of the three remaining extremes: that things do not exist, that they both exist and do not exist, and that they neither exist nor do not exist. Subsequently, thanks to meditating in accordance with the extraordinary certainty wherein the conceived objects of the extreme ontological positions have no place, the point will come where all conceptual extremes will stand refuted in a single stroke, and the practitioner will behold the dharmadhatu clearly. It is as the great and omniscient Gorampa Sonam Senge has said: "The intellect of ordinary people, which investigates ultimate reality, cannot refute in a single stroke all four conceptual extremes. But by refuting these extremes one after the other and by meditating properly, one reaches the path of seeing. This is called the view that sees the dharmadhatu."

The learned and accomplished masters of the Old Translation school take as their stainless view the freedom from all conceptual constructs of the four extremes, the ultimate reality of the two truths inseparably united. In addition, they possess the profound pith instructions of the Vajrayana. They actualize the ultimate nature by developing certainty in it through the path of perfect reasoning—the arguments of the four realizations.[268] And then by their meditation, they achieve unshakable confidence in the inseparability of the two truths—the indivisibility of primordial purity (*ka dag*) and spontaneous accomplishment (*lhun grub*). This is how they have gained, and continue to gain, accomplishment. Hundreds of thousands of treasures of Dharma burst forth in their minds, and many have reached the realization of the all-penetrating rainbow body. Such is the result of their perfect view, which guides them on the path.

One might think that such a view is confined to the Nyingmapas alone, but this is not so. The absence of the four conceptual constructs was repeatedly taught by the Buddha in the profound sutras and tantras. Scholars (for example, the six ornaments of India) have elucidated this teaching both directly and indirectly, and it has been the inner practice of all the great accomplished vidyadharas. It is the sole path to omniscience and is the very heart of the views of both the Sarmapa and Nyingmapa.

MEDITATING ON MADHYAMAKA—ADVICE FOR THE STUDENT, FROM MIPHAM'S ANSWER TO DRAKAR TULKU

I would like to say a few words just as they come to mind and with the intention of helping all those—whether of our own or other schools—who are trying to realize suchness. On the basis of correct reasoning, beginners must achieve certainty that phenomena are without intrinsic being, and that "absence of real existence" and "dependent arising" are actually the same thing. It is of the highest importance simply to generate an extraordinary conviction that appearance and emptiness are inseparably united—just as with the moon reflected on the water.

By relying on this and growing used to it, you will gain an understanding that will indeed correspond to the fundamental mode of being of things. Be that as it may, whatever is apprehended conceptually cannot go beyond the figurative ultimate. You should never say that this and this alone constitutes the meaning of the prajnaparamita and that there is no higher ultimate than this. If you do this, you will be taking as definitive what is but a semblance of prajnaparamita, the mere object of an ordinary consciousness. The result will be that you will not enter that wisdom that is utterly nonconceptual and is the authentic meaning of prajnaparamita, and you will be turning your back on the unmistaken way of penetrating it, namely, an uncontrived resting meditation in which nothing is removed and nothing is added. As long as you fail to relinquish your attachment to the supremacy of your view, actual primordial wisdom beyond all conceptual constructs will not take birth in your mind stream.

Therefore, the mind that understands with certainty that dependently arising phenomena are without inherent existence understands also that all things are like a moon reflected in water. And yet this is no more than an approximation to the certainty enjoyed by noble beings in their postmeditation, when they see that everything is like an illusion. The ultimate reality of suchness is indeed to be scrutinized closely. Nevertheless, the realization of the nonfigurative ultimate itself, the experiential sphere of meditative equipoise, is free from conceptual constructs. It is beyond the reach of thought and word and is therefore the way of being of the ineffable ultimate that cannot be revealed by examples. All this is to be recognized by distinctly self-cognizing primordial wisdom and is an experience that is still to be cultivated. This is something that you should think about.

Now it might be thought that such a fundamental mode of being is the field of experience of noble beings, who are in possession of distinctly self-cognizing primordial wisdom, but that it cannot in any way be experienced by ordinary beings.

True, the actual nonfigurative ultimate is by no means experienced by ordinary beings, but only by the Aryas. The understanding of ordinary beings can realize and taste the ineffable nature only by means of a meaning-generality or mental image (*don spyi*). This is referred to in the sutras as the "acceptance of the nature of phenomena,"[269] and in the tantras as "example wisdom." In either case, this is a state of mind attuned to the final and perfect ultimate. A state of freedom from conceptual constructs that is in accordance with this state may indeed be induced in the mind by virtue of no more than the certainty arising from analytical investigation. This, however, is a very lengthy process and takes birth in connection with, and thanks to, an extraordinary accumulation (of wisdom and merit). It can, on the other hand, be realized swiftly and without much difficulty in dependence on the profound methods of Mantra, and especially through the power of the pith instructions that introduce one directly to the nature of the mind. It is thus that the experience of the fundamental mode of being occurs.

When this happens, if the person concerned is someone who has already acquired—through an examination based on study and reflection—a strong conviction of the inseparability of emptiness and dependent arising, he or she will be in a position to compare the experience that occurred in the course of analysis with the experience occurring now, which does not derive from analysis but from resting in the natural state of mind free from all apprehension and clinging. On both occasions, there is no difference whatever in what is taken as the object, namely, the fundamental nature in which emptiness and dependent arising are indivisible. However, when you are analyzing, it is like having your eyes closed and thinking about something in front of you, whereas when you are in the state that is free of clinging, it is like having your eyes open and seeing the thing directly. That is the difference. And once you have experienced this, then no matter how much other people may denigrate your practice that is free from all apprehension, and no matter how much they may explain to others the flavor of the treacle that you yourself have actually tasted, you will never have any doubt.

If, on the other hand, you have studied only a little, if you have not, by means of reasoning, gained certainty in the fundamental mode of being, and if you are not in possession of the key points of the pith instructions, you may rest without fabrication in a completely blank state of mind (without understanding or perceiving anything), but how could you possibly come anywhere near the state of absence of conceptual construction? By contrast, if you have managed to perfect your investigation of the fundamental mode of being, or if you are in possession of the pith instructions for settling the mind, the light of wisdom, in which all four extremes are simultaneously discarded, will become clear.

Therefore, the realization through certain knowledge of the nonfigurative ultimate is, generally speaking, to be posited as the realization of the ultimate, in just the same way that all objects understood through inferential reasoning (which understands by way of mental images or object-generalities) are to be referred to as "realizations." For instance, through reasoning, one comes to the realization that there are past and future lives. Through the testament of scripture, one realizes the existence of the karmic law of cause and effect. And through the evidence of smoke, one realizes that there is a fire, and so on.

10

THE LION'S ROAR

A Comprehensive Discourse on the Buddha-Nature

TEXTUAL OUTLINE

1. The sugatagarbha is present in the minds of beings
    2. The assertions of earlier Tibetan masters
    2. The assertion of our own position
        3. The meaning of the first line of the stanza from the *Uttaratantra*
            4. The general approach
            4. The uncommon approach
                5. The argument based on scriptural authority
                5. The argument based on reasoning
                5. A refutation of objections
        3. The meaning of the second line of the stanza
            4. A refutation of objections
        3. The meaning of the third line of the stanza

1. The manner in which the sugatagarbha is present in the minds of beings

1. A refutation of certain false positions regarding the buddha-element
    2. A refutation of the view that the buddha-element is not empty
        3. A refutation based on scripture
        3. A refutation based on reasoning

THE LION'S ROAR

The nature of the mind, primordially immaculate,
Is the ultimate Manjushri, bodhisattva hero,
Who with the sharp blade of the path of reasoned certainty
Cuts through the webs of confusion and existence.

The heart of the teachings of all victorious ones past, present, and to come, the core of their enlightened mind, the single crucial point of all the teachings of the sutras and the tantras, is exclusively the all-pervading buddha-essence, the sugatagarbha.[270] This matter is exceedingly profound, so much so that the Buddha said that even for the great and powerful bodhisattvas on the tenth ground, it is as difficult to realize the sugatagarbha correctly as it is to discern a form in the dark of night. This being so, what need is there to speak of the capacity of ordinary beings?

Moreover, in some of his discourses, the Sugata, our teacher, elucidated the nature of the sugatagarbha by speaking about its emptiness. On other occasions, he elucidated its character by saying that it is primordially endowed with the [ten] strengths and other enlightened qualities. Now even though these two aspects are necessarily united without contradiction, some people—through their failure to find confidence in the crucial point of the inseparability of the two truths (which is more profound than the profound)—consider that the sugatagarbha is permanent and not empty by its nature. Others, by maintaining that it is mere emptiness, fail to assert that it is primordially endowed with the inalienable qualities of the kayas and wisdoms. They thus adopt a nihilistic view and make the mistake of underestimation. And in the hope of substantiating their opinions, they proclaim their refutations and assertions with all the clamor of a tempestuous sea.

By contrast, those who are fortunate enough to be guided by their teacher's essential instructions—a perfect nectar whereby their hearts are satisfied—have faith in primordial wisdom, the noncontradictory union of the expanse of emptiness and the wisdom of luminosity. They bring to rest any kind of fixation on the extremes of either appearance or emptiness. It is in accordance with their position that I shall now speak.

As a general principle, the words of the Tathagata, which are utterly trustworthy, are expressed in scriptures that are perfectly correct and reliable. The undeceiving and definitive character of these same scriptures is generally established through three kinds of examination.[271] Specifically, the explicit meaning revealed in the words of the texts should be held as definitive when it is shown that reasoning does not disprove it and that it is moreover supported by valid demonstration. It is a mistake to neglect the reasoning by which the scriptures are substantiated and to proceed simply on the basis of a trust that one may feel in their regard. For there are in general scriptures that are true and scriptures that are false. And among those that are true, one cannot deny that some scriptures are of definitive meaning while some are of provisional meaning.

Consequently, ordinary beings are able to cut through their misconceptions by means of study and reflection, and thanks to the three types of valid cognition, they are able to ascertain the points that should be assimilated. And it is thanks to this that they acquire irreversible conviction. If, on the other hand, they fail to ascertain through valid cognition the truth of their position for themselves, and they are unable to prove it to those who contest it, they are like those who, though unsure about the presence of [an invisible] flesh-eating spirit, proclaim that it is there in front of them. They are unable to convince either themselves or anyone else. Therefore, the learned should adopt a procedure of speaking in a way that accords with reason. If their position is logically established, their supporters will be filled with irreversible enthusiasm and the tongues of dissenters will be cut short. By contrast, when a path is not established by reason, then no matter how much it is decorated by all manner of assertions, a host of doubts will proliferate like water welling up from a spring.

Therefore, if we engage in the path that has been expounded by the buddhas and the bodhisattvas and their lineage, and that has not been muddled by mere intellectuals, and if we set biased partisanship aside and honestly assess the correct reasons that establish the sugatagarbha, we will see that there are no arguments for, and many arguments against, two false assertions. The first is that the sugatagarbha is permanent, truly existent, and not empty by its nature; the second is that it is simply emptiness and is devoid of qualities. Conversely, we will see that there are excellent arguments that support, and none that undermine, the assertion that the buddha-essence exists within sentient beings, and that, though empty by nature, it has the character of being primordially endowed with enlightened qualities.

1. The sugatagarbha is present in the minds of beings

Let us begin, therefore, by examining the arguments that demonstrate the presence of the buddha-essence, the sugatagarbha, within the minds of beings.

The *Uttaratantra* contains the following text:

> Because the kaya of perfect buddhahood radiates,
> Because in suchness there is no division,
> Because they have potential for enlightenment,
> All beings have at all times buddha-essence.

Now in order to establish the meaning of this text through the use of logical arguments, we will first mention the position of other traditions and then state the position of our own perfect tradition.

2. The assertions of earlier Tibetan masters

In Tibet, certain masters of former times understood the first line
of the stanza, "because the kaya of perfect buddhahood radiates,"
to mean that all objects are simply pervaded by the dharmakaya
wisdom. They understood the second line of the stanza, "because
in suchness there is no division," to mean that suchness is similar
in kind to mere emptiness. And they understood the third line,
"because they have potential for enlightenment," to mean that sentient beings simply have the ability to become enlightened. These
statements, however, are very summary and fail to capture the crucial and essential meaning of the *Uttaratantra*.

With regard to the first point (the kaya of perfect buddhahood
radiates), the authentic buddha-potential is not established by the
mere fact that objects are pervaded by the dharmakaya. For even
though the wisdom of buddhahood, which is present within the
mind stream of an [enlightened] being, embraces all [other] objects
and is therefore present in all things, this does not mean that those
same objects have themselves the cause for becoming buddhas.
Furthermore, since the dharmakaya is not for the moment manifest in our minds, we may doubt that there is any evidence of its
presence.

Regarding the second point (in suchness there is no division),
the meaning of the buddha-potential is not at all to be equated
with just the figurative ultimate, the mere concept of emptiness
[as presented by these earlier masters]. These masters say that the
buddha-potential is like a seed that will transform into a shoot.
They say that this potential has no enlightened qualities at the
moment but that these will develop when the potential is associated with the conditions of the path. In affirming this, however,
they are saying that the emptiness of true existence—a conceptual
aspect that is a nonimplicative negation, in other words, something
uncompounded—is capable of performing a function. But it is
completely illogical to ascribe such a characteristic to an emptiness
of this kind. A seed that is a compounded entity is perfectly capa-

ble, on the conventional level, of transforming into a shoot. But it can never be possible for an absence of true existence superimposed onto a seed to transform into a shoot.

Furthermore, to claim that it is through the fact of being empty of true existence that one is able to attain buddhahood is to speak carelessly. For whereas it is quite true to say that if the mind exists truly, it cannot attain buddhahood, there is no certainty in saying that it is simply through the absence of true existence that buddhahood can be attained. All phenomena lack true existence, including earth and stones, but who could maintain that this gives them the ability to attain buddhahood?

Again, it is senseless to posit the buddha-potential as the lack of true existence just because focusing on the absence of true existence is able to remove the obscurations [of defilement]. For those who say this also say that the cognitive obscurations *cannot* be removed just by focusing on emptiness. They moreover think that [in any case] one must also be adorned with an infinite accumulation of merit.

It is pointless to give the name "sugatagarbha" to such a kind of nonimplicative negation [emptiness as defined by the earlier scholars]. A "potential" of this kind is the same as what the shravakas and pratyekabuddhas meditate on. On the contrary, the ability to attain buddhahood is not established by this means and, as far as concerns a sugatagarbha seen as a mere nonimplicative negation, it is quite untenable to say that, after removing the cognitive obscurations, the primordial wisdom of omniscience arises. For since within the very nature of a nonimplicative negation there is no element of knowing, it is impossible for any kind of knowledge to be present even at the time of enlightenment.

Therefore, [instead of an uncompounded absence of true existence], it would fit the position of our opponents better to think of the buddha-potential in terms of a kind of compounded nature that is able to evolve—saying that within the mind streams of all beings there are, present from beginningless time, the seeds of wisdom, love, and power. After all, even wild beasts and demons feel love for their young; and they have the ability to recognize the difference between helping and harming. And if this capacity were to be informed by the path, and if it were gradually freed from hindrances and made to develop, such beings would eventually possess boundless knowledge, love, and power. If our opponents were to say that this is what the capacity for enlightenment is, it would be a far better position than to say that the buddha-potential is a nonimplicative negation. For it necessarily implies a causal sequence giving rise to a result; and to abandon this result-producing factor—which cannot but be a momentary entity—and say that the cause [of enlightenment] is an uncompounded nonthing, incapable of giving rise to anything at all, is truly an astonishing position to adopt.

Some people, reflecting upon such problems, say that the buddha-potential is not the absence of true existence in all things. Only the mind's absence of true existence is tenable as the buddha-potential. But even if we grant that the buddha-potential is the mind's lack of true existence, the fact remains that a "lack of true existence" is unable to perform the activity of giving rise to something, whereas the moments of the mind can quite rightly be said to perform the function of generating successive moments. An uncompounded buddha-potential [as they understand it] thus becomes irrelevant and our opponents should abandon it.

Now they may think as follows. They could say that they are not positing the buddha-potential on the basis of the separation of the two truths each on its own side but that, on the contrary, this same buddha-potential is the nature in which the luminosity of the mind (the phenomenon, *chos can*) and its emptiness (its ultimate nature, *chos nyid*) are inseparable. In answer to this, we would say that if, of the two—ordinary consciousness and primordial wisdom—our opponents are referring to primordial wisdom, which is unchanging and uncompounded, then what they are saying is proved by reasoning and scripture and is certainly true. But if, by the phenomenon that is to be united with emptiness, they mean the ordinary consciousness, which is momentary, then to think that *this* can be gradually transformed into buddhahood is very foolish. For it follows in that case that there are two aspects to the potential: one that is compounded and one that is uncompounded. This being so, the aspect that is uncompounded—and consequently powerless [to produce the enlightened qualities even at the stage of buddhahood]—is the buddha-potential only in name. On the contrary, the real buddha-potential must be the compounded aspect—which is able to produce results. But by such a thing, the wisdom intention of all the Mahayana sutras, which declare that the naturally present buddha-potential is the uncompounded dharmadhatu (the expanse of ultimate reality), is reduced to nothing. Since the buddha-potential, posited in terms of something produced and something that produces, is inevitably a matter for the [ordinary] mind, one may *refer* to this naturally abiding potential as the pure dharmadhatu, but in that case, what one believes and what one says are in blatant contradiction.

When one affirms that the potential for buddhahood is the unchanging dharmadhatu, one must recognize that the basis for the imputation of "dharmadhatu" must be the nonfigurative ultimate truth, the great union of the two truths, the very meaning of the middle way that is in no way found [in any ontological extreme]. If, failing to recognize this, one states that it is just the figurative ultimate, then the situation is like someone who sees a troop of monkeys in the forest and deludedly thinks that they are the gods of the Heaven of the Thirty-Three! For if one takes as the dharmadhatu something that is not the dharmadhatu and claims that it is the buddha-potential, and if focusing on this, one thinks that one is meditating on the prajnaparamita and thinks that it is the cause of the *svabhavikakaya*, one is simply inventing a path and claiming that it is the Great Vehicle—as the wisdom sutras themselves say.

The naturally pure dharmadhatu, or emptiness, is the expanse of the two truths free from all the webs of mental elaboration, and it is known by self-cognizing primordial wisdom. This is the authentic buddha-potential and is that which becomes the svabhavikakaya endowed with the twofold purity—as all the Mahayana sutras and their commentaries proclaim. This being so, the naturally present potential is uncompounded, and it is improper to say anything that suggests otherwise. It is unacceptable to say anything to deny that the qualities of the dharmakaya are a result that comes about through elimination. For it is untenable to say that something uncompounded can give rise to a result other than itself and then cease to exist—in the same way that a productive cause gives rise to a produced effect. This the Regent [Maitreya], a mahasattva abiding on the tenth ground, has declared in the *Uttaratantra*. And the glorious lord, Arya Nagarjuna, has also clearly said it in his *Dharmadhatu-stava*. For this reason, we in our tradition follow these texts and affirm that the buddha-potential is the uncompounded dharmadhatu.

This very expanse is the ultimate way of being of all phenomena and is in itself devoid of birth or cessation. It abides as the very essence of the inseparability of appearance and emptiness and never falls into either of these two extremes. So it is that compounded phenomena, which do appear to arise and cease, do not exist in the way that they appear. Consequently, the nature of the dharmadhatu is never stained by them. The causal process [that gives rise to] samsara is pure from the beginning; it is completely inseparable from the immaculate appearances of spontaneously present luminosity. By means of this crucial point, we should recognize the character of the sugatagarbha correctly.

2. The assertion of our own position

3. The meaning of the first line of the stanza from the *Uttaratantra*, "Because the kaya of perfect buddhahood radiates"

The meaning of this first line is as follows. The dharmakaya, the kaya of utterly perfect buddhahood, possesses qualities equal to the vastness of space. Therefore, if the dharmakaya is able to appear, to radiate, or to manifest at some later stage within the mind stream of a person who is at present ordinary and completely fettered, this shows that the sugatagarbha is present *at this very moment* in the mind streams of sentient beings. This proof is supported by arguments that are both common and uncommon [that is, belonging to the teachings in general and to the Nyingma tradition in particular].

4. The general approach

First of all, if there are sentient beings who have actualized the dharmakaya wisdom, it necessarily follows that the potential for enlightenment was already present in those beings' minds. For such an actualization would be impossible if the potential for it had been absent. As it is said in the *Dharmadhatu-stava*,

> When the element [containing gold] is there,
> Pure gold appears through work performed.
> But when that element is absent, nothing but exhaustion
> Will result from work performed.

4. The uncommon approach

It may be thought that while the above argument is tenable, it shows only that, following the example of crops growing in a field, the mind is indeed able to *become* buddha, but only in the manner of a [material] cause[272]—how does it establish the presence of a special potential that is primordially endowed with the qualities of enlightenment? The latter is nonetheless established. The bhagavan buddhas possess the wisdom kaya, the nature of which is very clearly uncompounded. As both scripture and reasoning demonstrate, it is neither compounded nor impermanent.

5. The argument based on scriptural authority

As far as the scriptures are concerned, the *Nirvana-sutra* says, "O monks of excellent discipline, the tathagata is uncompounded. If you say that the tathagata is compounded, you will become tirthikas, and it would be better for you to die!" And in the same text we find, "O son of the lineage, the tathagata is a body of permanence, an indestructible body, a body of adamant. It is not a body of flesh. Look upon it as the dharmakaya." And again, "Rather than to say that the tathagata is impermanent, it would be better for your tongue to be touched by the blazing flames of a fire. It would be better to die! Do not allow such words to be heard!"

Moreover, in order to show that a nonimplicative negation (mere emptiness) cannot be nirvana, the state beyond all suffering, the same text says, "Emptiness, emptiness! The meaning is that though we search, we find nothing at all. But 'nothing at all' is an idea shared even by the Jains. Liberation is not at all like that." And the same text goes on to say, "What therefore is liberation? It is the [buddha] element, something uncontrived. It is the sugatagarbha."

The *Vajracchedika-sutra* also says,

> Whoever sees me as a form,
> Whoever knows me as a sound,
> Has strayed upon the path of error.
> Such beings see me not!
>
> For the buddhas should be viewed as dharmata,
> The guides are dharmakaya.
> Since dharmata cannot be known,
> Me these beings cannot know.

As these quotations indicate, this point is extensively explained in all the sutras of definitive meaning.

5. The argument based on reasoning

From the point of view of reasoning, the following may be said. If the primordial wisdom of omniscience—the final result that is nondual and of the same taste as primordial dharmadhatu—were impermanent, if it were newly produced from causes and conditions, it could not be self-arisen primordial wisdom. It would not be freed from the torment of change. It would constantly arise and cease. It would be unreliable, for by nature it would be destructible. It could not be a sure refuge, for as soon as it arose, it would be destroyed. It would remain only a little while when all the causes for it were assembled. Neither could it be of one taste with all phenomena. It would not be beyond all ontological extremes. The conceptual mind could not be prevented from arising. Finally, the [primordial wisdom of omniscience] would not be independent but would depend upon conditioning factors. The faults of all these consequences would be entailed. And since by making such a statement, the error of holding the view that the vajra body is impermanent is so enormous, one should abandon this evil path and say instead that the kaya of nondual primordial wisdom is uncompounded and supremely permanent.

Now if one assesses the matter just by reasoning based on ordinary perception, and if one objects that it is impossible for primordial wisdom to be uncompounded because it is impossible for cognition and permanence to go together, this is a very poor argument to make. There is indeed a lesser kind of knowledge that cognizes objects and is necessarily impermanent. But this is not the same as primordial wisdom, in which the knower and the things known are of a single taste, and which is endowed with the all-pervading indestructible expanse. For this is a state of unchanging luminosity, an uncompounded radiance—in which the phenomena of both samsara and nirvana are contained. This primordial wisdom is, from the very beginning, beyond both arising and cessation. This is established by the reasoning of final analysis.[273]

Moreover, a primordial wisdom of this kind abides neither in the extreme of compoundedness nor in that of uncompoundedness. It is, so to say, "the great nonabiding uncompounded" and is utterly unlike something that is just "nonexistent."[274] For existent things and nonexistent things are both relative phenomena: they either arise dependently or are designated dependently. And if they are examined correctly, they are found to be compounded, fallacious, illusory, and deceptive. By contrast, the sugatagarbha is the great uncompounded nature of all phenomena, the dharmata of all dharmas, both existent things and nonexistent things, and is itself perfectly incontrovertible. As it is said in the *Mulaprajna*,

> Intrinsic being is not fabricated,
> Is not contingent upon something else.

And,

> Nirvana is an uncompounded state,
> While both existing things and nonexisting things are
>   composite.

Ultimately, therefore, the primordial wisdom of the dharmakaya pervades [the phenomena of] both samsara and nirvana. It is an uncompounded state, the state of equality, or evenness. It is unchanging, ultimate truth. This is established by the sutras of definitive meaning and by the reasoning that investigates the ultimate status of phenomena.

Within the mind, and endowed with the capacity to become manifest, the dharmakaya wisdom is already present from this very moment; and in the manner of the dharmata, it abides free of increase and decrease. Whether or not it is manifest, and however it may appear as being free or not free of adventitious stains, there is absolutely not the slightest difference in its actual way of being, whether in terms of bad or good, before or after [the removal of the said obscurations]. And this is so because it has the nature of being uncompounded and immutable. As it is said in the *Uttaratantra*,

> As it was before, so later it will be,
> It is unchanging dharmata.

And,

This nature of the mind, this luminosity,
Like space, is without change.
Craving and the rest are adventitious stains
Deriving from deluded thought, and they do not defile it.

As this and other texts show, all the phenomena of samsara are changing and unstable. But though they appear to change within the sphere of dharmata, nevertheless the pure essence of the mind, the sugatagarbha, is like space; it is unchanging. This should be clearly understood, for it is affirmed again and again in the scriptures.

Accordingly, the vast expanse of uncompounded luminosity is not stained by delusion; it is intrinsically pure. Within the self-radiance of the undeluded nature, the [ten] strengths and so on,[275] all the qualities of the resultant state, are spontaneously present and as inseparable from it as the sun's rays are from the sun itself. So it is as the *Uttaratantra* says,

The buddha-element is void of what is adventitious
And has the character of something separable.
The element is not itself devoid of supreme qualities,
Which have the character of what cannot be parted from it.

All the faults of samsaric existence derive from the deluded mind that clings to the personal and phenomenal self. But from the very beginning, the original and luminous nature [of the mind] is never stained by these deluded mental states and is never mixed with them. For they are entirely adventitious to it, like the clouds in the sky. For this reason, it is possible to distinguish these individual defects from the buddha-element and to separate them from it. The buddha-element in itself is empty of these defects and is unstained by them.

Moreover, being unaffected by the damage wrought by delusion, this element is not empty of the perfect qualities that are inseparable from self-arisen primordial wisdom—which is luminous by its very nature and is the very essence of all phenomena. The buddha-element is never without these qualities, for they belong to it in the same way that the rays of the sun belong to the sun itself.

Accordingly, given that the naturally present buddha-potential is established as the very dharmakaya—uncompounded and primordially endowed with its qualities—and given too that beings are able to attain enlightenment, it follows that the dharmakaya wisdom must of necessity subsist stably without increase or decrease within the mind streams of sentient beings. For it is established by the power of manifest fact that beings are able to attain enlightenment when they train on the path. And since the dharmakaya that manifests when buddhahood is attained is uncompounded, it cannot be something that is newly produced through causes and conditions. It is, therefore, proved that, from this very moment, the dharmakaya wisdom abides within beings as the nature of buddhahood.

5. A refutation of objections

Now regarding this assertion, certain people have objected that if the dharmakaya wisdom subsists right now in the present moment as the nature of buddhahood in beings, how is it that the primordial wisdom of omniscience does not [immediately] dispel the obscurations of these same beings? And clinging to the theory expounded in the common vehicle to the effect that *buddhahood* is the result of which the state of *sentient being* is the cause, such people also think that if the result is actually present in the cause, this is the same as saying that when one eats one's food, one eats one's excrement.[276] And with these and other arguments, they think that they can undermine our position.

The minds of our opponents, however, are not trained in the meaning of the extremely profound sutras of definitive meaning; they are guided only by an interpretation supplied in texts of common understanding.[277] It is not surprising, therefore, that doubts arise in their minds. But the truth of the matter is otherwise. Although the dharmata, the luminous primordial wisdom, is present equally in all beings, when the deluded mind arises adventitious to it, it is precisely this mind together with its object that supplies the basis for the designation of samsara. Because beings are deluded in this way, they do not cognize the dharmata as it is. The situation is analogous to the time of sleep when through the power of the mental consciousness alone, the appearances of bodies, objects, the visual consciousness, and so forth arise without limit. [The mind of the dreamer] perceives, and fixates upon, the subject and object [seen in the dream] as being separate. The mental consciousness is unable to understand that its nature does not correspond to a separate apprehender and something apprehended. But even though the mental consciousness fails to realize this, its nature does not change. In just the same way, even though all phenomena subsist in the nature of emptiness, people do not automatically realize this. Delusion is always possible owing to the fact that the way things are does not correspond to the way they appear.

Consequently, the ordinary mind (*sems*) and the primordial wisdom of the sugatagarbha are shown to be related in terms of a phenomenon (dharma, *chos can*) and the nature of that phenomenon (dharmata, *chos nyid*). Likewise, the state of buddhahood and the state of beings are shown to be related in terms of the way of being and the way of appearing, respectively. Thus, the refutation just referred to, which uses the reasoning of the result's being present in the cause, is completely wide of the mark.

So it is that our argument is proved: the dharmakaya, clearly manifest at the time of the result, is the evidential sign that shows that, at the time of the cause, the buddha-potential is present and primordially endowed with perfect qualities. In terms of the actual mode of being (the way things are in their nature), there is no such thing as a cause and fruit distinguished in terms of a chronological sequence. Nevertheless, from the standpoint of the appearing mode (when we consider the way things appear), we are obliged to speak in terms of cause and result. This is the so-called reasoning of dependency,[278] which deduces [the existence of] a cause from [the existence of] a result.

3. The meaning of the second line of the stanza, "Because in suchness there is no division"

All phenomena of both samsara and nirvana are of one taste, for in their ultimate way of being, the great primordial luminosity of emptiness, there is no division between them. The same is true for buddhas and sentient beings. Ultimately, there is no division between them. This is the equality of samsaric existence and the peace of nirvana. As a consequence, the reasoning of the nature of things[279] shows that, owing to adventitious delusion, beings seem to exist even though they do not diverge in the slightest from the dharmata, the ultimate way of being. This being so, it is certain that beings possess the buddha-essence. It is said moreover in the sutras that all phenomena are primordial luminosity; they are beyond suffering and have the nature of manifest buddhahood.

4. A refutation of objections

Now our opponents could complain that previously when we were responding to others' objections, we said that the mere fact that suchness is indivisible proves that the buddha-potential is present [in things].[280] This being so, they argue [turning our previous argument against us] that it follows that the buddha-potential is present even in earth, stones, and so on.

To this we reply as follows. What we call the buddha-potential must be posited as the faultless cause of buddhahood: the full flowering of the mind that is undeluded with respect to the nature of knowledge objects. This occurs with the complete removal of the two obscuring veils, which have arisen through the power of the deluded mind. And since the ability to accomplish the path [to buddhahood] is not found in material, inanimate things like earth and stones, the latter should not be posited as having the buddha-potential, even though, on the conventional level, they are indivisible from suchness. Earth, stones, and so on appear through the power of the mind. It is not the mind that has arisen through the power of outer objects like earth and stones. This should be understood in the sense indicated by the example of dream visions and the dreaming consciousness.

Now within this mind—the creator of the three worlds—there dwells the dharmata, the sugatagarbha, endowed with the nature of ultimate and immaculate purity, in the same way that moisture inheres in water. With this understanding, we can say that the phenomena of samsara and nirvana are simply the display of the ordinary mind and of primordial wisdom, respectively. Thus it should never be thought that samsara and nirvana are separate. And furthermore, we hold strongly that all phenomena, which on the ultimate level never stray from the condition of the dharmata, primordial buddhahood, are likewise never beyond the sphere of tathagata.

As it is said in the *Ratnaguna-samchaya-gatha*,

> The purity of form should be known as the purity of the result.
> The purity of both result and form becomes the purity of omniscience.
> The purity of omniscience, result, and form is like
> The element of space: there's no dividing it.

What is the purity that consists in the cognitive subject's freedom from obscuring veils? It is the purity, or nature, of the object—namely, form and so on. This is because the obscurations that veil the subject's or mind's own experience[281] only seem to be removed gradually, whereas from the point of view of its actual nature, the mind is primordially free of such obscurations. Accordingly, when the impurities within the cognitive subject, the mind, are exhausted and buddhahood is attained, no objects or things are left to be purified. It is just as when the defect in the eye is cured, the black lines [which are a symptom of the defect] automatically disappear.

Now it might be thought that when one individual attains buddhahood, all impure appearances should cease [right across the board]. This, however, is not the case because individual beings are obfuscated by the obscurations of their own particular subjective experience. Every being has a kind of perception in which the way things are is at odds with the way that they appear.

Another question may also be raised. On the level of buddhahood, when the way things appear corresponds in all respects to the way they are, is there an experience of all the impure appearances [perceived by unenlightened beings] or not? If there is, it follows that perfect and manifest enlightenment with regard to all things has not been attained. On the other hand, if there is no such experience, it follows that [enlightened beings] are unable to have knowledge of the paths and so on of wandering beings.[282] The answer to this is that the primordial omniscient wisdom of the buddhas knows all phenomena of samsara and nirvana spontaneously and without effort as being of equal taste with itself. From the buddhas' own point of view, they see everything as great purity; and yet without ever diverging from this vision, they see all that appears to beings of the six realms exactly as these same beings perceive them. Because all the obscurations of dualistic perceptions are exhausted for them, all phenomena are contained—in a manner that is entirely complete and without being confused—within the expanse of the dharmata. Thanks to this crucial point, the primordial wisdom, which is beyond arising and cessation, sees them instantaneously and in a state of equal taste with itself. This is hard to understand even for those who are residing on the levels of realization; there is no need to speak of those who perceive phenomena in the ordinary manner.

It is said in the *Bodhisattvapitaka*,

The equality of all phenomena
Is understood as equal by the self-arisen wisdom.
Wherefore the manifest and perfect Buddha,
Tathagata, sees all equally.

And

Because it knows the naturally luminous character of
the mind as it is, the wisdom of a single instant of mind
is called the unsurpassable, genuine, perfect enlightenment of buddhahood.

In accordance with this, the master Chandrakirti has said,

Vessels may be different, but their space is one and
undivided.
Just so, phenomena are many, but their suchness is beyond
all multiplicity.
In understanding perfectly their single taste, such beings in
their perfect wisdom
Know all knowledge objects in a single instant.

Thus, the great primordial wisdom, which is indivisible from
the vast expanse, embraces all phenomena and sees them in the
same effortless way that the moon and the stars appear reflected in
the ocean; it pervades them and sees them in the state in which all
thoughts are stilled. And this is the self-arisen primordial wisdom
of luminosity, the dharmata residing in the ground, which—once
the obscuring veils have been removed—will manifest just as it is.
On the basis of the correct reasoning of the nature of things, which
examines the ultimate, one can acquire an irreversible conviction
that this is so. By contrast, [if one is confined] to the assessment of
the lesser, ordinary mind, one would have to conclude either that
there is no wisdom in the state of buddhahood or that even if there
is such a wisdom, it would be the same as the ordinary changing

mind. One would have to conclude either that the buddhas are incapable of seeing the world of beings or else that they have impure perceptions. It would be impossible to establish the single taste of the wisdom that sees the nature of phenomena and the wisdom that sees phenomena in all their multiplicity. One would encounter only a chaos of turbulent contradictions and worries.

3. The meaning of the third line of the stanza, "Because they have potential for enlightenment"

The meaning of these words is that all sentient beings have a potential thanks to which they are able to attain buddhahood. It is established that adventitious defilements are, by definition, removable and that the dharmakaya, primordially endowed with the qualities of enlightenment, is present in all sentient beings without distinction. Conversely, the presence in beings of this potential for enlightenment means that they have the buddha-essence. For it is present at the time of buddhahood itself; and since the dharmakaya of the buddha is uncompounded, there can be no qualitative variation in it in terms of bad or good, before or after [defilements are removed].

The third of the three reasons [given in the stanza from the *Uttaratantra*], by which one understands that a result is generated from a cause, constitutes the argument of efficient causation. Nevertheless, owing to the crucial fact that no change occurs in the buddha-potential (that is, dharmata or suchness), this is not just a matter of deducing a result from the simple presence of a cause. When the result is gained, no change occurs within the nature of the buddha-potential. [It is not improved when enlightenment happens, nor is it worse beforehand.] Moreover, however long adventitious obscurations are present, it is always possible for them to be removed and therefore the potential is never deprived of the capacity for enlightenment.

There are, therefore, three arguments that prove that all beings possess the tathagata-essence—a conclusion that derives from the perfect path of reasoning based on the power of objective fact.[283]

The first is that there is no difference in nature between the buddha-potential at the time of the cause and the dharmakaya at the time of the result. The second is that because the dharmakaya is present when one attains the result, it must also be present at the time when one is a sentient being—without there being any increase or diminution [whether in the enlightened, or the unenlightened, state]. The third argument is that even if one makes a nominal distinction between the earlier cause and the later result, in reality, they are of one taste in the nature of the unchanging dharmadhatu.

The reasoning that proves that the tathagatagarbha is present in all sentient beings shows also that there is no difference between final liberation, the tathagata, and the ultimate nature of all phenomena. And if one understands that this happens thanks to the tathagatagarbha itself, a single final vehicle (the Mahayana) will be established.

There are, on the other hand, those who say that the sugatagarbha is not present in the state of sentient beings but that it is present at the time of buddhahood, and those who say that the qualities of enlightenment are not present at the causal stage but are newly acquired at the time of the result. All such people turn their backs on the meaning of the Mahayana, and the arguments they use to establish it as a single perfect vehicle become incoherent speculation. Consequently, those who aspire to the teachings of the supreme vehicle must make considerable use of their intelligence in order to understand this point.

This assertion that the buddha-element primordially endowed with enlightened qualities is present even at the time when one is a sentient being is indeed a profound point, beyond the reach of the conceptual mind. And it was for this reason that the Buddha told his disciples to trust his teaching, saying that it was undeceiving, however difficult it was for them to understand it using their own strength. This, therefore, is a doctrine of the utmost profundity.

Scholars of limited intelligence, however, produce a stream of objections to it. It follows, they say, that buddhas and sentient beings have the same kind of mind, and so on. But all their arguments and refutations, based as they are on conventional reasoning, are futile. As is it said in the *Sandhinirmochana-sutra*,

> The ultimate and the compounded sphere
> Are by nature neither different nor the same.
> Whoever understands them to be different or the same,
> Engages in them incorrectly.

So it is that the nature of the mind, the buddha-essence, and the mind that is a relative phenomenon must not be asserted as being either the same or different. As to their mode of being, they are never beyond the condition of the dharmata. As to their appearing mode, however, it is always possible for delusion to arise. And not only is there no contradiction here, but if one were to say otherwise, such a position would be defective, since it would mean either that there is no possibility of liberation or that no one could ever be deluded. It is precisely because there is a discrepancy between the way things are and the way things appear, that it is established, on the one hand, that beings are deluded and, on the other hand, that they can enter the path, discard delusion, and achieve buddhahood. Through the kind of reasoning that examines the ultimate, it is established that all phenomena are emptiness. Nevertheless the qualities of the sugatagarbha are not invalidated thereby, for as the Buddha affirmed, although the unsurpassable qualities are present, they are—by that same reasoning—found to be, by nature, empty.

The meaning taught by the scriptures of the second turning of the dharma wheel is that *all* phenomena of both samsara and nirvana are empty—for these scriptures say that even the sugatagarbha is of the nature of emptiness. By contrast, the particular and essential teaching that the sugatagarbha is inseparable from the appearances of the kayas and wisdoms (which themselves possess an empty nature) corresponds to the wisdom intention of the sutras of definitive meaning belonging to the final turning of the dharma wheel—which, from this point of view alone, is superior to the second turning. This is why the *Sandhinirmochana-sutra* praises the meaning of the final turning as supreme—not as a general assessment but with reference only to the definitive teaching that sets forth the buddha-essence. This point can be clearly ascertained from other sutras such as the one that speaks about the buddha-element using the example of the cleansing of a jewel.

We therefore need to keep together the aspects of appearance and emptiness—that is, the teachings on emptiness as revealed in the scriptures of the second turning and the teachings on the kayas and wisdoms as revealed in the scriptures of the third turning. The omniscient Longchen Rabjam held that the meanings of both the second and third turnings—together and without separation—constituted the definitive teaching, and this is precisely the position that we too should hold.

There is no conflict between the second and third turnings of the dharma wheel. There is no need to say [as some do] that one turning is definitive while the other is provisional. What is more, when the two turnings are brought together and when it is understood that the causal [ground] continuum is the sugatagarbha, this becomes the crucial point of the essential instructions of the Vajrayana. One must therefore understand that all such teachings of the Buddha come together into a single point. Regarding this final meaning, Nagarjuna, Asanga, and all the aryas are of one mind—as we may understand clearly from such writings as (Nagarjuna's) *Dharmadhatu-stava* and *Bodhichittavivarana* and (Asanga's) *Uttaratantra*. Moreover, as master Nagarjuna has himself said,

> Emptiness expounded in the sutras
> And everything the Conqueror has taught—
> All serve to take away defilement;
> They do not cause the buddha-element to change.

As this text says, when one investigates with the kind of reasoning that examines the ultimate, the vajra-like inseparability of the [two] truths is established. And since this is the vast expanse, which cannot be broached by merely intellectual understanding, there is—with regard to the ultimate [in itself]—no basis for engaging in controversy.

1. The manner in which the sugatagarbha is present in the minds of beings

It is now time to explain the way in which the element is present in the minds of beings. From the standpoint of their own nature—their way of being—all phenomena are encompassed by the expanse of the dharmata. The dharmata rests in a state of equality, or evenness, without arising or ceasing. It is beyond the categories of good or bad, of samsara or nirvana, and so on. It is beyond the distinctions of transcendence and ordinariness, self and other, great and small—as well as differences of time, past, present, and so on. It is just the unchanging, unmoving, one and only sphere of the dharmadhatu. Although this is the case with regard to the nature of things, deluded adventitious perception nevertheless occurs—in accordance with which the bodies, minds, and all the objects of the three worlds appear. Even when the nature of the dharmata is not perceived, the dharmata is not absent. It is present without diverging even slightly from its own nature. Thus, the dharmata, or nature of the mind, is, as it were, unmanifest, enclosed within a sheath of adventitious defilement. It is present in the midst of it like a kernel, an essential core, and is referred to as a "potential" or "essence." We are told to understand this by means of nine examples: the treasure hidden beneath the earth and so on. Moreover, the scripture speaks of how, in relation to adventitious defilement, the buddha-potential is found to be in three different situations—of impurity, of partial impurity, and finally, of complete purity. Nevertheless, in all these three situations, there is no difference whatever in the buddha-potential itself. As it is said in the *Uttaratantra*,

> Because the wisdom of the Buddha resides in beings,
> They are never parted from that stainless nature.

And since potential for enlightenment is named according
    to the fruit,
It's said that beings all possess the buddha-essence.

It is also said in the same text,

This also is by nature dharmakaya;
It is suchness and potential.

And also,

As impure, impure-and-pure,
And completely pure
Are described respectively,
Beings, bodhisattvas, tathagatas.

If, failing to understand this, one thinks that the sugatagarbha is tucked away somewhere in the five aggregates, like a juniper berry in a metal basin, so that there are in effect two minds, one deluded, one undeluded, accompanying each other like light and dark—and if in this way one affirms or rejects the sugatagarbha, one succeeds only in making a lot of noise without getting any closer to the view of the Mahayana.

On the other hand, it serves no purpose to proclaim a teaching on the buddha-essence to a band of mere intellectuals whose minds are untrained in the meaning of the Great Vehicle. Indeed, a profound teaching such as this is not to be taught to those who are spiritually immature or to those who are outside the Dharma. For such people are unsuitable vessels for the reception of this profound doctrine. One should instead explain the Dharma to them beginning with the teachings on no-self, impermanence, and so on, demonstrating it with logical proofs. It is pointless to teach them the doctrine of the buddha-essence. For since it cannot be proved on the basis of ordinary valid cognition alone, it simply becomes an occasion for defective intellectual positions (affirming what is not the case and negating what is). On the other hand, when the minds of people are trained from the lower tenet systems of the Buddhist teaching onward, and when an extraordinary conviction arises in their minds regarding the nonfigurative ultimate of Great Emptiness—if, at that point, the teaching on the buddha-essence is gradually revealed to them, they will experience confident faith in its regard. Therefore one should avoid the mistake of thinking, on the one hand, that although this path is true, it cannot be proved by reasoning and can be realized only by experience, or of thinking, on the other hand, that since it cannot be proved on the basis of ordinary valid cognition, it is not a true path. [Avoiding this mistake,] one should become expert in the crucial ways of the practice of the path.

1. A refutation of certain false positions regarding the buddha-element

Certain wrong ideas about the nature of the buddha-element should now be dealt with. These are, first, the view that the element is not empty but truly existent; second, the view that the element is no more than an empty void; and third, the view that the element is impermanent and compounded.

2. A refutation of the view that the buddha-element is not empty

3. A refutation based on scripture

Regarding the first of these ideas—namely, that the buddha-element is not empty, we find the following text in the noble *Lankavatara-sutra*:

> The Bodhisattva Mahamati addressed the Lord, the Blessed One, and asked, "The Buddha has said in the sutra that the sugatagarbha, which abides within the sheath of impurity, is permanent, firm, and unchanging. How

then is this different from the self [or *purusha*] proclaimed by the tirthikas? For they speak of a self [or
purusha] that is devoid of the qualities, or *gunas*." The
Lord, the Blessed One, replied, "They are not the same.
The buddhas taught the sugatagarbha in terms of the
three doors of perfect liberation,[284] of nirvana, and of
the unborn nature. In order not to alarm the childish,
who fear the absence of self, they taught an approach to
the sugatagarbha, speaking of it as something beyond
ordinary thought—the sphere beyond appearance.
Regarding this, O Mahamati, the bodhisattvas, the
great beings of the future as well as those of the present
time, should not fixate on it as though it were a self. . . .
Indeed, there is no liberation for those who entertain an
idea of real existence."

The sutra also says,

If [this essence] is not empty by nature, then even if
[you say that] it is empty of something other than itself,
this does not count as its emptiness. Of the seven kinds
of emptiness, the least is that of a thing's emptiness of
something else. Among a myriad other assertions they
made about it, [the buddhas] said that this should be
discarded. Furthermore, O Mahamati, the Tathagata is
not permanent, nor is he impermanent. And the reason for saying this is that there are faults in both these
alternatives.

And,

These ideas are upheld by demons;
Existence, nonexistence—both should be transcended.

And,

If there is something higher than the supreme state of
nirvana, this too is like a dream and an illusion.

3. A refutation based on reasoning

In accordance with the meaning of these and other scriptures,
and thanks to the crucial point that the sugatagarbha is by nature
empty, logical analysis shows that it is appropriate for this same
sugatagarbha to be the nature of the mind. It shows too that it
pervades all objects, that it is permanent for as long as time lasts,
that it is inconceivable, and that it arises impartially as all qualities.

By contrast, it is altogether impossible for a sugatagarbha that is
not empty and exists truly to be the nature of other things. Neither
could [a truly existent sugatagarbha] be the outcome of the kind of
reasoning that investigates the ultimate. For something established
as both one and truly existent to be the result of an investigation
that establishes all phenomena as devoid of true existence is as contradictory as light and dark. But neither is true existence established by conventional valid cognition. For even though, from the
latter's point of view, [things seem to be] truly established, it can
never be shown that these same things are not empty. An argument
to establish the existence of something that cannot be established
by either of the two investigations is as unreal as a flower growing
in the sky—it is a meaningless waste of energy.

2. A refutation of the view that the buddha-element is an empty void

Now with regard to the second of the three views just mentioned,
those who fail to grasp the point that the vast and ultimate expanse
is the union of appearance and emptiness understand the buddha-
potential (the dharmadhatu or emptiness) only in terms of a nonimplicative negation—in other words, the figurative ultimate.
They contradict the texts that affirm the primordial presence of its
enlightened qualities. This is completely incorrect.

3. A refutation based on scripture

As it is said in the sutra of the *Jnanamudra-samadhi-sutra*,

> In times to come, there will be those
> Who do not wish for truth but only profit for themselves,
> Who neglect their vows yet say they strive to gain
>   enlightenment,
> Who love to talk and say that all is emptiness.

And also,

> Emptiness is unborn; no one fabricated it.
> It is unseen; it neither comes nor goes.
> "In emptiness we're trained," some say, yet fix upon it as an
>   object.
> Those who speak like this are dharma thieves!

And,

> Concepts about nonexistence
> Are distractions that ensnare the childish.

And as it is said in the *Prajnaparamita-sanchaya-gatha*,

> Bodhisattvas, even if they think "These aggregates are empty,"
> Are still engaged in concepts; they have no faith in the
>   unborn.

Finally, in the *Samadhiraja-sutra*,

> Existence, nonexistence—these are two extremes.
> Impure and pure are likewise two extremes.
> Utterly rejecting both extremes therefore,
> Even in the middle do the wise forbear to dwell.

And also in the *Angulimalya-sutra* we find,

> *Kye ma*! In the world there are two kinds of people who destroy the holy Dharma: those who have an extreme view of emptiness and those in the world who proclaim a self. These are the ones who destroy the holy Dharma; by them the holy Dharma is upturned. . . .

> . . . Emptiness indeed is the remedy that uproots every view. To grasp at emptiness itself—whether as a thing or a nonthing—is said to be a view for which there is no remedy. . . .

> . . . Emptiness and the denial of emptiness do not transcend concepts and must be abandoned. This is repeatedly said in both the sutras and the shastras.

3. A refutation based on reasoning

Let us now subject this point to logical examination. The assertion of a nonimplicative negation (which simply counters the *idea* of true existence) is no more than an ascription contrived by the conceptual mind fixating on an object of refutation. It does not bring one into the very nature of things [the ultimate truth in itself], a state that is beyond all conceptual misapprehension. This point is easy to understand, and there is no need to discuss it in any great detail. Although the understanding of the emptiness of true existence, in the form of a nonimplicative negation, is not itself the authentic way of being of the dharmadhatu, beginners are quite right to contemplate it as the point of entry (but no more than the point of entry) into that same authentic nature. As we find in the sutra,

> O Manjushri, compared with a bodhisattva who supplies the needs of the Triple Gem for a thousand years as calculated in the realm of the gods, if another bodhi-

sattva were to examine and think—just for the time of a finger snap—that all compounded things are impermanent, that all compounded things are suffering, that all compounded things are empty, and that all compounded things are devoid of self—such a bodhisattva would generate far greater merit.

2. A refutation of the view that the buddha-element is impermanent and compounded

Now with regard to the third false view, it may be asked whether the ground, the sugatagarbha, the wisdom of omniscience fully manifest like the unclouded sun, is permanent or impermanent. After all, some sutras say that omniscience is permanent, while others say the contrary. For so it is that—in harmony with the outlook of beings to be trained, whose condition has not yet been completely transformed—the scriptures do say that omniscience is impermanent. The reason for this is given in the *Pramanavarttika*, which says,

> Valid cognition is not permanent
> For it validly cognizes entities.
> Since knowledge objects are impermanent,
> Cognition likewise is impermanent.

It is from a cause—namely, the path, the cultivation of bodhichitta and meditation on emptiness and so on, that omniscience arises. For it would be inappropriate for it to arise without a cause. Omniscience, moreover, is the valid perception of all phenomena, and if valid cognition is an unmistaken state of mind, it follows that it is the assessment of things just as they are. And none of these things is permanent. Since its objects are knowable phenomena, and since the latter are impermanent, it follows that the valid cognition that assesses them must also be impermanent, arising in sequence, stage by stage. If valid cognition were permanent, then it would be logically established as being void of any function—certainly void of any activity such as that of assessing objects. Therefore, it is highly inappropriate [in such a context] to say that omniscience is permanent; its impermanence is established. Likewise, all existing things are impermanent, and even though nonthings (general ideas and so on) are labeled as being permanent, they have no basis for permanent existence. Therefore, genuinely permanent entities cannot in any sense be found. It is necessary to demonstrate matters in this way for the tirthika philosophers outside the Dharma, as well as for those of the common vehicle whose minds have not been trained in the way in which the [ordinary] mind is transformed into the inconceivable dharmata. Indeed, there is no other way for things to appear to [ordinary] consciousness. However, from the point of view of the knowledge of primordial wisdom, which is the outcome of the complete transformation just referred to, omniscience is established as permanent. Objects of knowledge that arise and cease momentarily and that are set forth as the proof of impermanence, on the one hand, and wisdom as the knowing subject that also arises sequentially and momentarily, on the other, are no more than what appears in the perception of ordinary minds that have not been transformed. This is not the actual mode of being of things. If there are no phenomena that are born even in one instant, it goes without saying that there is no temporal sequence inaugurated by them. For example, in the case of a dream, although various aspects of a temporal sequence (earlier and later) or of space may endlessly appear, they do not exist in the way that they seem.

Consequently, when the dharmata, which is free of arising and cessation, and also the primordial wisdom of buddhahood (in which the ordinary mind is completely transformed)[285] are perfected, this is the wisdom body in which the knower and the known are inseparable. Even at the time of sentient beings (when the mind is not transformed), the fundamental condition of the ordinary mind, or dharmata, which is naturally united with luminosity, is unchanging. And this unchanging nature of the mind, referred to as the naturally present buddha-potential, is not different before or after [the removal of] the defilements, which are changing, adventitious, and removable—and occur sequentially, arising and ceasing momentarily. The inequality of samsara and nirvana, good and bad, and so on (all of which are the dualistic perceptions of the untransformed ordinary mind) appears ineluctably and undeniably. Yet dualistic phenomena, as well as arising and cessation, have no place in the fundamental nature itself, which abides in the state of great equality, or evenness. Within that nature, all distinctions of spatial and temporal location are encompassed. This nature is the object of the self-cognizing primordial wisdom enjoyed by the aryas. And since it is unspoiled, unaltered by change in the course of time, why not label it with the conventional name of "great permanence"? For it is there—unaffected by the momentary process of arising and cessation.

So it is that all functioning things, which change, as well as space and other nonthings—in other words, all objects of knowledge, whether in time or space—are contained in, and encompassed by, the dharmata. It is not the dharmata that is encompassed by phenomena—just as it is the sky that contains the clouds, not the clouds that contain the sky.

Therefore, the fundamental nature of the luminous expanse, the great equality of the dharmata, is the single, self-arisen primordial wisdom that naturally embraces all things, abiding innately within them. Nevertheless, people conditioned by adventitious impurity do not realize this nature. And yet when these impurities are removed through the elimination [of obscurations] and the realization [of qualities] included within the five paths, and when great primordial wisdom, in which there is no separation between knower and known, is attained, all knowable objects of that unchanging, self-arisen primordial wisdom are cognized—nonconceptually, effortlessly, and spontaneously—as being of equal taste with the dharmata. And thus the wisdom of omniscience is achieved.

Nevertheless, this manner of knowing does not imply that self-arisen wisdom is born from causes. The dharmakaya, which is completely free of adventitious defilement, is the result of elimination. Though it seems to arise newly from causes, it is only perceived in this way by those who have yet to transform their minds. According to how things really are, however, within the dharmata, the nature of the dharmakaya, there is neither arising nor destruction: all phenomena are equally, and from the very beginning, manifest buddhahood. From the very beginning, they are the peace beyond suffering; they are luminosity by their nature and so on. This ultimate view of the profound sutras is something difficult to conceive of even for the bodhisattvas on the pure grounds. There is no need even to mention ordinary beings. On the other hand, if an authentic confidence that this is how things are arises in one's mind, it is praised as being comparable to the reception of the prophecy that one has become a nonreturner.[286] It is something to which we should aspire. Moreover, if one considers that the wisdom kaya of the Tathagata is permanent, this is itself a source of merit.

As it is said in the *Prashanta-vinishchaya-pratiharya-samadhi-sutra*,

> O Manjushri, sons or daughters of the lineage may give whatever is desired by the four ordained assemblies in every region of the world in the ten directions for ten million kalpas as calculated in the realm of the gods. But other sons or daughters of the lineage who, acting appropriately, declare that the Tathagata is permanent, that the Tathagata is changeless, will generate far more merit.

And also we find in the *Mahanirvana-sutra*,

> O Kashyapa, at all times and with one-pointed mind, the sons and daughters of the lineage should persistently declare two things: the Buddha is permanent; the Buddha remains. . . .
>
> Anyone who acts on the understanding that the inconceivable is permanent is an object of refuge.

By contrast, the scriptures tell us that in considering the kaya of the Tathagata to be impermanent, one fails even to take refuge and that to think that the indestructible kaya is impermanent is a source of boundless defects. With this understanding, one should cultivate respect for the perfect teaching.

So it is that the sugatagarbha, according to its own nature, is free from all mental elaborations: existence and nonexistence, permanence and annihilation, and so on. It is the union of the two truths, the state of equality, or evenness, the one and only sphere [of the dharmakaya]. Within such a way of being, all phenomenal existence is of the single taste of suchness. To see this as it is amounts to reality in itself, from which there is nothing to remove and to which there is nothing to add. It is the perfect view, free from every kind of grasping, that realizes the ultimate truth.

As we find in the *Bodhipaksha-nirdesha-sutra*,

> O Manjushri, anyone who sees that all phenomena are not unequal, that, being nondual, they are not two, possesses the perfect view.

And in the *Gaganaganja-paripriccha-sutra* it is said,

> Things and nonthings both are objects of consciousness,
> But the learned who dwell in utmost purity
> Forbear to grasp at them
> By viewing them as things and nonthings.

And as it is said in the *Bodhisattvapitaka*,

> Ultimately speaking, for the aryas' wisdom (in their postmeditation experience) and primordial wisdom (in their meditation), there is not a single thing that can be known, that can be discarded, that can be meditated upon or actualized.

However, when we make correct distinctions by means of valid conventional reasoning, we understand as true what *is* true—for example, that the path of the aryas is an undeceiving path. We understand as false what *is* false—for example, that one is liberated through meditating on the *atman*. We understand as impermanent what *is* impermanent—for example, that all compounded things are momentary. We understand as permanent what *is* permanent—for example, that the sugatagarbha, self-arisen primordial wisdom, is unchanging in all its aspects. We understand as nonexistent what *is* nonexistent—for example, that the self and dualistic perceptions do not exist. To uphold the existence of what does exist is like understanding the way in which dependent arising appears—namely, the ineluctable law of cause and effect. It is like understanding that the spontaneously present qualities of the sugatagarbha, or dharmata, abide by their very nature within all sentient beings. These and other distinctions are means whereby unmistaken wisdom perceives the nature of things on the conventional level. Therefore, from understanding it and from assimilating it, great and excellent qualities are attained. For this is the root of a virtue that is free from all confusion.

Generally or specifically, the sutras provide us with many teachings. In particular, they say that the personal self does not exist, and yet they speak of the sugatagarbha, which is beyond the two conceptual elaborations of self and no-self, calling it the "great self." They say that this great self has supreme transcendent qualities of purity, bliss, and permanence. They do so in order that we might know of the existence of the great nonabiding nirvana that possesses the unchanging perfect qualities of peace, solace, and excellence. It is as we find in the *Mahanirvana-sutra*,

> That which is true and perfectly permanent is called "self." That which is sovereign, which does not change and does not pass, is called "self."

Therefore, when one hears an explanation of this profound sugatagarbha, unbounded benefit accrues from merely taking a devoted interest in it. As it is said in the *Uttaratantra*,

> The wise who yearn for this domain of the victorious ones
> Will be vessels for a host of buddha qualities.
> Rejoicing in this mass of inconceivable perfection,
> They rise above the merit of all living beings.

> Some there are who, wishing for enlightenment,
> Present both gold and jewels
> In number equal to the dust in all the buddhafields,
> And offer them each day to all the dharma kings.

>> Others, who, hearing but one word
>> Of such a teaching, long for it,
>> Attain far greater merit
>> Than the virtue that derives from such a gift.

> The wise who yearn for many kalpas
> For an unsurpassable enlightenment
> Without effort keep in body, speech, and mind,
> Their discipline unstained.

>> Others, who, hearing but one word
>> Of such a teaching, long for it,
>> Attain far greater merit
>> Than the virtue that arises from such discipline.

> There are those who through absorption cool the fires
> Of the defilements in the three worlds of existence—
> Perfecting the samadhis of the gods and the abodes of Brahma
> As a means for perfect and unwavering enlightenment.

>> Others, who, hearing but one word
>> Of such a teaching, long for it,
>> Attain far greater merit
>> Than the virtue gained from such absorption.

The teaching in question is indeed hard to fathom, but it is very important to know about it and to aspire to it. Because the irrevocable lion's roar, the doctrine of the sugatagarbha, the essence of the supreme vehicle, is exceedingly profound, those of inferior mind, whose previous training is slight, find it hard to take an interest in it. As we find in the *Tathagata-sangiti-sutra*,

> Regarding this my wisdom,
> Those of childish mind have doubts.
> [My wisdom] does not change its state.
> It is like space in which an arrow flies and falls.

Also the *Sarvavaidalya-sangraha-sutra* says,

> Through the blessing of the maras, these foolish people fall into the lower realms. For they have blamed and criticized this teaching. They even want to blame and criticize those who set forth the Tathagata's teaching.

And it is written in the *Brahmadatta-paripriccha-sutra*,

> When this well-turned teaching of the Dharma is expounded,
> Those of evil conduct think that it is incorrect.
> When without faith they harbor doubts,
> They're driven mad for myriads of kalpas.
> Through thoughts bereft of faith, they turn to evil deeds.
> The minds of those with angry thoughts are uncontrolled.
> Repudiating all things that are meaningful,
> Through lack of faith they cling just to the dregs.
> Puffed up with pride, forever arrogant,
> These faithless ones bow down to none. . . .
>
> They contradict with words devoid of virtue,
> Defiling thus the doctrine of victorious ones.

Like tirthikas, they waver and have doubts.
They go against the Dharma, which they bring to ruin—
The Dharma that these faithless ones forsake.

And in the *Dushila-nigraha-sutra* it is said,

> O Shariputra, this world of ours will be completely filled
> with unholy beings who sink to pursuing nothing but
> their own livelihood, who are addicted to controversy,
> harming both themselves and others.

When I reflect on all these texts, [I cannot help thinking that]
the age of dregs is well advanced and that the beings born now,
when the teachings are at their end, have a distorted understanding
of the four reliances. As a result, the crucial point of the tradition of
the supreme vehicle [that is, the teaching on the tathagatagarbha]
has greatly declined and a contrived and counterfeit teaching has
arisen. It is indeed rare to find people who treasure this doctrine,
the very life force of the Mahayana path.

Simply through the fact of being born in the end-time of the
teachings of the vidyadhara lineage of the Old Translation school,
I have seen and heard many precious teachings of that same lineage.
Thanks to my good fortune, I have been able to place upon my
head the lotus feet of several perfect spiritual friends, notably the
omniscient Dorje Ziji (Jamyang Khyentse Wangpo], who, as the
regent of the powerful Buddha Padmasambhava, is Manjushri ever
youthful appearing in human form. And though I am immature
in years and intelligence, a certain slight capacity regarding these
profound teachings has, as a result, been born in me.

Therefore, this well-turned explanation of the naturally present
buddha-potential, the dharmadhatu—in the manner of a nonabiding union [of appearance and emptiness] free from all extremes—
constitutes a lion's roar.

Now, as we find in the *Brahma-visheshachinti-paripriccha-sutra*,

O Devaputra, teachings that speak of nonattachment
constitute the lion's roar. Teachings that speak of
attachment are not a lion's roar but the yapping of foxes.
Those who teach with some secondary purpose in mind
do not express the lion's roar.

And we find too in the *Mahanirvana-sutra*,

The lion's roar is the definitive teaching that the
buddha-nature lies within every sentient being; that
the tathagata constantly abides without fluctuation. . . .

However extensive the explanations given in solitary
places may be, do not, O son of the lineage, refer to them
as the roaring of a lion. A great lion's roar occurs only
when something is proclaimed in the midst of many
scholars endowed with wisdom. Moreover, the lion's
roar is not an explanation of the fact that all phenomena
are impermanent, that they are suffering, that they are
without self and utterly impure. It occurs only when the
tathagata is explained as permanent, as blissful, as self,
and as utterly pure.

The scriptures speak about the lion's roar with many examples,
and we should understand the matter accordingly.

Now if this clear description of the Sugata's own path is not in
accordance with the opinions of certain people, it is nevertheless
a statement of the perfect path and therefore it should not disturb
their minds. As it is said in the *Madhyamakavatara*,

The arguments contained within our treatises were not
contrived through love of disputation.
They set forth suchness only for the sake of freedom.
They are not to be blamed if while expounding emptiness,
They show the falseness of discordant doctrines.

This is how to protect the teachings. As we find in the *Samadhiraja-sutra*,

> What does it mean to protect the Dharma? It means to demolish any attack against the Dharma through the application of what is in agreement with that Dharma.

It is also the way to uphold the teachings as this is described in the *Gaganaganja-paripriccha-sutra*,

> Those who gain the true enlightenment of the victorious
> ones,
> Perfectly uphold the authentic Dharma.
> Those with perfect understanding of this unstained
> state
> Uphold the teaching of all enlightened beings.

To uphold the Dharma is a way of repaying the kindness of the buddhas as well as of accumulating unbounded merit. The *Tathagata-mahakaruna-nirdesha-sutra* says,

> Those who keep close company with Buddha's teaching,
> And thereby have renunciation, uninterested by worldly
> things,
> Will be upholders of the teaching of the Blissful One
> And will repay the kindness of the buddhas.

And as it is said in the *Gaganaganja-paripriccha-sutra*,

> Even if he taught throughout a hundred million kalpas,
> Never would the Buddha's wisdom reach its end.
> Those who hold the teachings of the Tathagata
> Will likewise have immeasurable merit.

1. Conclusion

Although I may have gained some slight proficiency
In speaking of the scriptural tradition of the supreme vehicle,
I am still young and immature in training.
So who would trust the chatter of a silly shaveling?

People these days follow those who are well known,
Bereft of the intelligence to test what's good and bad.
And most are utterly disturbed by demons of their envy.
So I readily admit, it's not the time for well-turned discourse.

And yet because my supreme teacher and my yidam deity
I constantly revere within the lotus of my heart,
An explanation of the words and meanings of the perfect
    scriptures
Clearly dawned within the space of my awareness.

Long-lasting joy arose and lively interest
In the practices of well-turned explanations—
A delight that in my later lives and other realms
Will grow and increase like the waxing moon.

The joy arising in the hearts of the intelligent
That comes from this discussion of the ultimate profundity
Is not the bliss of those who fall in the extremes that are samsara
    and nirvana.
It is indeed a joyous feast for those of perfect fortune.

The lion's roaring of the supreme vehicle—the union
Of appearances and emptiness, beyond all clinging—
Subjugates the herd of savage beasts, all evil views.
May the essence of the Buddha's teaching spread in all the ten
    directions!

My dharma brother, who bears the name of Guna (Khenpo Yönten Gyatso), a holder of the jeweled treasury of the three trainings,
once said to me, "Writing down whatever comes into your mind,
please compose an explanation of the stanza in the *Uttaratantrashastra* beginning 'Because the kaya of perfect buddhahood
radiates.'" So in order to comply with his request, I bhante Lodrö
Drime[287] wrote this text just as it occurred to me. May virtue
increase!

———————

After lying unnoticed for two whole cycles of years (twenty-four
years)[288] among the Lord Mipham's papers, this text was at length
discovered. As the great master Lungtok was arranging for woodblocks to be carved for it, the master Yönten Gyatso, who had first
requested the text, visited and with the learned Lekpa'i Lodrö
inquired whether any additions or modifications were to be made.
Therefore Lodrö Drime Jampel Gyepe Dorje (Mipham Rinpoche
himself) spent two days preparing a new copy, bringing into focus
several passages from the original text and adding several important points that had not been previously mentioned. This was done
on an auspicious date in the second half of the fourth month (Saga
Dawa) in the iron hare year of the fifteenth rabjung cycle (1891) at
the retreat place of Dule Namgyal Ling.

An Explanation of the Seven-Line Prayer to Guru Rinpoche according to the Teachings of the Path of Liberation

Hung

In Orgyen's land, upon its northwest rim,
On lotus, pistil-cup, and stem,
Wondrous, supreme mastery you found
And as the Lotus-Born you are renowned.
A ring of many dakinis encircles you,
And in your footsteps practicing we follow you.
To grant your blessings, come, we pray.

Guru Padma Siddhi Hung

Hung, the seed-syllable of the enlightened mind, symbolizes the ultimate status of samsara and nirvana: the naturally luminous, self-arisen primordial wisdom. **Orgyen's land** is the source par excellence of the Secret Mantra teachings. From the point of view of the inner meaning, however, we should understand that the nature of our own mind is the wellspring of the Secret Mantra.

In the Tibetan word for **northwest** (*nub chang*), the element *nub* (west) also conveys the idea of sinking—into the mire, for example—whereas *chang* (north) also means to extricate or free oneself. Therefore, "west," here, signifies samsara, whereas "north" refers to the pure state of nirvana. Consider the text in the *Mahaparinirvana-sutra*:

> The seven steps in the western direction that the Tathagata made on being born indicated that there would be no further birth for him, no more aging and death, and that this was to be his last embodiment [in samsara]. The seven steps made in the northern direction indicated that he was to be liberated from samsara.

Rim, or frontier, symbolizes a nonabiding in extremes (such as samsara or nirvana). That which is referred to as a rim or frontier is indeed impossible to pinpoint. It is like the "path of the Middle Way," a term used to refer to the absence of ontological extremes. This rim, therefore, indicates the nature of the mind, unaffected by either the defects of samsara or the excellence of nirvana, the ultimate primordial ground. This is, in a general sense, the object of the view.

What is the primordial ground like when it is unerringly realized? The ground, symbolized here by the word **lotus**, is emptiness, the ultimate expanse of primordial purity. From the very beginning, it is utterly beyond conceptual ascription and is, like a lotus flower, free from every defect. Beyond all location, this ultimate nature is posited as an object of realization. The subject that realizes the ultimate nature is the naturally luminous, self-cognizing primordial wisdom, radiant and in full flower. This is the vajra of awareness and is represented by the **pistil-cup**.

These two (subject and object, lotus and pistil-cup) are not different entities; they are indivisible like a vajra. And the wisdom of equality, which realizes this, is indicated by the **stem**, which holds the lotus flower and its pistil together. The ultimate expanse and primordial wisdom are thus inseparably united. As an aid to our understanding, however, they are provisionally described in terms of subject and object, though this does not mean that awareness actually realizes emptiness as if it were an object placed before it. For from the very beginning, primordial wisdom and the ultimate expanse are indivisible.

This is the self-arisen wisdom of great bliss, also called the "nature of the mind," or the "mind of uncontrived luminosity." It is **on** this ground that all phenomena of samsara and nirvana, both compounded and uncompounded, rest. This ground, which is recognized by self-cognizing primordial wisdom alone, is beyond all extreme positions of existence, nonexistence, both, or neither. It is beyond all language and conception, all formulation. As it is said in one of the *dohas* (songs of realization),

> The nature of the mind alone is seed of everything;
> From it samsara and nirvana both arise.
> I venerate this mind, which like a wishing gem
> Brings forth the fruits that we desire.

And in the *Praise to the Mother*, it is said,

> No name, no thought, no formulation is there for the
>   Wisdom That Has Gone Beyond;
> Unceasing and unborn, the very nature of the open sky;
> The purview of primordial wisdom self-cognizing:
> To this the mother of the Buddhas past, present, and to
>   come, I bow.

The tantra *Self-Arising Awareness*[289] says, "If you know awareness, the root, you also know all phenomena, the stem." And,

> Awareness, dharmakaya, transcending birth and death,
> Is known nondually within the thought-free state.
> All-embracing, it is boundless light.
> Within the vastness of the universal ground encompassing
>   all things,

Awareness, which pervades it, manifests as primal wisdom's
    play.
This primal wisdom unconfined you have within you.

In the Great Perfection tantra *Revelation of Bodhichitta: The Perfect Pure Reality*,[290] it is said,

Self-arisen Buddhahood, endowed with the essence of the
    lotus,
Appears as two and yet it is not two. It is a bliss-pervading
    space.
Teacher, place, attendance, teaching—all are indivisible.
Throughout the three times, all is perfect.
Everything appears, through blessings gained, in
    nonduality;
And all things have the nature of great bliss. . . .

The *Manjushrinamasamgiti*, the recitation of the names of
Manjushri, who is the personification of the wisdom body of all
the buddhas, declares,

Consciousness is utterly transcendent by its nature;
It is primal wisdom in the guise of nonduality.
It is free of thought, spontaneously present,
Performing all the actions of the buddhas of the triple time.
There are no buddhas first or last.
Primordial Buddha lists to neither side.
Wisdom is the only eye that is immaculate.
The one who has the wisdom body is the Tathagata.

And,

Definitively freed from every obscuration,
It rests in evenness like space itself.

Transcending all defiled emotion,
It is the knower of the no-time of the triple time.

In these and other ways, the tantras of the Vajrayana indicate the ultimate primordial wisdom, the coemergent wisdom of the fourth empowerment. Since this wisdom, in transcending every object of thought and word, is by nature inconceivable, it is **wondrous**. It is referred to in expressions like "luminous great perfection" and "ultimate coemergent [bliss]." Herein lies the principal realization of all the buddhas; the **supreme mastery** whereby the sovereignty of the primordial and spontaneously present state of union of the great Vajradhara is **found**. The three kayas are naturally present within this state, which is itself referred to as the self-arisen, ultimate **lotus**.

As it is said,

Awakened from the sleep of ignorance,
Their minds made vast with every knowledge object,
Buddhas are compared with lotuses in blossom.

Self-arisen primordial wisdom, free from all attachment, is called "Buddha" or "lotus."

All the tathagatas of the past and present and those who will gain enlightenment in the future are indivisible within the realization of ultimate reality, or suchness. They cannot be distinguished. As it is said in the tantra *The Auspicious Cuckoo of Awareness*,[291]

Of one taste in the dharmakaya, equal in their work for
   beings,
They appear quite differently to those who might be
   trained.
But since within the dharmadhatu all are one,
When a single Tathagata is accomplished, so too are all the
   buddhas.

Consequently, it is said that, on the level of ultimate truth, the wisdom kayas of all the buddhas cannot be differentiated; they are one and the same.

On the level of conventional truth, however, the buddhas of the three times practice their respective paths and gain their fruit—they burst into flower, like lotus blossoms. They are, so to speak, **born** from the fundamental ground of ultimate reality, the dharmata. In other words, this ultimate reality is **renowned** as their "source." On the level of ultimate meaning, therefore, this is recognized as "Buddha Padmasambhava."[292] According to the different points of view expressed in various texts, this ultimate reality is also known by the following names: Samantabhadra, primal Buddha, dharmadhatu, utmost perfect purity, ultimate bodhichitta, suchness, ultimate truth, self-arisen primordial wisdom, sugatagarbha, the primal wisdom that pervades samsara and nirvana, the uncontrived mind of natural luminosity, wisdom unsurpassed, coemergent great bliss, and the cause-heruka. The ultimate truth established in the three great traditions of Mahamadhyamaka (the Great Middle Way), Mahamudra (the Great Seal), and Mahasandhi (the Great Perfection) and the ultimate truth indicated by expressions found in the sutras and tantras are none other than this primordial wisdom.

From this primordial wisdom, there emanates an inconceivable illusory display of the five wisdoms and the other qualities of enlightenment (which are simply aspects of primordial wisdom distinguished conceptually). This is the **ring of many dakinis**, primordial self-cognizing wisdom's unhindered display, which moves and **encircles** it in the immaculate space of the ultimate expanse. For the one primordial wisdom manifests as an inconceivable display, an illusory tapestry of emanations: the principal Buddha, the retinue, and all the rest.

As it is said in the tantras,

> Within a single family are assemblies of tathagatas,
> And in each assembly of one such family are many families.

In one sole family are unnumbered families,
All arising from the family of Great Joy.

Though this ultimate reality is the primordial nature of the mind of every being, it is nevertheless something that has to be actualized on the Mahayana path—specifically through the power of the profound maturation [occurring through the empowerments received] and thanks to the liberating instructions of the Vajra Vehicle of the Secret Mantra. While one remains in an ordinary state of mind, this nature is like a beautiful statue hidden inside a lotus and is called the "sugatagarbha."

In order to indicate ultimate reality as it actually is, the teachings of the middle (that is, the second) turning of the Dharma wheel describe it as emptiness, set forth in terms of the three doors of perfect liberation. The sutras of ultimate meaning belonging to the third turning, however, refer to this reality as the primordially and spontaneously present kayas and wisdoms. These two views complement each other without any contradiction and are taught in such texts as the treatises on reasoning and the hymns composed by the lord Nagarjuna, as well as the *Sublime Continuum* (*Uttaratantrashastra*) and the *Ornament of Clear Realization* (*Abhisamayalamkara*) of the regent Maitreya. Elucidated in this way, the authentic ultimate nature may be actualized thanks to the pith instructions of the Vajrayana. When this occurs, we arrive at the heart of a myriad sutras and tantras.

It is through supreme knowledge free from doubts that we come to an irreversible certainty about ultimate reality, the primordial wisdom of the inseparable union [of appearance and emptiness]. This is what is referred to by the words **in your footsteps practicing we follow you.** If, by means of the view, we become convinced of this ultimate reality—the supreme goal of all paths and tenets— and if, by means of meditation, we gain skill [in recognizing it], we will come to realize it. The naturally luminous primordial wisdom will manifest. All impure, ordinary perceptions will be transmuted into pure wisdom and will thus be blessed.

If this has not happened, however, and if the dreamlike experiences of samsaric suffering continue without interruption, [we invoke the Guru with the words] **to grant your blessings**. And by this we mean that in order for our mind stream to be blessed by the path, we pray that, through the teachings we receive and reflect upon, and through the pith instructions of the teacher, the realization of ultimate reality may **come** to us. For as it is said in the *Pramanavarttika*, "to come" means "to realize." Within that state of ultimate nature, subject and object, like the ocean and its waves, are not separate. That we might come to this state and attain to its realization, **we pray**, thereby expressing our aspiration.

The various stages of the path, beginning with the views of the Vaibhashikas and proceeding right through to the view of the luminous vajra-essence, are progressively more effective for the realization of ultimate reality, until finally the primordial wisdom transcending the ordinary mind is reached. The empty nature of this primordial wisdom, the dharmakaya beyond all conceptual description, is **Guru**. Its character is luminosity, the unobstructed display. It is the spontaneously present sambhogakaya—which, however, is not different from the ultimate expanse itself and is thus unstained by conventional attributes. This is **Padma**. The indivisibility of these two is all-pervading cognitive potency, which arises as the display of samsara and nirvana. Like a wishing jewel, it fulfills the hopes and wishes of an infinity of beings. This is **Siddhi**. The syllable **Hung**, endowed with the five wisdoms, is the seed-syllable of the enlightened mind and symbolizes the self-arisen primordial wisdom.

A LAMP TO DISPEL THE DARK

An Instruction That Points Out the Nature of the Mind
according to the Way of Old and Realized Yogis

———

To my teacher and to the wisdom-being Manjushri, I bow down!

No need is there for study or reflection, or extensive practice.
Ordinary mantrikas living in the villages,
Who, according to the pith instructions, stay
Within the recognition of the nature of their minds,
Will attain without much hardship
To the state of vidyadharas.
Such is the profound path's power.

When you leave your mind in its natural flow without thinking of anything—while nevertheless remaining attentive—you will experience a stagnant, indeterminate state, blank and withdrawn. Because there is no deep insight of discerning knowledge, the teachers refer to this state as *ignorance*. Because it is indefinable in terms of being "this" or "like this," they refer to it as an *indeterminate state*. And since you can't say where you are or what you are thinking about, they refer to it as a state of plain vacancy. What is happening is that you are simply resting in the state of the universal ground. On the basis of such a way of meditating, you are to give rise to a state of wisdom beyond ordinary cognition. But since *self-cognizing* primordial wisdom does not arise, a meditation of this kind is not itself the main practice. As we find in the *Aspiration of Samantabhadra*,

> Oblivious and blank, they have no mindfulness.
> This itself is ignorance, the cause of their delusion.

While the mind is experiencing this blank condition devoid of mindfulness and mental movement, if you suddenly look at the one who is perceiving this state without thinking, there manifests the awareness that is free of any movement of thought, a state of openness in which there is no "outside or inside," a state that is bright and limpid like the sky. There is neither "experiencer" nor "experienced," and yet you have a clear and certain sense that this is your own nature, and you feel that, apart from this, there is nothing else.

Since that state cannot be thought about or described with words as being this or that, we can just as well call it "a state that is beyond all conceptual extremes and beyond expression," "uncontrived luminosity," or "awareness." Primordial wisdom that recognizes its own nature has arisen. The blank and murky state clarifies; and just as when the interior of a house becomes visible at dawn, you have a definite certainty regarding the nature of your mind. This is called the "pith instruction that breaks the eggshell of ignorance."

When you have this realization, you will understand that this nature [of the mind] has been spontaneously present from the very beginning, that consequently it is not produced by causes and conditions, and that throughout the course of time it is beyond all movement and change. Apart from this, you will not find even an atom of some other so-called mind. Previously, the state of blankness was inexpressible because you did not know how to describe it—for you had no certainty about it. By contrast, the nature of awareness is also inexpressible, and yet with regard to this ineffable state, you do have a decisive certainty free of doubt. There is therefore a great difference between these two indescribable states. In the first case, it is as if you had no eyes; in the second, it is as though you had them. Herein is also contained the key distinction between the universal ground and the dharmakaya.

So-called ordinary mind, absence of mental activity, ineffability, and so on may be either pure or impure. If you gain certainty in the key instructions related to the pure exalted meaning of these ambivalent terms, you will gain experience and realization of the profound and ultimate nature.

While resting in the spontaneous flow of the nature of the mind, some people think that all they have to do is simply maintain a state of clarity and an awareness of this. And thinking in this way, they settle in a state of clarity that is in fact a construction of their mental consciousness. Other people stay fixed on a completely empty mental state, as if their mind had become completely void. In both cases, there is a clinging to the dualistic experience of subject and object, of perceiver and perceived. And this is a feature of the mental consciousness.

When this occurs, you should watch the nature of this consciousness that is tightly mindful both of the clarity and of the perceiver of that clarity, of both voidness and the perceiver of voidness. If by this means, the "tent peg" of the mind's dualistic clinging is pulled out, a decisive certainty is gained regarding the natural state of the mind—nakedly, lucidly clear, luminous and empty, devoid of center and circumference—a state of utter freshness and purity. This is the "face of awareness." Free of the husk of fixing onto meditative experiences, awareness (the naked state of primordial wisdom) has arisen. This is the pith instruction that cuts through the web of samsaric existence.

Now that it is freed from the various shells of mental experience—like a grain of rice separated from its husk—awareness recognizes the natural flow of dharmata in nondual self-illumination or cognition.

A mere recognition of the nature of awareness is not enough. You have to acquire a stable habit of resting in it. It is therefore important to maintain undistracted mindfulness and to leave your mind in its natural state. When you are resting in this way, sometimes there will be moments of dull thoughtlessness and sometimes there will be a thought-free state of all-penetrating openness that brings forth the lucidity of deep insight. Sometimes there will be an experience of bliss to which you feel attached, sometimes there will be a bliss that is free of attachment. Sometimes there will be various experiences of luminosity to which you cling and sometimes a clear, stainless luminosity that is free of attachment. Sometimes there will be unpleasant feelings of discomfort, sometimes pleasant feelings of comfort. Sometimes there will occur a powerful whirlwind of thoughts that will carry you away and destroy your meditation. Sometimes there will be a thick dullness devoid of any clarity. And so on. All sorts of mental states that you have grown used to from time without beginning, together with the movements of karmic wind, will arise unpredictably and without limit. They are just like the sights and scenes of various places, pleasant or rugged, seen in the course of a long journey. Nevertheless, you should just keep to the path without getting engrossed in whatever may manifest.

In particular, while you are still unused to this practice, you will experience turbulent movement when thoughts blaze up like a fire. Don't let them discourage you. Instead, keep a good balance in your practice, neither too tense nor too slack. If you do this, *achievement* and the rest of the five experiences will come.[293] It is also at this time that usually, and thanks to the pith instructions of your teacher, you will confidently recognize, on the basis of your own experience, the difference between awareness and the lack of awareness, or ignorance, and between the universal ground and the dharmakaya, between ordinary mind and primordial wisdom.

Keeping to this practice, you should let your consciousness rest within itself. And all by itself its nature will manifest as primordial wisdom, just like water that becomes clear when it is left to stand. You should take this pith instruction as the main one. Moreover, don't increase your mental activity by indulging in hesitant questions like "Is what I'm meditating on ordinary consciousness or primordial wisdom?" or by theories you have read about in books.

These are just hindrances to your calm abiding and deep insight (respectively, shamatha and vipashyana).

When you have gained a firm habit of the natural union of shamatha (a continuous, steady, mindful resting in the natural state of mind) and vipashyana (knowledge of the luminosity of your own nature), you will recognize that shamatha (the mind's primordial and natural rest) and vipashyana (the mind's luminous nature) have never been separate from the very beginning. And self-arisen primordial wisdom, the state of the Great Perfection, will be realized. This is a pith instruction on resting in the space-like state of equality.

Regarding the method for meditation, the glorious Saraha has said, "Completely give up the thinker and the thing thought about. Just be like an unthinking child." And when you receive the pith instructions that introduce you to the nature of awareness, it is as Saraha has said: "If you apply yourself to the instructions of your teacher and make an effort, there is no doubt that coemergent wisdom will arise."

The nature of the mind—that is, awareness, self-arisen primordial wisdom—is manifest from the very beginning, coemergent with your mind. And it is not different or separate from the ultimate nature of all phenomena. This is the meaning of the expression "uncontrived ultimate luminosity."

Therefore, to rest in the natural flow and to maintain awareness (the nature of the mind or the ultimate nature of phenomena) that has been recognized is an essential instruction that gathers a hundred crucial points into one. This is what must be continually maintained in practice.

The signs of progress in one's meditation can be gauged by the occurrence of luminosity at night. The signs of the perfect path are faith, compassion, wisdom, and so on. These develop spontaneously, and it is in turn thanks to them that realization is attained easily and with a minimum of hardship.

This you will discover from your own experience. And it is certain that it will be profound and swift because you will have the same degree of realization as that of practitioners who have entered other paths that require a great deal of effort and diligent practice.

The result that is gained through meditating on the luminosity of the mind will be that when the veils of discursive thought and their associated habitual tendencies are drawn aside, twofold knowledge (of the nature and the multiplicity of all things) will come effortlessly into flower. You will attain to the primordial realm where the three kayas are spontaneously present.

This is a profound teaching. *Guhya Samaya.*

———

For mantra practitioners living in the villages, who do not strive in study and reflection but who still desire nevertheless to practice on the nature of the mind, this profound instruction, deriving from the experience of old and realized yogis, is a quintessential instruction in a language of Dharma that can easily be understood. It was set down in writing by Mipham Jampel Dorje on the twelfth day of the second month of the fire horse year (1906).

Virtue. *Mangalam.*

NOTES

1. For a translation of Kunzang Pelden's biography of Mipham, see the *Essential Hagiography*, in John W. Pettit, *Mipham's Beacon of Certainty: Illuminating the View of Dzogchen the Great Perfection* (Somerville, MA: Wisdom Publications, 1999), 23–39.

2. Kunzang Pelden's account is in fact an extensive introduction to the index (*dkar chag*) of Mipham's works drawn up by Shechen Gyaltsap Rinpoche and Kunzang Pelden himself.

3. This event is recorded in the Tibetan editor's preface to the recently published biography translated here.

4. In this book, all Sanskrit names and terms have been rendered phonetically and without diacritics. This is normal practice for "popular biography." In the interests of editorial unity, phonetic spelling has also been used in the excerpts from Mipham's more technical writings included in the second part of this volume, regardless of the conventions adopted in the books from which these excerpts were taken.

5. See Gene Smith, *Among Tibetan Texts: History and Literature of the Himalayan Plateau* (Somerville, MA: Wisdom Publications, 2001), 230–31. Readers will also find a useful overview of Mipham's scholarly interests and compositions in Douglas S. Duckworth's *Jamgön Mipam: His Life and Teachings* (Boston: Shambhala Publications, 2011).

6. See p. 81.

7. See, in particular, *The Land of the Lamas: Notes of a Journey through China, Mongolia and Tibet* (London: Longmans, Green, 1891), chap. 5, and his *Diary of a Journey through Mongolia and Tibet in 1891 and 1892* (Washington, DC: Smithsonian Institution, 1894).

8. Excerpts are from the following previously published books: Padmakara Translation Group, trans., *The Adornment of the Middle Way* (Boston: Shambhala Publications, 2005); Jamgön Mipham, *The Wisdom Chapter* (Boulder: Shambhala Publications, 2017); and Jamgön Mipham, *White Lotus*, trans. Padmakara Translation Group (Boston: Shambhala Publications, 2007). Details about the previously published material can be found in the sources section at the back of the book.

9. A fairly extensive bibliography has been supplied in Mipham, *Wisdom Chapter*. Readers who are completely unfamiliar with Madhyamaka may derive some help from the elementary presentations in the translators' introductions in the following: Padmakara Translation Group, trans., *Introduction to the Middle Way* (Boston: Shambhala Publications, 2002); Padmakara Translation Group, *Adornment*; and Mipham, *Wisdom Chapter*.

10. See p. 169.

11. See p. 167.

12. Skt. *jina*, Tib. *rgyal ba*. "Victorious one" and "conqueror" are commonly used synonyms of the term *buddha*.

13. Tib. *zho 'thung gyi mtshon*, lit. "the weapon of the drinker of curd." This is a poetic reference to the vajra (thunderbolt) of Indra, which was made of the bones of the Rishi *Zho 'thung* (drinker of curd).

14. Tib. *ye shes kyi rang snang*.

15. For an explanation of the six special characteristics, or features, of Samantabhadra, see Jigme Lingpa and Longchen Yeshe Dorje, Kangyur Rinpoche, *Treasury of Precious Qualities*, trans. Padmakara Translation Group (Boston: Shambhala Publications), 2:240–41.

16. It is thanks to Manjushri that all the buddhas have attained enlightenment.

17. Tib. *Rig pa rang shar chen po'i rgyud*.

18. Skt. *Manjushrijnanasattvasyaparamarthanamasamgiti*, Tib. *'Jam dpal sgyu 'phrul drwa ba*.

19. For the seven qualities of union, see Jigme Lingpa and Longchen Yeshe Dorje, Kangyur Rinpoche, *Treasury of Precious Qualities*, 2:229, 2:462n542.

20. Tib. *grangs med bskal pa*. The expression "measureless kalpa" does not mean infinity; it denotes a specific period of time defined by Vasubandhu in the *Abhidharmakosha* as 10^{59} kalpas.

21. Skt. *Sahaloka*. There are several explanations for this way of referring to the world system in which Buddha Shakyamuni appeared. See Jigme Lingpa and Longchen Yeshe Dorje, Kangyur Rinpoche, *Treasury of Precious Qualities*, 1:366–67, 1:485n260.

22. Skt. *Susthitamati-devaputra-pariprccha-sutra*, Tib. *Lha'i bu blo gros rab gnas kyis zhus pa'i mdo*.

23. Skt. *Manjushribuddhakshetragunavyuha*, Tib. *'Jam dpal gyi sang rgyas kyi zhing gi yon tan dkod pa'i mdo*.

24. Tib. *Bstod pa glur blang pa'i rgyud*.

25. Tib. *Jam dpal sgyu 'phrul drwa ba'i rgyud phyi ma.*

26. These are actually Manjushri's names and symbolize the six wisdoms.

27. Tib. *Jam dpal rtsa ba'i rtogs pa.*

28. That is, the wisdom that sees the nature of phenomena (*ji lta ba'i mkhyen pa*) and the wisdom that knows phenomena in all their multiplicity (*ji snyed pa'i mkhyen pa*).

29. Tib. *Jam dpal rtsa ba'i rgyud.*

30. Manjushriyashas (sometimes, Manjushrikirti) was the eighth sovereign of Shambhala and the first of the twenty-five *Kalki* (or *Kulika*) kings. He composed the *Laghutantra*, a commentary on the *Kalachakra Tantra*, which is the only surviving scripture of that tradition. Because he initiated his entire kingdom into the Kalachakra, his subjects were organized into a single caste, the *vajrakula*. According to the Kalachakra reckoning of time, he is considered to have lived in the second century BCE.

31. Probably Lochen Dharmashri of Mindroling.

32. Guru Rinpoche is understood to be an emanation of Manjushri as indicated by the names of his eight manifestations, which are the same as the names of Manjushri given in the *Samgiti.*

33. Skt. *Uttaratantrashastra*, Tib. *Rgyud bla ma.*

34. Tib. *Yon tan rin po che'i mdzod.*

35. Tib. *Shing rta rnam gnyis.*

36. "Red rituals" are so called because they involve the offering of meat and blood, which, in principle, is frowned upon in the Mahayana.

37. Tib. *rkyang.* Endowed with a gleaming, russet coat of almost flame-like purity, this kind of horse is a creature of exceptional beauty.

38. That is, until he was about three years old.

39. Tib. *Sdom gsum rnam nges* by Ngari Panchen Pema Wangyal.

40. As its name suggests, the "black" astrological system (*nag rtsis*) is the tradition from China (*rgya nag*, the black expanse), while the "white" system (*dkar rtsis*) derives from *Jyotish*, the astrological system of India (*rgya dkar*, the white expanse). The black system is associated with a form of divination based on the five elements and is used to make predictions and calculate auspicious dates.

41. Skt. *Jatakamala*, Tib. *Skyes rabs.*

42. The four visions of *thögal*, the highest level of practice in the tradition of the Great Perfection. Mingyur Namkha'i Dorje was the subject of many stories. It was said that he had reached such a high level of accomplishment that when he tied his belt, it would pass through his body; he would eat indifferently whatever was placed before him—or nothing, as

the case may be. When he took off his dharma robe (*chos gos*), he could hang it on a sunbeam.

43. Tib. *Dpal chen 'dus pa*. This is the gathering of four wrathful male yidams of the Longchen Nyingtik cycle: Yamantaka ('Jam dpal gshin rje), Hayagriva (Rta mgrin), Vishuddha (Yang dag), and Vajra Kilaya (Rdo rje phur ba).

44. Ziltrom is located on the high mountain slopes above Dzogchen Monastery.

45. Tib. *'Jam dpal stod sgrub kyi rig gtad*.

46. Tib. *'Jam dpal smra ba'i seng nge'i rjes gnang*.

47. Tib. *dbyangs 'char*. A system of divinatory practice. See Jamgön Kongtrul, *The Treasury of Knowledge, Book Six, Parts One and Two: Indo-Tibetan Classical Learning and Buddhist Phenomenology* (Boston: Snow Lion, 2012), 356, 826n894.

48. Jamyang Khyentse Wangpo seems to be implying (as we read a few lines later) that Mipham Rinpoche would naturally acquire an understanding of Svarodaya when he accomplished his yidam deity.

49. The text that Mipham Rinpoche borrowed was the *Yuddhavijaya Tantra*, the principal text on Svarodaya. His extensive commentary is entitled *Kun gzigs dbyangs 'char chos pa shel gyi me long*. See *Mipham's Collected Works*, Shechen edition (Paro, Bhutan, 1984), vol. *dhih*, pp. 777–1118.

50. In connection with his consecration of the pills during his retreat, it is said that Mipham placed a bean under his tongue for the duration of an eclipse. When the eclipse was over, the bean had sprouted—an indication of accomplishment.

51. *Vajratikshna*, "vajra-sharpness," is an epithet of Manjushri.

52. Tib. *Dkon mchog 'byung gnas kyi mdo*.

53. The twelfth Lap Kyabgön (Lab skyabs mgon) (1832–88) of the Gelukpa monastery of Lapgön at Yushu, Khams.

54. "Born in Dhakpo'i Lhagyari, this tertön was the immediately preceding incarnation of Minling Terchen Gyalse Rinchen Namgyal." This is a note inserted by Kyabje Dilgo Khyentse Rinpoche himself. Sengchen Dorje Tsegyal is a name of Gesar of Ling, the folk hero of Tibet, whom Mipham considered to be one of his protector spirits.

55. See note 50.

56. Tib. *dgra lha*, a kind of wrathful protector.

57. Skt. *Bodhicharyavatara*, Tib. *Byang chub sems dpa'i spyod pa la 'jug pa*.

58. That is, the *Norbu Ketaka*, Mipham's commentary on the ninth chapter of the *Bodhicharyavatara*. See Mipham, *Wisdom Chapter*.

59. Skt. *Manjushrinamasamgiti*, Tib. *'Jam dpal mtshan brjod*.

60. The three kinds of service pleasing to the teacher are the making of material offerings, physical service, and finally (and most pleasing) the putting of his or her teachings into practice.

61. Tib. *bka' babs chen po bdun*. These are (1) the long lineage of orally transmitted teachings (*bka' ma*), (2) earth treasures (*sa gter*), (3) mind treasures (*dgongs gter*), (4) rediscovered treasures (*yang gter*), (5) the teachings of the hearing lineage (*snyan brgyud*), (6) pure vision teachings (*dag snang*), and (7) recollections from former lives (*rjes dran*).

62. Skt. *Madhyamakalankara*, Tib. *Dbu ma rgyan*.

63. That is, the two *Vibhaga*: the *Differentiation of the Middle and Extreme Positions* (Skt. *Madhyanta-vibhaga*, Tib. *Dbus mtha' rnam 'byed*) and the *Differentiation of Phenomena and the Nature of Phenomena* (Skt. *Dharmadharmata-vibhaga*, Tib. *Chos dang chos nyid rnam 'byed*). Both these scriptures are numbered among the five famous texts of Maitreya-Asanga.

64. Tib. *Man ngag lta ba'i phreng ba*.

65. Skt. *Chandra-vyakarana*, Tib. *Brda sprod rig pa'i gzhung*.

66. That is, in the preparation of medicines.

67. That is, *Bka' brgyad bde gshegs 'dus pa*, a terma of Nyang Nyima Özer.

68. The fifth Shechen Rabjam, 1864–1909.

69. Tib. *Tshe sgrub gsang ba 'dus pa*.

70. Tib. *Sgyu 'phrul drva ba*.

71. Tib. Gshin rje khro chu'i skor.

72. Tib. *Ye shes bla ma*. A text on *trekchö* and *thögal* belonging to the Longchen Nyingtik cycle.

73. Skt. *Abhidharmakosha*, Tib. *Mngon pa mdzod* by Vasubandhu.

74. Tib. *Tshad ma'i rigs gter* by Sakya Pandita.

75. Tib. *Snga 'gyur rgyud 'bum*.

76. That is, respectively, *bka' ma, gter ma*, and *dag snang*.

77. Taken together, these texts are often referred to as *Mdo rgyud sems gsum*. Individually, they are the *Spyi mdo dgongs pa 'dus pa* (*The General Scripture of Summarized Wisdom*), which is the main tantra of Anuyoga; *Sgyu 'phrul drwa ba* (*Net of Illusory Manifestations of Vajrasattva*, the *Mayajala Tantra*), which is the main text of Mahayoga; and *Sems sde* (the *Mind Class Teachings*)—namely, Atiyoga, the Great Perfection. These texts are contained in the collection of textual transmissions (Kama, bka 'ma).

78. That is, the *snying thig* teachings of Longchenpa and Jigme Lingpa, respectively.

79. Skt. *Lalitavistara*, Tib. *Rgya cher rol pa*.

80. Skt. *Madhyamakavatara*, Tib. *Dbu ma la 'jug pa*.

81. The four perfect knowledges (*so so yang dag par rig pa bzhi*) belong to the qualities of buddhahood. They are the perfect knowledge of each and every aspect of the Dharma—that is, all the words of limitless teachings without confusion; the perfect knowledge of the meanings of all such words without confusing them; the perfect knowledge of how best to express such teachings, and a knowledge of all languages; and the perfect knowledge of unbounded intelligence and ability. See Jigme Lingpa and Longchen Yeshe Dorje, Kangyur Rinpoche, *Treasury of Precious Qualities*, 1:389.

82. Tib. *chags thogs las 'das pa*, a reference to the obscurations of defilement and the cognitive obscurations.

83. This insert is quoted almost verbatim from Khenpo Kunzang Pelden, the *Essential Hagiography*. See Mipham, *Wisdom Chapter*; Pettit, *Mipham's "Beacon of Certainty,"* 26.

84. That is, Shechen Gyaltsap Gyurme Pema Namgyal (1871–1926).

85. These eight treasures, listed in the *Lalitavistara*, are specified by Khenpo Kunzang Pelden in the *Essential Hagiography*. See Pettit, *Mipham's "Beacon of Certainty,"* 25.

86. That is, beings other than the bodhisattvas residing on the grounds of realization of the path of meditation.

87. See Jamgön Mipham, *Dbu ma rgyan gyi rnam bshad*, 90. For an alternative rendering, see Jamgön Mipham, *A Teaching to Delight My Master Manjugosha*, in *Adornment of the Middle Way*, 144.

88. That is, the *Madhyamakalankara* of Shantarakshita. See Mipham, *Dbu ma rgyan gyi rnam bshad*, 56. For an alternative rendering, see Mipham, *Teaching to Delight*, 120.

89. See Mipham, *Dbu ma rgyan gyi rnam bshad*, 56. For an alternative rendering, see Mipham, *Teaching to Delight*, 115.

90. See Mipham, *Dbu ma rgyan gyi rnam bshad*, 28–29. For an alternative rendering, see Mipham, *Teaching to Delight*, 100.

91. This is probably a reference to Rongzom Pandita and Longchenpa, as mentioned on page 97.

92. See Mipham, *Dbu ma rgyan gyi rnam bshad*, 78. For an alternative rendering, see Mipham, *Teaching to Delight*, 135.

93. Skt. *Kalachakra Tantra*, Tib. *Dus kyi khor lo rgyud*.

94. Tib. Drag po lcags kyi 'khor lo can (Fierce Holder of the Iron Wheel): the twenty-fifth Kalki and last of the thirty-two kings of Shambhala.

His reign is expected to begin in the year 2327, and it is prophesied that he will appear to the whole of humanity in 2424. He will wage an apocalyptic war, defeat the corrupt and degenerate rulers of the world, and will usher in a golden age.

95. Skt. *Samadhiraja-sutra*, Tib. *Gting 'dzin rgyal po'i mdo*.

96. Tib. *Rtsa ltung gi 'grel pa*.

97. Tib. *Yid bzhin rin po che'i mdzod*.

98. Lozang Palri Rabsel (1840–1919) of the monastery of Kumbum in Amdo.

99. That is, Tsongkhapa.

100. In all probability, Tashi Özer was the khenpo of Palpung Monastery, who became a close friend of Mipham (see p. 29). Khangmar Geshe is undoubtedly the Lozang Chöpel of Drepung just mentioned. The earlier and later answers to refutation were, respectively, Mipham's reply to Drakar Tulku of Drepung (see Mipham, *Wisdom Chapter*) and his reply to Lozang Rabsel of Kumbum.

101. Tib. *Gzhan gyis brtsad pa'i lan mdor bsdus pa rigs lam rab gsal de nyid snang byed*. Although the title declares that Mipham's response is brief, it is in fact a text of 332 pages in the Sichuan edition. See Mipham, *Shes rab le'u'i tshig don go sla bar rnam par bshad pa nor bu ke ta ka*, in *Mipham's Collected Works* (Chengdu: Si khron mi rigs dpe skrun khang, 1993), vol. 19 (*dza*), 1–117.

102. Mipham composed the *Norbu Ketaka*, his commentary on the "Wisdom Chapter" in 1878 when he was thirty-two years old. The subsequent debate with Japa Dongak (1824–1902) must have taken place some time in the following decade—that is, before 1878, when Patrul Rinpoche died. We should note that Mipham's commentary on the *Madhyamaka-lankara* was written in 1876 when he was thirty; *The Lion's Roar: A Comprehensive Discourse on the Buddha-Nature*, included in the present volume, was written around 1867, when he was twenty-one; while the *Beacon of Certainty* is said to have been dictated by Mipham at the age of six! By his own standards, therefore, he was not particularly young when he composed the commentary on the "Wisdom Chapter," and his remark to Patrul Rinpoche about his youth and immaturity was perhaps more an expression of humility than a statement of fact. It should perhaps be mentioned that, in the debate with Japa, Mipham was debating with a scholar twenty-two years his senior.

103. Kunzang Pelden identifies Pema Benzar (or Padmavajra) as a khenpo from Dzogchen Monastery. See Pettit, *Mipham's "Beacon of Certainty,"* 31.

104. Tib. *Phyogs bcu'i mun sel.*
105. Tib. *Rin chen gter mdzod.*
106. An alternative name of Gyurme Pema Namgyal, the third Shechen Gyaltsap.
107. Skt. *Maitrisimhanada-sutra*, Tib. *Byams pa seng ge'i sgra chen po'i mdo.*
108. Tib. *stag tshang.*
109. Tib. *Rgyud lugs 'jam dpal zhi sgrub.*
110. Tib. *Khro bo phyag rgya zil gnon gyi zla gsang.*
111. Tib. *Gshin rje khro chu dug gdong.*
112. Tib. *Kim kang dmar po.*
113. Tib. *yang zlog.*
114. Tib. *Gter stön gsum tshogs kyi rta mgrin yang gsang.*
115. Tib. *Rta nag lcags ral.* Nyangrel Nyima Özer (Nyang ral nyi ma 'od zer) was one of the first great tertöns. He revealed the *Bka' brgyad bde gshegs 'dus pa* and *mani bka' 'bum.*
116. Tib. *Dpal chen yang dag ru lu gsang ba'i dgongs pa.*
117. Tib. *Rgyud lugs ltar bkral pa'i dpal chen rdo rje gzhon nu.*
118. Tib. *Gsang bdag dregs pa kun 'dul.*
119. Tib. *Drang srong lokatri'i sngags rgod.*
120. Tib. *Nyang gter khros ma nag mo.*
121. Tib. *Tshe bdag phyag rgya zil gnon.* This appears to be the wrathful sadhana of Manjushri mentioned above.
122. Tib. *Gsang ba 'dus pa.*
123. Tib. *'Jam dpal dmar po longs spyod tshe 'phel.*
124. Tib. *Dus 'khor lhan skyes.*
125. Tib. *Dbyangs can dkar mo.*
126. Tib. *'Jam dpal bdud rtsi gcud lan zhes od ldan gyi man ngag.*
127. Tib. *'Jam dpal dmar ser las thams cad sgrub pa'i rgyun khyer shes rab ye shes.*
128. Tib. *'Jam dpal mchog sbyin rdo rje la bsten ba'i bcings grol gyi gdams pa 'kha' dri med.*
129. Tib. *'Jam dpal gzungs sgrub.*
130. Tib. *'Jam dpal rdo rje'i rnon po'i gsang grub.*
131. Tib. *'Jam dpal bde ba chen po'i sgrub thabs.*
132. Tib. *'Jam dpal dhi sgrub.*
133. Tib. *'Jam dpal a yig 'bru gcig.*
134. Tib. *Gzhin rje gshed dgra 'joms nag po.*
135. Tib. *'Jam dpal na' ga raksha pha lam rdo rje'i ral dri.*
136. Tib. *King dmar rgyun khyer ya ma'i snying thig.*

137. Tib. *Drak po sum sgril gyi sgrub thabs khro chu khol ma.*
138. Tib. *Tshe sgrub 'dus kyi rgyun gyi nyams len.*
139. Tib. *Khro gyal gtsug tor byi byad bkrol.*
140. Tib. *Mnga' bdag nyang gi khro bo sme brtsegs.*
141. Tib. *Gu ru chos dbang gi mkha' 'gro sme brtsegs.*
142. Tib. *Shin tu zab pa yi ge gcig pa'i sgom bzlas.*
143. Tib. *'Jam dpal dhi sgrub.*
144. Tib. *Rin chen tog.*
145. Tib. *'Jam dpal mu sgrub.*
146. Tib. *Rnam snang dkar po.*
147. Tib. *'Jig rten dbang phyug* (Avalokiteshvara).
148. Tib. *Sems nyid ngal gso* (Avalokiteshvara).
149. Tib. *Rdo rje khu tshur.*
150. Tib. *Gu ru mkha' 'gro bzhi bskor.*
151. Tib. *'Jam dpal bdud rtsi'i zhun thig.*
152. Tib. *'Jam dpal bde ba chen po.*
153. Tib. *bka' brgyad gsang sgrub hung rgya can.*
154. Tib. *Rdo rje chos kyi sgrub thabs pad ma ra ga.*
155. Tib. *Rta bgrin sgrub thabs le'u tshan gnyis.*
156. Tib. *'Jam dpal rdo rje srog sgrub.*
157. Tib. *'Jam dpal na ga rak sha.*
158. Tib. *'Dod rgyal sgrub thabs.*
159. Tib. *Rta mgrin sgub thabs phrin las lhun grub.*
160. Tib. *Bde mchog dmar po.*
161. Tib. *Lha chen sgrub thabs pad ma ra ga'i phreng ba.*
162. Tib. *Rma bya chen mo.*
163. Tib. *Rgyal mtshan rtse mo'i dung rgyan.*
164. Tib. *So sor 'brang ma.*
165. Tib. *Gdugs dkar mo.*
166. Tib. *Dsam bha la ser po.*
167. Tib. *Nor rgyun ma'i sgrub thabs che chung gnyis.*
168. Tib. *Gtsug tor 'bar ma.*
169. Tib. *Lha yi bla ma.*
170. Tib. *Mdo dgongs pa 'dus pa.*
171. Tib. *Jo bo'i lugs kyi mi 'khrugs pa.*
172. Tib. *Mi 'jigs pa sbyin byed rig pa'i lha mo chen mo lnga.*
173. Tib. *Rig pa'i rgyal mo gsum.*
174. Tib. *Sa lugs 'jam dpal dmar ser dpa' gcig.*
175. Tib. *'Jam dpal shes rab 'khor lo'i sgrub mtha' jnanachakra.*

176. Tib. *'Jam dpal ngag gi dbang phyug sgrub thabs prajnachakra.*
177. Tib. *Dbang gi 'jam dpal yan lag med pa'i rdo rje.*
178. Tib. *Dbyangs can dmar po'i gsang sgrub jnanadarsha.*
179. Tib. *Spyan ras gzigs seng ge sgra yid bzhin re skong.*
180. Tib. *Spyan ras gzigs yi ge phyed dang bzhi pa'i sgom bzlas.*
181. Tib. *Khro bo stobs po che.*
182. Tib. *Yum chen mu kha le.*
183. Tib. *Dam tshig rdo rje'i sgom bzlas che chung gnyis.*
184. Tib. *Phyag rdor bdag bskyed leu' tshan gnyis.*
185. Tib. *Gnyan 'joms 'jam dpal nag po.*
186. Tib. *Rdo rje 'jigs byed phyag gnyis pa.*
187. Tib. *Rwa lugs 'jigs byed.*
188. Tib. *Dus 'khor lhan skyes.*
189. Tib. *Gshin rje gshed dmar.*
190. Tib. *Bde mchog.*
191. Tib. *Kye rdor lhan skyes.*
192. The city of the vajra aggregate is a poetic name for the subtle aspect of the physical body, which is composed of the channels, winds, and essence-drops, and forms the basis of the advanced yogic practices of the perfection stage.
193. Tib. *kha sbyor yan lag bdun.* The enlightened body endowed with seven qualities of union is the supreme accomplishment of the path of learning. See Jigme Lingpa and Longchen Yeshe Dorje, Kangyur Rinpoche, *Treasury of Precious Qualities,* 2:229.
194. See note 53.
195. A mani wall is a structure made up of flat stones on which are carved mantras (not only the mani mantra) and other sacred texts. They serve as the supports for the meritorious practice of circumambulation.
196. For further information on Sherab Yarphel and a presentation of some of his teachings, see Shechen Gyaltsap Gyurmé Pema Namgyal, *Practicing the Great Perfection: Instructions on the Crucial Points,* trans. Padmakara Translation Group (Boulder: Shambhala Publications, 2020).
197. That is, Lochen Dharmashri, the brother of Terdak Lingpa and cofounder with him of the monastery of Mindroling.
198. Tib. *Sangs rgyas dang byang chub sems dpa'i mtshan 'bum nor bu'i phreng ba.*
199. Skt. *Mahayanasutralamkara,* Tib. *Theg pa chen po mdo sde rgyan.*
200. *Ornament of the Mahayana Sutras.* See chapter 18, stanzas 1 and 2.
201. Skt. *Maitreyaprasthana-sutra,* Tib. *'Phags pa byams pa 'jug pa'i mdo.*

202. The five levels of meditative experience in the generation stage are mentioned in the *Treasury of Precious Qualities* in the context of the first of the "four life-fastening nails." *Habituation* is the third of the five levels of experience. See Jigme Lingpa and Longchen Yeshe Dorje, Kangyur Rinpoche, *Treasury of Precious Qualities*, 2:151, 398n238.

203. Of the nine stages of calm abiding, "one-pointed mind" (*sems rtse gcig pa*) is the eighth. See Dalai Lama, *Opening the Eye of New Awareness*, trans. Donald S. Lopez Jr. (Boston: Wisdom Publications, 1990), 66.

204. Pelden Lhamo is traditionally regarded as one of the principal protector deities of Tibet. Her life force is connected with the sacred lake of visions (Lha mo'i bla mtsho) in which the signs of the incarnations of the dalai lamas were sought.

205. The details of the circumstances of the composition of this commentary are given in the colophon. See Mipham, *White Lotus*, 91. For the guru yoga practice just mentioned, see also *White Lotus*, 93.

206. It seems that there are some words missing from the text here.

207. Tib. *Tshe sgrub gsangs ba 'dus pa.*

208. The identity of the mysterious foreigners and the purpose of their visit is a matter of speculation. The collection of earth samples suggests either scientific research or prospecting for mineral deposits. As we have said, the travelers may have belonged to the party of William Rockhill, who passed through Kham at that time. It is well documented that the presence of foreign explorers and researchers was generally viewed among the Tibetans with distrust and hostility. See Charles Bell, *Tibet Past and Present* (Oxford: Oxford University Press, 1924), 263.

209. Tib. *Rdo rje nyi ma'i snang ba.*

210. That is, four reasons why Mipham Rinpoche received his name.

211. Tib. *Bkra shis mi 'gyur ma.*

212. Tib. *Gnyug sems skor gsum.* Compiled after Mipham's death by Shechen Gyaltsap, this cycle of three texts is a comprehensive expression of Mipham's teachings on the Great Perfection.

213. Tib. *Snying Thig.*

214. Tib. Lopön Pawo (Slob dpon dpa' bo), another name for the second-century Indian Buddhist poet Ashvaghosha.

215. Skt. *Udanavarga*, Tib. *Ched du brjod pa'i tshoms.*

216. Traditionally, it is said that if mules, which are normally sterile, become pregnant, the condition will kill them.

217. Skt. *Pramanavarttika*, Tib. *Tshad ma rnam 'grel.*

218. Padmaraja, or in Tibetan, Pema Gyalpo (Pad ma rgyal po) is the name of

one of the eight manifestations of Guru Rinpoche. Padmaraja is inseparable from Manjushri.

219. This rather obscure expression (despite the author's assessment) seems to refer to Mipham's actual life span, which by Tibetan reckoning was supposed to be sixty-seven years. In fact, he died on the last day of the fourth month of his sixty-eighth year.

220. Skt. *Bodhisattvajataka*, Tib. *Byang chub sems dpa'i skyes rabs*.

221. That is, the system of the profound view (Madhyamaka) associated with Manjushri and Nagarjuna (second century) and the system of vast activities (Yogachara) associated with Maitreya and Asanga (fourth century). These two traditions correspond, respectively, to the collections of scriptures and teachings of the second and third turnings of the dharma wheel.

222. That is, the *mandal rten gsum*, a mandala offering in which a statue, a scriptural text, and a small stupa are used to symbolize (respectively) the vajra body, speech, and mind.

223. In other words, the practice of the Great Perfection.

224. In other words, there were eight of them.

225. Tib. *Dpal g.yul las rnam par rgyal ba'i rgyud*.

226. Tib. *'Od gsal snying po*.

227. Tib. *Phyogs bcu'i mun sel*.

228. Skt. *Mayajala-guhyagarbha-tantra*, Tib. *Sgyu 'phrul gsang ba snying po*.

229. Skt. *Abhisamayalamkara*, Tib. *Mngon rtogs rgyan*.

230. Tib. *Rgyal po lugs kyi btsan bcos sa gzhi skyong ba'i rgyan*. See Jamgön Mipham, *The Just King*, trans. José Ignacio Cabezón (Boulder: Snow Lion, 2017).

231. Tib. *Mkhas 'jug*.

232. Tib. *Rdo rje nyi ma'i snang ba*.

233. Tib. *Dpal dam pa dang po'i sangs rgyas kyi rgyud*—that is, the *Kalachakra Tantra*.

234. Tib. *Sems kyi spyod pa rnam par sbyong ba so sor brtag pa'i spyad sgom 'khor lo ma*.

235. In other words, the great monastic foundation of Kumbum in Amdo.

236. The Shiwalha and Phakpalha lamas, important hierarchs in the Geluk school, both had their seat at the monastery of Jampa Ling in Amdo.

237. The Svarodaya is a form of divination based on the sound of the vowels and consonants. See note 49.

238. Tib. *Don rnam par nges pa shes rab ral gri*.

239. Tib. *Ye shes bla ma*.

240. The briny ocean is thereby rendered pure and fresh.

241. Tib. *Spyi mdo dgongs pa 'dus pa.*

242. In the sense that Mipham would soon be going there.

243. See p. 90.

244. An abbreviation of the name "Kunzang Pelden" by which the great khenpo is widely known.

245. Khenpo Pema Sherab interprets this as meaning that Mipham's views on Madhyamaka are expressed with sufficient clarity in his commentary on the *Madhyamakalankara* (*Adornment of the Middle Way*).

246. See note 212.

247. Terdak Lingpa and Lochen Dharmashri, the founders of the great monastery of Mindroling.

248. As Khyentse Rinpoche recorded in his autobiography, in the days following Mipham's death, Lama Ösel went almost mad with grief. See Dilgo Khyentse Rinpoche, *Brilliant Moon*, trans. Ani Jinba Palmo (Boston: Shambhala Publications, 2008), 18.

249. This is possibly a reference to the elder brother of Dilgo Khyentse Rinpoche. See John Pettit, *Mipham's "Beacon of Certainty,"* 38, 473n138.

250. Presumably created by the requests of his closest disciples.

251. The fourth month of the Tibetan year, regarded as sacred because it contains the anniversaries of the Buddha's birth and of his mahaparinirvana.

252. According to Matthew Kapstein (in an oral communication), it is said that toward the end of his life, Mipham Rinpoche's hands trembled so much that his handwriting had become illegible.

253. Tib. *sme brtsegs* and *rnam 'joms*, respectively.

254. Mipham Rinpoche passed away on the twenty-ninth of Saga Dawa, the fourth month. The bathing of the body by Gyaltsap Rinpoche and others began on the eleventh day of the fifth month. This suggests that Mipham Rinpoche remained in after-death meditation (*thugs dam*) for about twelve days.

255. That is, by reverently holding the books to their heads.

256. Tib. *Dpal rdo rje sems dpa' thugs kyi sgrub pa.*

257. In the previous mention of this event, it is stipulated, perhaps more plausibly, that the explanation of Kalachakra was bestowed by Mipham Rinpoche himself.

258. That is, Kyabje Dilgo Khyentse Rinpoche.

259. When giving their age, Tibetans traditionally include the year of pregnancy. Dilgo Khyentse Rinpoche, being born in 1910, completed his text at the age of twenty-nine by Western reckoning.

260. It should be remembered that the earlier tradition (*snga rabs pa*) mentioned here does not refer to the Nyingma school but to the earlier Madhyamaka tradition, represented by the Nyingma, Sakya, and Kagyu schools together, in contradistinction to the later tradition (*phyi rabs*) of Tsongkhapa.

261. *Madhyamakalankara*, v. 70. See Shantarakshita, *Madhyamakalankara*, in *Adornment of the Middle Way*, trans. Padmakara Translation Group (Boston: Shambhala Publications, 2005), 62.

262. *Madhyamakalankara*, v. 71. See Shantarakshita, *Madhyamakalankara*, p. 62.

263. Compare Mipham's remark in his commentary to the *Madhyamakalankara*: "The intelligent should ask themselves whether they would be able to realize the profound view of the glorious Chandrakirti (the Middle Way of primordial wisdom in meditative equipoise) without relying on the path set forth according to the present [that is, Svatantrika] approach." See Mipham, *Teaching to Delight*, 297.

264. That is, the "Wisdom Chapter" of the *Bodhicharyavatara*.

265. *Bodhichittavivarana*, v. 88.

266. In the *Adornment of the Middle Way*, the "figurative ultimate" (*rnam grangs pa'i don dam*) and the "nonfigurative ultimate" (*rnam grangs ma yin pa'i don dam*) were originally translated as the "approximate ultimate" and the "actual ultimate in itself," respectively. These renderings were used experimentally at a time when we had not yet found a more satisfactory translation. Subsequently, in later translations, we adopted the twin terms *figurative* and *nonfigurative*, which correspond more closely with the two Tibetan expressions. The figurative ultimate is so named because, while being a theoretical concept, it is nevertheless a type, or figure, that points to the actual nonfigurative ultimate in itself, the latter being not an intellectual idea but a profound experience that transcends the ordinary mind.

267. *Madhyamakavatara*, chap. 6, v. 89. See Jamgön Mipham, *The Word of Chandra*, in *Introduction to the Middle Way*, trans. Padmakara Translation Group (Boston: Shambhala Publications, 2002), 256.

268. Tib. *rtogs pa bzhi'i gtan tshigs*. This is a way, according to the Mahayoga tantra, of establishing that the phenomena of samsara and nirvana, the spontaneous display of the ordinary mind and of primordial wisdom, manifest within the indivisibility of the two truths.

269. Tib. *chos kyi rjes su mthun pa'i bzod pa*, attained on the level of acceptance, the third of the four levels of the path of joining. This is the point beyond which, it is said, the mind can no longer fall into the lower realms.

270. In this translation, we have consistently rendered the Tibetan terms *rigs* as "buddha-potential," *khams* as "buddha-element," and *sangs rgyas kyi snying po* as "buddha-essence."

271. That is, investigations based on the three types of valid cognition: direct perception, inference, and the authority and consistency of scripture.

272. That is, in the same way that clay is the material cause of the earthenware vessel that it becomes.

273. The reasoning of final analysis refers to the conventional valid cognition of pure perception (*dag gzigs tha snyad kyi tshad ma*).

274. That is, something that is designated as simply nonexistent in the ordinary sense.

275. For a full account of a buddha's qualities of realization, see, for example, Jigme Lingpa and Longchen Yeshe Dorje, Kangyur Rinpoche, *Treasury of Precious Qualities*, 1:387–90.

276. This is a reference to the *satkaryavada* view of the Samkhya school of Indian philosophy, which states that effects preexist in their causes. This theory is refuted by Shantideva in the ninth chapter of the *Bodhicharyavatara* in the same terms as the objection given here (the view has the consequence that when one eats one's food, one eats one's excrement).

277. The teachings of the first and second turning of the dharma wheel.

278. Tib. *ltos pa'i rigs pa*.

279. Tib. *chos nyid kyi rigs pa*.

280. See p. 151.

281. Tib. *rang snang*.

282. This is a contradiction, since the knowledge of the paths on which beings find themselves is one of the ten strengths that are the marks of buddhahood.

283. Tib. *dngos po'i stobs kyis zhugs pa'i rigs pa*.

284. The three doors of perfect liberation are a central notion of the Mahayana teachings of the second turning of the dharma wheel. They are a means of approach to ultimate reality through an understanding of three qualities implicit in all phenomena. The three doors are (1) all phenomena are empty, (2) they are beyond all attributes, (3) they are beyond all aspiration or expectation.

285. Here and a few lines later the state of buddhahood is referred to simply as the "totally transformed state [of the mind]" (*gnas yongs su gyur pa*). In the same vein, the condition of sentient beings is referred to as the "untransformed state" (*gnas ma gyur pa*).

286. In the course of their training on the path, bodhisattvas receive a prediction of their irreversible attainment of enlightenment. Bodhisattvas of

the highest capacity receive this even while they are still on the path of joining; those of medium capacity receive it on the path of seeing; those of least capacity receive this prediction only when they have attained the eighth bodhisattva level, that is, the first of the pure grounds.

287. One of Mipham's names.

288. The "cycle of years" (*lo skor*) referred to here obviously does not refer to the sixty-year rabjung cycle but to the cycle of twelve animals by which the years are identified.

289. Tib. *Rig pa rang shar gyi rgud.*

290. Tib. *Rdzogs chen chos nyid byang chub sems rnam dag ston pa'i rgyud.*

291. Tib. *Bkras shis rig pa'i khyu byug.*

292. In other words, the name Buddha Padmasambhava (like Padmakara) is interpreted as meaning "the source of lotus[-like] buddhas."

293. These are the five experiences of the generation-stage practice. For more information on this, see Jigme Lingpa and Longchen Yeshe Dorje, Kangyur Rinpoche, *Treasury of Precious Qualities,* 2:15 and 398n238.

Bibliography

Primary Sources in Tibetan

Dilgo Khyentse. *Gsang chen chos kyi shing rta ' jigs med spra ba'i seng ge kun mkhyen bla ma mi pham ' jam dbyangs rnam rgyal rgya mtsho'i rnam thar snying po bsdus pa ngo mtshar bdud rtsi'i snang ba.* Edited by Dwags po Rinpoche, Adzom Gyalse Rinpoche, and Khenpo Tashi Tsering. Kathmandu: Shechen Publications, 2013.

Drakar Tulku. *Zab mo dbu ma'i gnad cung zad brjod pa blo gsal dga'i ba'i gtam.* In *Collected Works*, vol. 12. Block print. Chengdu: Dmangs khrod dpe dkon sdud sgrig khang, 2001.

Kunzang Pelden. *Gangs ri'i khrod kyi smra ba'i seng ge gcig pu ' jam mgon mi pham rgya mtsho'i rnam thar snying po bsdus pa dang gsung rab kyi dkar chag snga 'gyur bstan pa'i mdzod rgyan.* In *Collected Writings of 'Jam mgon 'Ju Mi-pham rGya-mtsho*, vol. 7. Gangtok: Sonam T. Kazi, 1976.

Mipham Gyatso, Jamgön Ju. *Bde gshegs snying po'i stong thun chen mo seng ge'i nga ro.* In *Mipham's Collected Works*, vol. 4 (*pa*), 441–85. Chengdu: Si khron mi rigs dpe khrun khang, 1993.

———. *Brgal lan nyin byed snang ba.* In *Mipham's Collected Works*, vol. 19 (*dza*), 118–227. Chengdu: Si khron mi rigs dpe skrun khang, 1993.

———. *Dbu ma rgyan gyi rnam bshad ' jam dbyangs bla ma dgyes pa'i zhal lung.* Mysore: Ngagyur Nyingma Institute, 1998.

———. *Guru tshig bdun gsol 'debs kyi rnam bshad padma dkar po.* In *Mipham's Collected Works*, vol. 25 (*ra*), 463–525. Chengdu: Si khron mi rigs dpe skrun khang, 1993.

———. *Rtogs ldan rgan po rnams kyi lugs sems ngo 'dzub tshugs kyi gdams pa mun sel sgron me.* In *Mipham's Collected Works*, vol. 33 (*e*), 68–73. Chengdu: Si khron mi rigs dpe skrun khang, 1993.

———. *Shes rab kyi leu'i tshig don go sla bar rnam par bshad pa nor bu ke ta ka.* In *Mipham's Collected Works*, vol. 19 (*dza*), 1–117. Chengdu: Si khron mi rigs dpe skrun khang, 1993.

PRIMARY SOURCES IN TRANSLATION

Chandrakirti. *Madhyamakavatara*. In *Introduction to the Middle Way*, translated by the Padmakara Translation Group, 55–114. Boston: Shambhala Publications, 2002.

Drakar Tulku. *A Pleasurable Discourse for Those of Clear Understanding: A Brief Exposition of the Key Points of the Profound Middle Way*. In *The Wisdom Chapter*, translated by the Padmakara Translation Group, 295–318. Boulder: Shambhala Publications, 2017.

Jamgön Kongtrul. *The Treasury of Knowledge, Book Six, Parts One and Two: Indo-Tibetan Classical Learning and Buddhist Phenomenology*. Boston: Snow Lion, 2012.

Jigme Lingpa and Longchen Yeshe Dorje, Kangyur Rinpoche. *Treasury of Precious Qualities*. Translated by Padmakara Translation Group. 2 vols. Boston: Shambhala Publications, 2010–13.

Kunzang Pelden, Khenpo. *Essential Hagiography*. In *Mipham's Beacon of Certainty: Illuminating the View of Dzogchen the Great Perfection*, 23–39. Boston: Wisdom Publications, 1999.

Mipham, Jamgön. *The Just King*. Translated by José Ignacio Cabezón. Boulder: Snow Lion, 2017.

———. *Ketaka Jewel*. In *The Wisdom Chapter*, translated by the Padmakara Translation Group, 77–193. Boulder: Shambhala Publications, 2017.

———. *Light of the Day Star*. In *The Wisdom Chapter*, translated by the Padmakara Translation Group, 195–294. Boulder: Shambhala Publications, 2017.

———. *A Teaching to Delight My Master Manjugosha*. In *The Adornment of the Middle Way*, translated by the Padmakara Translation Group, 67–383. Boston: Shambhala Publications, 2005.

———. *White Lotus: An Explanation of the Seven-Line Prayer to Guru Padmasambhava*, translated by the Padmakara Translation Group. Boston: Shambhala Publications, 2007.

———. *The Wisdom Chapter: Jamgön Mipham's Commentary on the Ninth Chapter of "The Way of the Bodhisattva."* Boulder: Shambhala Publications, 2017.

———. *The Word of Chandra*. In *Introduction to the Middle Way*, translated by the Padmakara Translation Group, 115–354. Boston: Shambhala Publications, 2002.

Padmakara Translation Group, trans. *The Adornment of the Middle Way*. Boston: Shambhala Publications, 2005.

———. *Introduction to the Middle Way*. Boston: Shambhala Publications, 2002.

Shantarakshita. *Madhyamakalankara*. In *The Adornment of the Middle Way*, translated by the Padmakara Translation Group, 49–66. Boston: Shambhala Publications, 2005.

Shechen Gyaltsap Gyurmé Pema Namgyal. *Practicing the Great Perfection: Instructions on the Crucial Points*, translated by the Padmakara Translation Group. Boulder: Shambhala Publications, 2020.

SECONDARY SOURCES

Bell, Charles. *Tibet Past and Present*. Oxford: Oxford University Press, 1924.

Dalai Lama. *Opening the Eye of New Awareness*. Translated by Donald S. Lopez Jr. Boston: Wisdom Publications, 1990.

Dilgo Khyentse Rinpoche. *Brilliant Moon: The Autobiography of Dilgo Khyentse*. Translated by Ani Jinba Palmo. Boston: Shambhala Publications, 2008.

Duckworth, Douglas S. *Jamgön Mipam: His Life and Teaching*. Boston: Shambhala Publications, 2011.

———. *Mipam on the Buddha-Nature: The Ground of the Nyingma Tradition*. New York: State University of New York Press, 2008.

Hookham, S. K. *The Buddha Within*. New York: State University of New York Press, 1991.

Mathes, Klaus-Dieter. *A Direct Path to the Buddha Within*. Boston: Wisdom Publications, 2008.

Pettit, John W. *Mipham's "Beacon of Certainty": Illuminating the View of Dzogchen the Great Perfection*. Somerville, MA: Wisdom Publications, 1999.

Rockhill, William Woodville. *Diary of a Journey through Mongolia and Tibet in 1891 and 1892*. Washington, DC: Smithsonian Institution, 1894.

———. *The Land of the Lamas: Notes of a Journey through China, Mongolia, and Tibet*. London: Longmans, Green. 1891.

Ruegg, David Seyfort. *The Literature of the Madhyamaka School of Philosophy in India*. Weisbaden: Otto Harrassowitz, 1981.

Smith, E. Gene. *Among Tibetan Texts: History and Literature of the Himalayan Plateau.* Somerville, MA: Wisdom Publications, 2001.

Thakchoe, Sonam. *The Two Truths Debate: Tsongkhapa and Gorampa on the Middle Way.* Boston: Wisdom Publications, 2007.

Vose, Kevin A. *Resurrecting Candrakīrti: Disputes in the Tibetan Creation of Prāsaṅgika.* Boston: Wisdom Publications, 2009.

Sources

Sources of previously published material are listed by chapter and, in some cases, by the headings found within the chapter.

Chapter 9. Selections on Madhyamaka

Mipham's Nonsectarian Attitude: Jamgön Mipham, *Light of the Day Star*, 197–99. Reprinted by permission of the publisher.

Great Emptiness, Freedom from Ontological Extremes: Jamgön Mipham, *Ketaka Jewel*, 82–84. Reprinted by permission of the publisher.

The Two Kinds of Ultimate and the Equal Status of the Svatantrikas and Prasangikas: Jamgön Mipham, *A Teaching to Delight My Master Manjughosha*, 101–10. Reprinted by permission of the publisher.

Conventional Phenomena Are Mind Only: Jamgön Mipham, *A Teaching to Delight My Master Manjughosha*, 111–13. Reprinted by permission of the publisher.

Freedom from the Four Conceptual Extremes: Jamgön Mipham, *A Teaching to Delight My Master Manjughosha*, 137. Reprinted by permission of the publisher.

Meditating on Madhyamaka—Advice for the Student: Jamgön Mipham, *Light of the Day Star*, 274–77. Reprinted by permission of the publisher.

Chapter 11. An Explanation of the Seven-Line Prayer to Guru Rinpoche according to the Teachings of the Path of Liberation

Jamgön Mipham, *White Lotus*, 19, 46–49, 53–58. Reprinted by permission of the publisher.

The Padmakara Translation Group Translations into English

The Adornment of the Middle Way. Shantarakshita and Mipham Rinpoche. Boston: Shambhala Publications, 2010.

Counsels from My Heart. Dudjom Rinpoche. Boston: Shambhala Publications, 2003.

Enlightened Courage. Dilgo Khyentse Rinpoche. Ithaca, NY: Snow Lion Publications, 2006.

The Excellent Path of Enlightenment. Dilgo Khyentse. Ithaca, NY: Snow Lion Publications, 1996.

A Feast of the Nectar of the Supreme Vehicle. Maitreya and Jamgön Mipham. Boulder: Shambhala Publications, 2018.

Finding Rest in Illusion. Longchenpa. Boulder: Shambhala Publications, 2018.

Finding Rest in Meditation. Longchenpa. Boulder: Shambhala Publications, 2018.

Finding Rest in the Nature of the Mind. Longchenpa. Boulder: Shambhala Publications, 2017.

A Flash of Lightning in the Dark of Night. The Dalai Lama. Boston: Shambhala Publications, 1993. Republished as *For the Benefit of All Beings.* Boston: Shambhala Publications, 2009.

Food of Bodhisattvas. Shabkar. Boston: Shambhala Publications, 2004.

A Garland of Views: A Guide to View, Meditation, and Result in the Nine Vehicles. Padmasambhava and Mipham Rinpoche. Boston: Shambhala Publications, 2015.

A Guide to the Words of My Perfect Teacher. Khenpo Ngawang Pelzang. Translated by the Dipamkara Translation Group in collaboration with the Padmakara Translation Group. Boston: Shambhala Publications, 2004.

The Heart of Compassion. Dilgo Khyentse. Boston: Shambhala Publications, 2007.

The Heart Treasure of the Enlightened Ones. Dilgo Khyentse and Patrul Rinpoche. Boston: Shambhala Publications, 1992.

The Hundred Verses of Advice. Dilgo Khyentse and Padampa Sangye. Boston: Shambhala Publications, 2005.

Introduction to the Middle Way. Chandrakirti and Jamgön Mipham. Boston: Shambhala Publications, 2004.

Journey to Enlightenment. Matthieu Ricard. New York: Aperture Foundation, 1996.

Lady of the Lotus-Born. Gyalwa Changchub and Namkhai Nyingpo. Boston: Shambhala Publications, 2002.

The Life of Shabkar: The Autobiography of a Tibetan Yogin. Ithaca, NY: Snow Lion Publications, 2001.

Nagarjuna's Letter to a Friend. Longchen Yeshe Dorje, Kangyur Rinpoche. Ithaca, NY: Snow Lion Publications, 2005.

The Nectar of Manjushri's Speech. Kunzang Pelden. Boston: Shambhala Publications, 2010.

Practicing the Great Perfection: Instructions on the Crucial Points. Shechen Gyaltsap Gyurmé Pema Namgyal. Boulder: Shambhala Publications, 2020.

The Root Stanzas of the Middle Way. Nagarjuna. Boulder: Shambhala Publications, 2016.

A Torch Lighting the Way to Freedom. Dudjom Rinpoche, Jigdrel Yeshe Dorje. Boston: Shambhala Publications, 2011.

Treasury of Precious Qualities. 2 vols. Boston: Shambhala Publications, 2010–13.

The Way of the Bodhisattva. Shantideva. Rev. ed. Boulder: Shambhala Publications, 2008.

White Lotus. Jamgön Mipham. Boston: Shambhala Publications, 2007.

Wisdom: Two Buddhist Commentaries. Khenchen Kunzang Pelden and Minyak Kunzang Sonam. Dordogne: Editions Padmakara, 1999.

The Wisdom Chapter: Jamgön Mipham's Commentary on the Ninth Chapter of "The Way of the Bodhisattva." Jamgön Mipham. Boulder: Shambhala Publications, 2017.

The Wish-Fulfilling Jewel. Dilgo Khyentse. Boston: Shambhala Publications, 1988.

The Words of My Perfect Teacher. Patrul Rinpoche. New Haven, CT: Yale University Press, 2010.

Zurchungpa's Testament. Zurchungpa and Dilgo Khyentse. Ithaca, NY: Snow Lion Publications, 2006.

INDEX